A DISTANT DRUM

Portrait of Ian Liddell VC, painted from a photograph taken by his mother.

A DISTANT DRUM

The story of the
5th Bn Coldstream Guards 1944–45

Captain Jocelyn Pereira

UNIFORM

I AM happy and proud to see a second edition to this book and must now offer it – not to my friends of the past but to present and future Coldstreamers.

Naturally I would like to rewrite much of it with more literary polish, but alas I cannot.

I can add one omission which was that, the principal leaders who were in command of the platoons under Ian Liddell's command and who had to rush the EMS bridge were Lump Windsor Clive, Robert Laurie, and Sergeant (now Major (QM)) Norman Duckworth. Of course there are other people involved in incidents whom I should have mentioned. Now I can only apologise to anyone whom I have by omission offended.

All that I can really add to my original introduction is that I do not retract one word. It was a plea for peace and I hope it will always be seen in this way.

CAPTAIN J. PEREIRA
1972

Photographs – & Credits

In this edition of *A Distant Drum* I have taken the liberty to include many more photographs than in earlier editions. These were taken by George Mackean who commanded support company. They were donated to the Imperial War Museum by Tim Bendix in an annotated album that belonged to his father. I have used information from the album, the text from *A Distant Drum* and the battalion diary to caption photographs. Every effort has been made to be as accurate as possible, however with the distance of time minor errors may have crept in for which I apologise.

I would like to thank Brian Liddell for allowing me to reproduce photographs of Ian Liddell VC from his family collection and the portrait in the frontispiece, Charles Lomer & Rodney Style for photographs of their fathers, George Windsor Clive for panoramic photo of Ems Bridge. Following Coldstream custom, I have not used title or rank unless that of commanding officer or above. These can be found in the order of battle in the appendices.

James Kerr (Editor for 75th anniversary edition)

Foreword to the seventy fifth
Anniversary edition by

LIEUTENANT GENERAL
SIR JAMES BUCKNALL
KCB, CBE

Colonel, Coldstream Guards

JOCELYN PEREIRA'S vivid and colourful narrative of the 5th Battalion's advance from Normandy to Cuxhaven in 1944-45 is a priceless piece of the Regiment's history and a tribute to those who served in that final, testing phase of the war. And yet its value to us is so much more. It is a story of war, an intensely human endeavour, with its bursts of extreme activity interspersed with long periods of relative inactivity; with its highs and lows, good times and bad. It is a story of Guardsmen, of professionalism and discipline in the most demanding of circumstances, of initiative and resourcefulness, of determination and stubbornness, of fortitude and stoicism in adversity, of comradeship and consideration for others, of humour and unbreakable morale, of extraordinary gallantry and sacrifice. These are characteristics which those who have served with the Regiment since the Second World War will recognise. With a light touch, a dose of irreverence, modesty and understatement, and an evidently healthy disregard for dress regulations, Jocelyn Pereira captures that enduring Coldstream spirit which continues to shine brightly today. On behalf of the Regiment, I would like to thank Edward Pereira for his permission to re-print this book; Simon Vandeleur, the Regimental Adjutant, for his encouragement of the project; Bill McLean, Rodney Style, Will Douglas and James Kerr for funding the re-print; and James Kerr himself for conceiving and driving the project through to completion, ensuring that this wonderfully rich story is made accessible to today's Coldstreamers and to many others. In Jocelyn Pereira's final words in the book: "War is only an incident in the history of the Coldstream Guards – but, my, what an incident!"

FOREWORD BY

General Sir Charles Loyd,
K.C.B., K.C.V.O., D.S.O., M.C.

Colonel, Coldstream Guards

JOCELYN PEREIRA is one of the very few who fought with the 5th Battalion Coldstream from Normandy to Cuxhaven. In 1944-45, he served his Regiment as efficiently and as faithfully as his illustrious father had done exactly thirty years before. He did so as intelligence officer, and his main duty was to predict from day to day to his Commanding Officer the situation and intentions of the enemy. This was no easy task, but in the process he displayed an uncanny intuition and cheerfulness rivalled only by an uncanny capacity to conceive new ideas for disregarding the Dress Regulations.

It is not easy to capture the interest of the ordinary person in the story of a battalion on active service. In this book, Jocelyn Pereira succeeds.

The mind of the reader is carried deep into the atmosphere of war. The mental stress caused by its seeming endlessness, the gallantry, the hardships and the uncertainties are all there to be absorbed. Above all such trials, the Coldstream spirit is seen to emerge triumphant.

In the winter of 1659, Monck's men earned the title of "Coldstreamers" from the way they endured the extreme rigours of the winter, and in 1944 and 1945, the men of the 5th Battalion proved themselves more than worthy of the title.

INTRODUCTION

DURING THE war, I used to think that I should like to write a book like *All Quiet on the Western Front*, so that people would be shocked and horrified by the ghastliness of war, and that even if it had to be forced down the throat of the public it would be a service to mankind that more people should appreciate the full misery of what was going on. But even if I were able to write like that there are a great many reasons that prevent one from describing what has actually happened in those terms and when the war was over, I thought I would limit myself to putting down a few personal memories for my own interest. I was the Battalion Intelligence Officer throughout the campaign so that necessarily I got a fairly overall picture of what went on, and someone who read the notes that I had made suggested that it would be an interesting way of recording the Battalion History, and on this idea I set out to write the rest of the story on a slightly revised plan. A formal Battalion history is bound to be a dull simulacrum even for those who can read between the lines and it is the hope of this book that by presenting a version which is strictly personal and unofficial it may be possible to give some life to what would otherwise be dry bones. As to what happened and what I saw, that is common to all, but as to the hopes and fears which are perhaps the most vivid part of all wars I can only say how things appeared to me, and trust that it was not so very different for everyone else.

So many different points of view have occurred to me as I have written that in the end the final product has come out rather a muddled collection of incidents and impressions; but even so I hope that it gives in some measure a slight reflection of the reality and will faithfully recall a portion of the great events of which it is a partial account.

Jocelyn Pereira
Monthey,
Switzerland,
August 5th,1946

This edition first published by Uniform in 2020
an imprint of Unicorn Publishing Group

Unicorn Publishing Group
5 Newburgh Street, London W1F 7RG

www.unicornpublishing.org

First published by Gale & Polden, 1949
Reprinted by S.R. Publishers, 1972

A catalogue record for this book is available
from the British Library

ISBN

Printed and bound in Great Britain

Cover design and typesetting by Uniform

Contents

Illustrations

GOOD-BYE, ENGLAND

FROM THE moment that the first envelopes arrived in the Orderly Room with the inscription "Top Secret" and their huge blobs of red sealing wax a distinctive atmosphere seemed to engulf one's life, giving it an air of indefinable adventure so that the brief summer days before the invasion were an experience all of their own, unlike anything that had ever happened before or anything that happened afterwards. And yet everything that occurred was as prosaic and methodical as though the whole routine were just another rehearsal, after which we would once more find ourselves sitting safely in an officers' mess in England and as far from the war as ever before.

Our marshalling area in Epping Forest was like any Army camp the world over, full of dusty cinder paths, acres of drab brown-canvas tents, and the universal smell of the cookhouse. Loud-speakers droned out endless announcements with tired indifference, ending with a "That is all" and a sort of strangled hiccough as someone switched the transmission over to the radiogram, and everyone went on with his own particular boredom to the nostalgic monotony of the latest dance tunes.

I spent most of the time sitting in my tent reading "Henry the Fifth" and thinking that I would have been wiser to have brought "The Hunting of the Snark" with me. It was definitely not a moment for Shakespeare, and I had to give it up in the end. Then I relapsed into checking over all the items that were supposed to be in one's small pack. We were issued with an unbelievable number of toys for the occasion – two twenty-four-hour pack rations sealed in cardboard boxes with adhesive tape, an emergency ration looking like a tin of sardines and said to contain liquid chocolate, a tin of water-sterilizing tablets, a Tommy cooker, a tin of hexamine fuel, two bars of chocolate, a tin of cigarettes, and two vomit bags. I resented the two vomit bags, not because I am a good sailor but because it seemed a typical piece of Army over-thoroughness, offending to one's sense of the fitness of things, rather like those notices in buses threatening one with "The penalty for spitting is £5," and then in the next corner proclaiming "Prepare to Meet Thy God." Almost every contingency has been foreseen by the Army, and it generally goes to the trouble of producing "Notes for Officers" on the subject. The only thing missing is a contribution from the Chaplains' Branch "How to behave when dead" – perhaps they are a little uncertain about the matter.

We were supposed to spend only twenty-four hours in the marshalling area, but there were delays and it turned out much longer. Endlessly the sun beat down on the withered yellow grass, on and on droned the loud-speaker calling up the serials due for embarkation, but we, it seemed, were destined to wait for ever. All through the day and the night long columns of men with all their worldly belongings strapped on to them formed up on the dusty parade ground and one after another went marching out of the camp. The ceaseless move of serial after serial had been going on ever since D Day – it was like a waiting room on a gigantic scale.

It was curious to think of the men who had sat there on D Day; I suppose that with them also boredom had outlived any other emotions and now we thought of them as aged veterans, heroes of many battles; in imagination their ghostly presence gave an air of glamour to the camp. Naively I was really looking forward to the excitement.

We almost gave up listening to the loud-speaker and then at last it was our turn: "Attention, please, attention, please. All serial numbers will now parade at the south entrance to the camp, where transport is waiting. That is all."

Strangely unexpected; to drive to war in a lot of smart, red London buses, down streets full of people unconcernedly shopping or queuing for the evening cinema. And yet that was how it happened. I thought: "Ah, if only they knew what we are thinking," but in reality my ideas went no farther than to feel "What an incongruous background to one of the dramatic moments of life! I could quite easily hail a taxi and drive home."

At the Victoria Docks we all formed up inside a vast shed beside the quay and Charles Lambton, the Adjutant, called the roll to make sure that everyone was present. "Guardsman Smith guardsmansmith – guardsmansmith sang out the echoes.

"Here, sir!" … heresir-heresir-heresir came the reverberating reply.

After this Charles gave out the regulations to be followed on board ship.

"If the ship sinks" … sinks-sinks-sinks said something up in the roof, as if to emphasize the matter. "You will be told what to do" … do-do-do – it was a sort of personal argument with an acoustic genie, and to the end I never knew what it was that I should be told if the ship sank.

We climbed on board. It was all very undramatic, but there is a timeless sense of excitement about one's first few hours on a ship. At a theatre the first rise of the curtain is a similar sort of moment – the thrill never tires – it was more like setting forth upon a holiday than upon the Invasion of Europe, and as we moved slowly down the river in the evening I was almost ashamed at how much I was enjoying myself. We watched the dome of St. Paul's grow smaller and smaller behind crowded lines of derricks and a jumble of masts. I threw my remaining English money into the Thames in the hope that it might have some magic homing influence like the fabulous fountain at Trevi. Quite smoothly and painlessly we were at last under way.

In the morning we found ourselves still in the Estuary and lying off Southend with the other ships of the convoy. During the night the storms on the Normandy beaches had become worse, and as a result we sat there for five days, going slowly round on the anchor as the tide changed and the wind blew. The land was so close you could pick out the line of the hedgerows and white, ribbon-like roads running over the hills, but psychologically it was as remote as the past years of training and all one's other memories of England that seemed so suddenly to belong to another world. And when I thought back to the day that the Battalion was formed it was like dropping stones into a long-disused well, causing the surface to ripple with half-forgotten associations that had become almost fabulous in their distant unreality. What a long chain of events lay between the autumn of 1941 at Elstree and a ship in the Thames Estuary on D15! I remember, on the first day, Mark Howard standing in the yard behind the school calling out names from endless pages of returns and lists. Multitudes of unfamiliar faces – there was hardly anyone one didn't know now – and a grey, blustering, autumnal afternoon with the leaves racing around the empty football field and piling up against the red-bricked school buildings. Deacons Hill, Pennymeade and Abbotsbury – time almost brought enchantment to the names of our dingy billets. It was a long, cold winter, full of anti-invasion exercises, and the summer when it came was also rather cold. We moved down to Devon to confer fleeting immortality upon Ilfracombe; in particular I remember a night that we spent in a park where everything grew like a carboniferous forest – the owner believed in something that prevented her from cutting anything down or killing the rabbits which burrowed deeply all over the lawns and worried the golden pheasants – we slept under trees festooned with Florida moss and in places they grew so thickly that the living propped up the dead. Then there was an inn called "The Pack of Cards" and another called "The Fox and Goose" which brought more hilarious memories – we made a lot of noise there; perhaps it still echoed on in a ghostly sort of way. Soon afterwards we moved to Salisbury Plain and joined the Guards Armoured Division. There were so many exercises that the constant coming and going over the wilderness of the plain came to impress the names of all the endless little places we captured or defended on one's brain as though there really had been a battle for Tinker's Firs and an heroic defence of Point 109. First we were at Knook Gamp, then in billets at Mere, where we received the first jeep and Charles tried it out up the Castle Hill where in days gone by Hardy used to sit and meditate on the Wessex scenery. Sometimes we went farther afield to Dorset and Somerset, filling the Vale of Avalon with the din of tanks and the noise of our mock battles – did we, one wonders, disturb King Alfred on his hill? It was probably quiet enough once more by now. Then there was Singleton, in Sussex, where we used to go to fire on the ranges; the camp was inconceivably uncomfortable, but now I seem to remember more clearly how in the spring the hazel woods were full of primroses and wild anemones. It's odd how the boredom and fatigue of those endless exercises seem to have become forgotten so that in retrospect one is left with nothing but pleasing memories of the English countryside almost as though we had enjoyed it all, and yet in a way we did.

In the winter we took part in Exercise "Spartan," which was a gigantic Army operation. There really should have been a medal for "Spartan"; it was a terrible ordeal of sleepless nights and hardship. One paper gleefully wrote that realism had been greatly added to by the loss of ninety lives and was severely reprimanded by *The Times,* but now I cannot even recall which side won or anything else very much about it except that afterwards we moved to Hunstanton, in Norfolk, where there was more training as energetic as ever. In the intervals we swam in the sea or caught crabs among the mud-flats; even Brigadier John Marriot used to join in, complete with rolled-up trousers and red hat. Most of the beaches were mined and the pier was all covered with barbed wire, but only the very dull of heart could have failed to enjoy Hunstanton. Despite all the training, there was always time off for amusement. After dinner in the mess we sometimes rather fancied our powers of singing; I wonder if any of the songs caught on in the neighbourhood. Perhaps they were a bit too Rabelaisian? I doubt whether the inhabitants of "The Red Lion" (our Mess) ever sing of "Mary … covered all over in tissue paper, tissue paper, marmalade and jam … ."

Next we moved up to Yorkshire and lived a rather troglodytic existence in Nissen huts widely separated and inconveniently placed among the intricacies of dark, damp pine woods. It was a very uncomfortable winter and we spent a lot of it getting cold and wet out on the Wolds with an interlude in Scotland at Castle Toward, where we practised landing and all the other types of training that go under the heading of "combined operations."

"Bon!" said the commandant of the camp, and he then proceeded to tell us what the wild waves were saying. It didn't sound very encouraging and when we came to put it into practice, wading ashore through the winter's surf from an L.C.I.,[1] we found that he had not exaggerated. It was definitely not an occupation for January and we were pleased when the next move came, which brought us to comfortable billets at Scarborough. Scarborough was the beginning of things; it was there that the first "Top Secret" letters arrived, that we first heard of Operation "Overlord," and it was there that censorship began. We moved down to Eastbourne amid a cloud of secrecy and with the unhappy realization that whatever there was to be said for or against the days of training that were now a period of the past, it was too late to change anything: the final test for which we had waited so long was upon us. But even in the busy days at Eastbourne there was still time for enjoyment. It seemed to be one of the most incredibly lovely summers that there had ever been: the trees were billowing clouds of greenery and the hills waves that danced upon the ocean swell. My birthday and D Day coincided – perhaps it was to be the last birthday one would ever have, and so we celebrated the twin events at a little inn in the Cuckmere Valley, but D

---

1   Landing Craft Infantry

On Board 'The Empire Gladstone' being transported to Normandy. The Battalion landed on Arromanche Beach on the 20th June 1944.

Day somehow kept the limelight and it was altogether rather a solemn affair. Now, all these events seemed so remote we no longer thought of them in terms of "last week" or "last year," but as distant, nostalgic recollections almost as one thinks of childhood. There was certainly time enough for recollection.

Our ship, the *Empire Gladstone,* was a cargo vessel converted for carrying troops, but the changes were only very rough and ready, such as might be necessary for a twenty-four-hour voyage, and after a few days the problem of passing the time became very considerable. There were about three hundred of us and eighty vehicles on board; the larger half of the Battalion having gone by a different route, and a small party being left behind until a later date; but even so the crowding was inconceivable. Fifteen of us shared a cabin barely ten feet by ten feet and with only one wash-place, so that a good deal of organization was needed to make life comfortable, and our daily routine became a complicated ritual as to whose turn it was to shave or who had to make their bed first so as to fit into the prearranged pattern. The unvarying order of events produced that same curious feeling that one has in a school, a hospital, and for all I know a prison – the sense that one is living in a world quite separately and apart from the rest of mankind and ticking through life like a well-balanced clock predestined to record hour after hour with unchanging exactness and complete indifference as to what may make the hours lag or speed away for other people. And yet it was not unpleasant. When there was nothing else to do we lay on the decks absorbing sun, studied the other ships in the convoy, or slept. I thought that I had seen the last of England, but this was not so, and by a curious turn of circumstances my last contact with land was destined to be, of all improbable places, Southend Pier. The evening before we sailed I followed Colonel Sandy (Lieutenant-Colonel The Lord Stratheden, the Commanding Officer) down a swaying rope ladder into a waiting tug and we were taken off to a room at the tip of the pier to hear the convoy commanders briefed for the voyage. If the days of whelks and bank holidays return I think I shall have to make a dignified pilgrimage there and drink a glass of beer in the room where we listened with such foreboding to all the dangers and difficulties that lay ahead of the convoy.

Whatever the potential dangers of the crossing, the actual voyage was a serenely untroubled affair. We passed quietly through the Straits during the night, at about midday we saw the last of the shores of England, and towards four o'clock we began to catch the first glimpses of the Normandy coastline. Within half an hour the faint outline of land, like a bank of mist with its cluster of pin-sized barrage balloons and miniature smudges of smoke, had come to take on the full appearance of "Gold Beach," with an armada of shipping lying off it that beggared all description. One might as well have tried to count the trees of a forest as get any idea of how many ships there were there. Towering over everything else in the anchorage, the doyen of the proceedings, was the *Rodney*, and everything in size and shape between it and a rowing-boat was represented in one form or another. There were cruisers, destroyers, corvettes, submarines and, more numerous than anything else, a vast assortment of landing craft. The sunken block-ships of the "Mulberry" harbour were already in position and the huge sections of the floating harbour were beginning to be assembled. Along the beaches one could just pick out the wrecks of a few amphibious vehicles that had been knocked out on D Day, and behind that the line of the hills that we had picked out earlier on – a low, gently rising lump of land with many hedgerows and straggling villages. It might have been Somerset. When it got dark we went to bed and there was an air raid. The next morning we got up while it was still dark; distant guns boomed away over the horizon, lighting up the line of the hills with a constant flicker of illumination. We stamped about in the cold trying to keep warm, and for the first time I was beginning to feel that perhaps it was not going to be quite so easy to go into battle as I had imagined. The sound of the far-away barrage bore an unmistakable suggestion: "It is the knell that summons thee to heaven or to hell." The intrusion that it made upon my breakfast of sausages and bacon was most unwelcome – definitely the uninvited guest. Perhaps it was the hour of the morning? Later in the day one might have found it exhilarating.

Much later than we had expected a party of Pioneers in L.C.Ts.[2] arrived to off-load our vehicles. They came clambering up the side of the ship in stocking caps like so many pirates and intimated that the less we tried to help the quicker things would go. I went off on the first L.C.T. to be loaded so as to try to get ahead to our area outside Bayeux in case it had been changed and to warn the other half of the Battalion which we expected to be already there of our imminent arrival. The L.C.T. touched the bottom about fifty yards out from the beach. Not a soul was to be seen anywhere; then a solitary figure in bathing shorts stood up in the shallows and came wading out to us. He said that there was about three feet of water in front of us and we would have to wait until the tide changed before we could reach the shore without swamping the vehicles. It was not

---

2   Landing Craft Tank.

at all what I had expected; dimly remembered training had prepared me for a whole hierarchy of people whom one expected to encounter on the beach and were said to regulate disembarkation. Countless pamphlets had stressed the importance of not holding things up and getting unloaded as fast as possible. I said that all our vehicles were properly waterproofed; it was unthinkable to hold up the unloading of the ship while the tide changed, and that anyway we had often tried them out in three feet before. In the end it was decided to try the first vehicle, which was a carrier. As it drove off the ramp into the sea I had a nasty feeling that it was going to be completely swamped, but all was well and we got off all the others without difficulty after it.

It was the 25th of June; we had been on our ship for a week, but it seemed much longer and not even Noah descending from the Ark can have looked upon the land with more eager curiosity. After the short belt of minefields and destruction along the foreshore we found ourselves heading for Bayeux on a road jammed to capacity with vehicles edging slowly along behind each other. In the fields on either side straw-hatted, blue-smocked Frenchmen were raking in the hay; and in Bayeux the normal pattern of any provincial French town seemed to be going on uninterrupted, only the constant streams of military traffic suggesting that there was a war on. There were plenty of divisional signs up to point out the way, and two miles farther on – delighted and relieved – I saw our own "Sixty-one" sign pointing into a hayfield. We had arrived.

I found Michael Willoughby, who had gone with the other half of the Battalion, sitting in the inevitable Normandy orchard under an inevitable Normandy apple tree. It was all very idyllic, and to mark the occasion I decided to make myself a meal out of the twenty-four- hour pack ration. It was all dehydrated stuff and I crumbled up about five different items with the idea of making a stew, but the result was disastrous. I never tried to be my own cook again.

We had two days in which to sample the Normandy of peace, and our discoveries can all very conveniently be summed up with the words "cream," "butter," "Camembert cheese," "artichokes," "cider" and "Calvados." After that we changed to the Normandy of war, and the contrast was startlingly and horrifyingly different.

"Baptism of fire" is a very apt expression. When you have never been in action an undefinable something seems to differentiate the experienced from the uninitiated almost as though a knowledge of war were some secret rite, and nothing that one can do in preparation or read into the accounts of others can wholly prepare one or convey the effect of the reality. It was particularly disturbing to sit one morning in a field marking up positions on the map as I had done so often on exercises with the realization that half an hour's drive would turn them into the inexorable life-and-death facts of battle, all the more startlingly evident by the very fact that so much of it was a routine I had followed so often and with such careless indifference and safety in the past.

I drove off in the scout car with the Commanding Officer and the "O" Group following us through Bayeux and then down the road to Caen. The first few miles were ordinary enough; then we came to the first war-destroyed village. Four years of blitz had accustomed one to ruins, but this was something different. Everything still lay in an extreme of disorder: household goods, doors, window frames, furniture, rubble and burnt-out vehicles were all mixed up in an incredible flotsam and jetsam of battle that

The Battalion on the move, somewhere in Normandy. The Guards Armoured Division sign can just be made out on the Bren carrier.

was strewn down every street. Nothing had been cleared up, for there was no one to do it, no owners to salvage what remained of their belongings, and no fire brigades to put out the smouldering fires. Every house was shell-torn, every roof a sort of crazy lacework of holes and collapse, and the pounded mortar formed a thick, white dust that lay over everything like a mantle of snow. At Bretteville l'Orgueilleuse we turned right off the main road where a signpost still proclaimed "Visitez l'eglise de Norrey en bessin. Miracle de XVIeme siecle," but when we passed it nothing remained but a finger of masonry more Gothic than its author ever dreamt.

We crested a slight rise in the ground and far away across the cornfields we could see the desolate hangars of Carpiquet aerodrome that was held by the Germans. I thought that something would be bound to fire at us, but nothing happened and we drove on down into the village of St. Mauvieux that we were to take over. It was very hot. The sun beat down on the dust-whitened ruins of the farmhouses and the flattened cornfields, producing a dazzling glare. The sickening stench of putrefying animals and corpses hung in the stillness like the Angel of Death. At first there seemed to be nobody about, but then we discovered the command post of the Wiltshires through a hole in the wall. Their commanding officer said that we would almost certainly be shelled and that we had better distribute ourselves between their various slit trenches while we discussed the take-over.

I sat in a trench with their intelligence officer. He said that they had only just come into action twenty-four hours before and that the whole thing was hell. They'd lost half of their company commanders already. The enemy opposite were the Adolf Hitler S.S. Division and they went in for sniping a lot. I would be well advised to remove my badges of rank, as the officers were definitely being picked out. At that moment they were clearing the village of Marcelet on the edge of the aerodrome, after which they would be more than glad to clear out and leave it all to us.

We sat there amid an air of uneasy expectancy; then suddenly I heard a distant umph, umph, umph, umph. Everyone in the open scuttled into trenches and something came singing through the air with a high-pitched "eeeeeee" that ended in a sort of angry "ssst" and a CRRUMP, CRRUMP, CRRUMP, CRRUMP, as four shells landed in the field just behind us. More came over, landing all round us. And even though the fragments went sizzling over our heads the deafening detonation of each shell seemed to have a force that nothing could stop and the concussions hit you almost as though the shell had been right on top of one. It was the most frightening thing that ever happened to me. I didn't want to die just then, just like that, and to sit there seemed to be like a sentence of death. The air was full of smoke and

Marcelet, near Carpriquet Airfield, late June, in contact with the enemy for the first time.

fumes. Someone shouted out for stretcher-bearers, and a more lightly wounded man went limping away towards the R.A.P. with another man helping him along. His ashen-white face streamed with sweat and he looked as though the shock had left him half-unconscious groping for he knew not what. Grimly we went on discussing the position. I was surprised to find that I could mark up the map with a steady hand; it was not at all a reflection of how I felt.

It was the most unpleasant day that I ever lived through. In retrospect the shelling was not as bad as many places we were in, but at the time every step down the sun-drenched lanes seemed to be haunted by the waiting tension between each stonk. At first we hardly knew the difference between the sound of our own guns firing and the Germans. I thought: This is barely endurable for a day; how can I go on for months and months? After a few days we learnt to recognize the sound of the German shells and could judge more or less where they were arriving. You can get used to something which is going to miss you, but a direct stonk is different: you can hardly become accustomed to a noise that may at any moment herald your death. If anything, as one gained in experience one's nerves seemed gradually to become less resilient under the strain, but the first day was the worst. After that I knew I wouldn't become bomb-happy, which was perhaps one's worst fear. In a defensive position like that there was little enough to do, but living in the open is a strain, constantly waiting for the next shell to arrive is a strain, and eventually imagination begins to run riot. In the end something gives. The modern doctor has stopped referring to "shell shock" and calls it an "extreme terror state," which is true enough; it isn't always a shell which actually starts people off. We had several cases in those first few days. There is something horrifyingly grotesque about seeing a sane individual suddenly turn into a gibbering idiot shaken by an uncontrollable hysteria. Confidence, morale and a certain amount of individual psychology are the safeguards against bomb-happiness, but, like all things in war, we had to learn this for ourselves and it required experience to give us the answers. I think it was easier for the officers than for the men; we had too much to do, and too much to think about, to become a prey to our imaginations. It was the long days of exposure in slit trenches open to the sun and the rain and the intense cold at nights that wore people down, and when you are physically exhausted it is only a small step on to nervous exhaustion.

Of the Germans we saw very little. One might peer out across the empty aerodrome for hours on end and see no one, or perhaps occasionally someone might run indiscreetly from trench to trench and there were some tanks that we now and then caught sight of, but on the whole they kept themselves very well hidden and we only knew where they were by patrolling. There were continual rumours that they had withdrawn and on these occasions we used to send out a few carriers to draw their fire. It nearly always worked, after which we would shell the place for a quarter of an hour or so. But the shelling probably did little damage, as the aerodrome was honeycombed with underground passages that they could shelter in which were partially the key to their invisibility. There was little of our position that could be seen by them, but it was easy enough to make good guesses, and I believe that they had a shrewd idea where our headquarters was.

After we had been there a week the Canadians attacked Carpiquet. It was a very large-scale attack supported by four hundred and twenty-eight guns and H.M.S. *Rodney*. Over eighty thousand shells were fired, and we had to change our positions to keep out of the way, as the Canadian start line coincided with a part of our area. Despite all this, it was a very costly attack and the fighting went on all around us for the next forty-eight hours, but once Carpiquet fell Caen was assured. It lay in the valley below and from some places we could even see the spire of Caen Cathedral sticking up behind the hill. Caen was captured a few days later, and by that time our position had become a backwater behind the lines. On the 11th of July we moved to a rest area at St. Martin-les-Entrees, just outside Bayeux. The 32nd Brigade which we were in was the only part of the Division which took part in the goings on before the capture of Caen, as the 5th Brigade, comprising the tanks of the Division, had only just arrived and we related our experiences of action to them almost as though we had been fighting all our lives. To people who inquired "What was it like at St. Mauvieux?" Guardsman Payne, the unofficial Battalion wit, coined the answer: "Oh, a very quiet place. All you ever heard was cries of *another stretcher!*"

NORMANDY

OPERATION "GOODWOOD" was an extensive affair; it involved several divisions, a large portion of the R.A.F. and the long and considered attention of Second Army Headquarters. Originally a minor breakout from the bridgehead was considered, but at this time the Germans were still reinforcing and building up their strength and eventually the more modest plan of enlarging the bridgehead south-east of Caen and generally discomfiting the enemy was adopted. Final results were even more modest than the revised plans, but the whys and wherefores of this belong to the role of higher tactics which I hope to steer carefully clear of, except when an occasional explanation cannot be avoided.

We spent the afternoon of the 18th in our orchard just off the main road by St. Martin les Entrees. It was a hot and sultry afternoon and we sat under the shade of the apple trees studying endless air photographs and planning how we would defend the various possible objectives that we had been given for the next day, none of which, incidentally, were ever reached by us, but in those days we were new to the game and firm believers in that mystical pre-battle performance known as planning. Dutifully we marked our

Major General Alan Adair, commander of the Guards Armoured Division briefing before Operation Goodwood.

maps with a series of meaningless traces designed to help us follow the cross-country route to Pegasus Bridge and the Orne River; studiously we studied every feature of the way down "Bomb Alley" between Couverville, Demouville, Touffreville and Sannerville (an unhappy little avenue of villages to be obliterated by the Air Force on the morrow so as to secure the flanks of the armoured sweep), and finally, primed with an immense amount of information that proved of no value, we rolled ourselves up in blankets and tried to get some sleep.

Trying to sleep at six o'clock in the evening is never very successful and eventually most of us gave up the idea altogether and loitered away the time until we were due to start by paying visits on the companies and having drinks with each other. I can't remember at what time we did leave, but by then it had become pitch dark and most of the drivers had gone to sleep; and therefore, although we had taken the precaution of parking all the vehicles so that they would be able to get away in correct order without sticking in the ditches, we had to do a great deal of shouting and shaking to get everyone on the move and by the time the whole Battalion column was under way everyone was feeling very ill-tempered. We couldn't, of course, use our headlights so that in the darkness of the night about all you could see ahead was the small, red tail-lamp of the vehicle in front swaying up and down over the bumps with hypnotic regularity. After the first ten minutes my driver ran into the parapet of a bridge; then a few moments afterwards he ran into a telegraph pole and announced that he suffered from night blindness, but by this time the whole column had come to a halt, so while another driver took over I walked up to the company ahead of us to see what was causing the delay.

Raymond Hubbard (the Brigade Liaison Officer) was at the head of the column and in a great state of excitement. Was there a squadron of the 2nd Welsh mixed up in our column? We hoped there wasn't. Well, there must be; they ought to be ahead of us, but they hadn't arrived; we would have to halt and let them pass. We protested that we couldn't, as we were in a very narrow stretch of road and there wouldn't be room. However, the argument was all rather in vain, as by this time the squadron had arrived and was already trying to push its way past us of its own accord. By dint of driving all our own vehicles into the ditch the tanks were eventually squeezed past us with a great deal of scraping and cursing and general ill-will. Then on we went. It was one of the most interminable journeys I've ever made. Mile after mile we crawled at snail's pace across fields, down narrow lanes, and over every conceivable type of bump and rut. The armoured half-track that I was in groaned and squeaked and rattled like a ship in a rough sea. Clouds of dust rose up all around us, making the night even darker than before and filling one's lungs with grit and petrol fumes. As dawn broke we reached a large hillside just short of the Orne, and I seized the opportunity to curl myself up in my seat and go to sleep.

I don't know how literally one is meant to take the admonition about "be not solicitous for tomorrow," but for my part I have always accepted it as it stood, with the result that in my whole war-time experience I never dug myself a trench, cooked a meal or brewed a cup of tea; these things just happened for me. When I woke up, the driver had a cup of hot tea ready for me, and some extremely cold and congealed bacon and beans. Someone else produced a tin of bully and some biscuits. Sergeant Westmacott (the Mess Sergeant) arrived with the chocolate and cigarette ration, and thus was solved the food problem.

As the last stars faded from the pale-blue sky and the landscape took on its colour of light-brown plough and yellow cornfields, the bombers came over to start the attack. It turned out to be one of the most useless pieces of destruction among many of this war. Few or no Germans were killed, but half a dozen harmless villages were obliterated, and a great number of civilians killed. Did it help the attack? It can't have helped much, as the 11th Armoured Division, who were in the lead, lost practically every tank they possessed and by the evening the Germans could claim to have knocked out over two hundred. The infantry got left far behind the armoured forces so that they couldn't be used when they were most needed in support of the tanks, and the results were far from satisfactory. This was the last of the great cavalcade of armour and a very costly one at that, but fortunately for us we were following up, not leading, and the Division had comparatively light casualties.

The day didn't go very well; it was far behind schedule by the time the 11th Armoured Division were sufficiently far on for our Armoured Brigade to move, and by the time we were ordered forward it was nearly midday. The day got hotter and hotter. Some German long- range guns shelled a little cluster of vehicles in the cornfields behind us. Idly we watched someone else going up in smoke, then started up and wound our way slowly down to the Orne. We crossed the famous Pegasus Bridge, passed through some very battered villages, passed big cross-roads, passed another village – a horrid idea was coming into my mind, another quarter of a mile and it wasn't an idea. I knew it: we were off our route. We had an elaborate *post-mortem* over the map, while everyone pleaded that in their innocence they had but followed the vehicle in front, and, anyway, they were quite sure the turning south wasn't marked or they wouldn't have missed it; but then the first few vehicles weren't ahead of us, so they must have found the right turning, added to which this was obviously not "the way to the battle." It was too hot and dusty to argue anymore, so eventually we agreed that it was just "one of those things" and started to turn the column back down the road again. When we eventually got on to the right route and re-joined the front bit of the Battalion we discovered that they were held up again and, anyway, hadn't noticed our unfortunate mishap, so that all was well.

By tea-time we found ourselves on the top of a hill overlooking Couverville and here we received orders to disperse off the road and prepare for a long wait. To the south of our hill the route ahead stretched out in one endless flatness, acres of cornfield and grass studded with little islands of greenery and houses that were villages. A very parched landscape it was, and rapidly turning to the monotonous, dun-coloured sameness of the clouds of dust that rose up from every road and track as the columns of vehicles slowly edged forward after the advancing battle. Added to the dust and haze of heat there were a great many fires burning. Houses that had been set on fire by the fighting, knocked-out tanks still smouldering away, and smoking wreckage on every scale from whole villages in flames to burning trucks and private fires that someone had lit to make themselves a cup of tea.

We felt very naked on our hillside; in fact, we were very naked and after a short while some shells started arriving in our area. It was one of those moments when no one feels really enthusiastic about digging in, as we were going to move on in due course. However, an order was sent round that everyone would dig in, so that was that, but not quite, as I managed to get the job of manning the rear-link wireless set in the half-track, which absolved me from digging. The heat in the back was almost unbearable, far hotter than the cactus-house at Kew, but on the whole it was preferable to digging a trench and I had the time to eat some bully and biscuits, though it was not a very appetizing meal, as the bully was by now almost liquefied and made me extremely thirsty – an uncatered-for contingency, as on principle I never carried a water-bottle.

At about tea-time we were ordered to move on again, pass through the minefield gap and go on as far as Demouville. "The minefield gap" part rather worried us, as we'd heard little about a minefield and still less about a gap; it was clear from the well-worn route ahead which way everyone else had gone and we presumed that in due course we should find the gap.

Before we moved off, I had a long dispute with Bunty Stewart Brown, our Second-in-Command, as to which of us should sit in the back of the half-track. Bunty said that it was my turn to be cool in front. I swore that I still hadn't done my fair share in the back; however, we spun a coin and I sat in the front. As it turned out, I owe my life to that coin.

Going through the minefield gap was far from pleasant, for, although we may have been ignorant about it, the Germans were well aware of it and as soon as we began driving through, they started to put down a most unnerving series of shots all around it. In the halftrack there is a certain amount of armour plating on either side, so that one is not worried by anything except a very close shot, but for the companies in completely unarmoured and extremely exposed T.C.Ls.[3] it must have been an agonizing ten minutes.

When we reached Demouville we found some of the Rifle Brigade creeping about from house to house, who told us that Germans were still holding out in the front of the village, which was not at all what we had expected, and No. 4 Company had to be hastily debussed to deal with the situation. While this was being done the Germans decided to shell the village. Two shells landed just in front of the halftrack, one of them right into a T.C.L. full of men, and then suddenly there was a deafening explosion and I found myself enveloped in dust and smoke. As the dust and clatter of slates from the house beside us subsided I shouted out: "Are you all right in the back?"

I could hardly have made a more stupid remark. It was obvious what had happened.

"No, sir; we've all been hit," came the answer.

---

3   Troop-carrying lorries.

The first man we got out had a nasty wound in the face. He was still quite conscious when we laid him in the ditch, but he didn't seem to feel anything at all – just sat there murmuring like a gramophone record: "Cor, what a do! ... Cor, what a do!" Bunty was unconscious and had been very badly wounded in the head; already his face had assumed that yellow pallor one associates with the dying and we never expected him to live as long as he did. The wireless operator was dead.

It was a costly incident and as soon as we could we backed all the vehicles out of the narrow village street into the more open fields behind.

I had no sooner got myself disentangled from Demouville when down the road came streams of prisoners in twos and threes. This is one of the things that eventually happen in every battle and are an intelligence officer's ever-recurring nightmare, as everyone automatically comes to the firm conclusion that the intelligence officer is the only person who can conceivably deal with the matter, and the unfortunate intelligence officer knows only too well that the situation is even in the best of circumstances only half-soluble.

The first step is to start shouting and gesticulating, preferably in German; this impresses the prisoners with the fact that you intend to do something about them. Next seize hold of the first three you can get and line them up side by side in the direction you want them all eventually to go; finally pick out a non-commissioned officer and murmur some parrot-phrase about forming up the remainder to him. You then have to move hurriedly on in case he asks a question and discovers that you can't really speak German at all. If all goes well, in a short while you have a neatly formed column all ready to march off. The formula works perfectly with any number from fifty to five hundred. If you are lucky the intelligence sergeant arrives at this stage and can start the process of counting, searching and recording their units, so that one is free to tackle the insoluble problem of getting a guard for them and the even more insoluble problem of whom they are finally to be dumped on. This may all sound very simple, and theorists will say that every unit ought to have some simple and elastic drill ready worked out to meet these occasions. Personally, I've never found that on any one occasion the circumstances permitted one to do the same things, and to the end of the war "what to do with prisoners" remained an unsolved nuisance.

By the time I had disposed of the prisoners we at last received our final orders. The armoured battle was drawing to a close with the capture of the village of Cagny, and we were to take up a position to the east of it.

Michael Willoughby came up to replace Bunty and together we set off to find a suitable site for Battalion Headquarters about a quarter of a mile short of Cagny while the companies debussed and marched up to their positions in the outskirts of the village.

Other people's battles always appear very confused, and the scene outside Cagny was no exception. The fields all around us were full of tanks churning about like herds of absent-minded elephants, and as far as one could make out some sort of battle was still in progress. Every now and then a tank would fire a shot at the distant woods to the left of Cagny. This would then start all the other tanks firing and a renewed series of manoeuvrings would begin all over again like an elaborate quadrille. What they were firing at I never found out, but it seemed a good idea, as at intervals a couple of German 88's would fire back ...ssst-bang, ssst-bang ... a disconcerting and ear-splitting noise that one never feels very happy about, as the whole thing is generally too fast for you to duck or jump into a ditch, added to which the A.P.[4] shots which are unlikely to hit anyone on their feet are liable to be mixed with air bursts which are a very different matter.

We had great difficulty in finding anyone who could tell us exactly what was happening, but eventually I found the Grenadier intelligence officer and together we swapped news and managed to make some sort of orderly picture out of the apparent chaos.

All this time I'm glad to say everyone else had been busy digging-in Battalion Headquarters, because as I was walking back one of the German 88's found its mark and hit a lorry, which immediately burst into flames. Within a few seconds the flames had spread to another lorry just by our command post, upon which everyone softly and suddenly vanished – it was the ammunition truck.

In theory one always feels that burning ammunition should go up in one sudden and cataclysmic bang; in practice nothing so convenient happens, and Michael and I in the command post were virtually imprisoned in our trench for the greater part of half an hour while the wretched thing burnt itself out. The performance opens with a great deal of crackling and popping as the small-arms ammunition explodes; then when things get properly alight the larger types of ammunition start to detonate, sending out a perfect hail of flying metal and burning pieces, rather on the blunderbuss principle. All this is interspersed by high-grade Guy Fawkes displays as boxes of Very lights or coloured smoke explode. By the time the fire had burnt itself down to safe dimensions of a rather vindictive bonfire the darkness was coming on and we began to prepare for the night.

---

4   Armour-piercing.

The Commanding Officer, Lt Colonel The Lord Stratheden, with Captain and Adjutant Charles Lambton.

As soon as I could free myself from the interminable chatter and messages coming over on the wireless I went off into the gloaming to find my intelligence truck and make arrangements for sleeping. Stumbling about in the cornfield I eventually saw a shape, solitary and motionless like a megalithic stone. "Is that you, Hobman?"

"Yes, sir. Your bed is all ready and made … ." He might just as well have said my grave. Like myself, Hobman, my orderly, was never very enthusiastic with a spade, and usually managed to under-estimate my length, so that I always had to fit myself into my slit trench rather like a corpse into too short a coffin, and once lowered beneath the ground the sensation was very much like I imagine a corpse feels.

"How are you fixed up – all right?"

"Oh, I'm all right, sir. You'll find me by that hedge just in front of the truck. Anything else you'll want tonight?"

"No, thank you. I'll be going round the companies at stand-to so I won't want any hot water until after breakfast. After that I shall probably want you and the truck to go back to Brigade Headquarters. Good-night."

"Good-night, sir."

After explaining to the duty officer how to find me in the night if necessary, I came back to my trench and got into bed, a very simple process, as my bed consisted of a mackintosh groundsheet laid on the bottom, then myself covered by a greatcoat, then a gas cape to keep off the dew, and finally a great deal of earth from the side of the trench which came in uninvited.

From the bottom I gazed upward at the sky, a rectangular patch of darkness framed by the side of the trench, and periodically lit up by gunfire, which caused the blackness above me to flicker, as with summer lightning when the more distant batteries fired, or suddenly to blaze with violet and orange light as something close at hand occurred. At times one seemed to be listening to a sort of orchestra of thunder; each noise having a meaning, place and purpose within the whole: the distant rumble-rumble drum-fire of a big programme being fired some five miles away, the closer, sharper "thump" from our own gun areas, and the occasional whine of a shell going the wrong way. But it was a quiet night with long intervals of almost unusual stillness, and, lying cramped in the bottom of my slit trench, my mind soon became detached from the endless quest of "What was that?" and I fell asleep. Almost immediately, it seemed, someone woke me up. Said it was 2 a.m. and my turn to take over at the command post.

"Are you sure you're awake?"

"Yes, absolutely sure. Anything happening?"

"No; it couldn't be quieter. Don't be long."

The figure vanished. I stirred in my trench, my grave with its air of "memento mori." At the back of my mind the associations revived the words of the Mass on Ash Wednesday ... "Memento, homo, quia pulvis est et in pulverem reverteris ... ." Was this some sudden consciousness of an elusive truth or was I being funny about it? I wasn't sure; divested of my greatcoat the night air seemed to take hold of every limb I possessed and shake me like an ague. Hurriedly I buckled on my revolver, fished for my cap, then stumbled over to the command post.

The command post is merely a rather larger and grander trench than the others; designed so that one can sit in it for comparatively long periods at a stretch without being overcome by claustrophobia or cramp. This particular model was L-shaped, one half being occupied by a signaller with the wireless set, the telephone exchange, and all the paraphernalia of signalling, while the other half was for the duty officer, who sits on a little ledge of earth and has the business end of the all-too-numerous assortment of headphones, telephones, etc. A canvas tarpaulin pulled over the top to hide the light completes things. The fog inside is as thick as a London fog, yet just as unwarming. And when, as eventually it must, one's small talk with the signaller dries up there is the incessant and maddeningly persistent noise of the wireless as company and commentary upon the endlessness of the hours. Most of the time one's headphones merely go zzzzzz-crackle- crackle-zzzz-crackle, etc., but at times they become suddenly animated into a quite different and even more tiresome sort of commentary that goes da di da di da di da di and so *ad infinitum.*

"Try renetting."

"Interference very bad tonight, sir; doubt if it'll do much good." Corporal Lyons was never a believer in anything doing much good.

"Try just giving them a call."

"Hullo, Oboe One. Report my signals. Oboe One over." Over the air from Brigade Headquarters comes the voice of Michael Rosse (the 32nd Brigade Intelligence Officer): "Hullo, Oboe One. O.K.; over." It's extraordinary what an essence of personality is conveyed by someone's voice on the wireless: the familiar tones suddenly fill me with a desire to be chatty, a practice frowned upon by the pundits of wireless procedure, but it passes the time. "Hullo, Oboe One. How are things going? Any news, Oboe One? Over."

"Not sending, sir. Give your mike a shake, it's got something wrong with it."

I try again after much shaking and tapping of the microphone. "Hullo, Oboe One. How are things going? Any news, Oboe One? Over."

"Good evening, my dear Acorn. No, no news; everything very quiet. Over."

"Hullo, Oboe One. I think I shall come over and visit you tomorrow, have you anything to drink, over."

"Hullo, Oboe One. I shall be delighted. I've got some maps for you if you'd like to fetch them at the same time. Over."

"O.K. Can I have the air photos too? Over."

"Hullo, Oboe One; very bad interference. What was it you said you wanted?"

"Hullo, Oboe One. I say again, air photos. Over."

"Hullo, Oboe One. Nothing heard; say again. Over."

I scream into the microphone: "I say again, air photos. Over!" "Hullo, Oboe One. Someone keeps cutting in. Say again. Over." Almost apoplectic I shout: "Hullo Oboe One. I say again, ABLE ITEM ROGER ... photos, Oboe One. Over!"

It's no good; the conversation becomes increasingly disconnected and has to be abandoned, as do so many wireless conversations. The genii of the ether resume their chatter zzzzz-crackle-crackle-zzzz; unknown voices on a different net call after unknown "Item sixes" and "Uncle niners" like absent-minded muezzins. Nobody answers. The hours creep by while I re-mark my map in six new ways, each more startling than the previous. Corporal Lyons finished the last chapter of "The Lady with a Mask." I won't look at my watch again because I looked at it five minutes ago. I know what time it must be: its 5 a.m., time of stand-to. Another day has begun.

Most of the morning was spent going round the companies with the Commanding Officer; then in the afternoon the Welsh Guards put in an attack on a little village just south of Cagny which proved to be practically unheld; in fact, all around us the enemy, who had seemed the day before to be so close in on us, were curiously silent, as if not there at all. We were much happier and expanded from our trenches like butterflies to take the sun and drink a little whisky. We sat about on empty packing cases discussing the strategy of the battle in an offhand way and generally rising to the stimulus of not being bothered. Then to our dismay Colonel Sandy arrived back from Brigade Headquarters with the news that we were to put in an attack at dawn the next day to capture the high ground east of Cagny and the village of Frenouville.

By this time we felt we knew all about defence and the dangers of taking over a position from another battalion – how much more dangerous was it going to be taking over a position from Germans? My heart sank and had to be revived by more whisky. I remember the whisky, as, in the ensuing rush to collect maps, warn Sergeant Todd (the Intelligence Sergeant) of some necessary preparations, and board the scout car with Colonel Sandie, my only bottle was irrevocably lost for all time.

Our start line was to be behind a small track running south from Cagny parallel to the village of Frenouville about half a mile away from us and mostly hidden by a rise in the ground. Behind the track there was a high stone wall and a narrow belt of trees surrounding what had once been a paddock but was now cratered and battered beyond recognition. In one place a bomb had dug a gigantic hole, nearly fifty feet across, and while Colonel Sandie took a quick preview at the inscrutable countryside we were to attack over I assembled the "O" Group in the crater. It was a large "O" Group, as, besides the company commanders, we had a multitude of supporting arms, each with a representative present – S.P. anti-tank guns, 17-pounders,

George Mackean, Support Company commander at Frénouville after Operation Goodwood

Frénouville, captured by the Battalion on 19/20thJuly. 1944

a troop of tanks, a section of R.E. with petards, a section of the field ambulance, a gunner officer, representative from a medium battery, and others besides.

By the time everyone had received their orders it was getting dark, and time to hurry back to pass on the plan of attack and make all the final preparations. We were to attack at first light, which, to allow for the time taken in getting everything together and marching to the start line, would involve starting the day at about 3.30 a.m.

Before a battle I always feel a little like a man about to have his appendix out. There is an unhappy sensation of sudden isolation before the rather frightening and unknowable ordeal to come. Anxiety – or, to be honest, fear – is something that you cannot share with anybody, however much they may be feeling the same way, and I'm sure that were anyone able to discuss the matter they would be of the opinion that there is no consolation in a mass execution versus a solitary death. The powers of detachment are heightened so that the mind seems to hover almost separated from the bustle and activity of the body, and one is filled with a rather factitious affability as though bursts of conversation could exorcise the unwelcome sense of isolation that has come upon one. At the same time it's rather pleasing to be able to escape to "Distant Self," who is able to speculate so dispassionately about what "Less Confident and Happy Self" will be doing this time tomorrow.

"Dear me; I suppose this time tomorrow he'll be sitting in Frenouville; or won't he? I wonder if anyone knows or cares just what he's thinking of – of course, they don't – but what fools. How interesting it is to uncover the very foundations of his superficial soul, his last and final dispositions, his hopes and fears! Who would miss the Olympian view of everything that is best and worst in mankind shown off to such dramatic advantage?"

"I may very possibly be killed – oh, intimate, subtle and revealing thought!" Some unknown sixth sense becomes activated by the stimulant so that everything is just slightly altered and strikes one with a curious significance that was invisible before as though some new lightning device were focused upon processes of one's emotions.

And all those who are not taking part in the attack the next day – is it imagination or do their faces express a whimsical question-mark which only tomorrow can answer: "I wonder if they'll come through all right? I expect they'll be all right. Poor old So-and-so; I hope he doesn't get killed." They appear to be a little more helpful, a little more courteous, than usual, as though dealing with someone who has just suffered a bereavement; on no account must the indecent nakedness of the soul become exposed at this embarrassing moment.

Distant Self says: "Of course he'd give anything to get out of it if he could. He'll possibly cling to any possibilities of cancellation like a leech, but, then, in the end I expect he rather enjoys thinking what a hero he's going to make of himself when it is safely over. He shouldn't be deprived of that at least."

But whatever the introspective and X-ray researches of Distant Self may reveal, the body of Grosser Self knows the value of having all feet on the ground – the importance of getting everything tied up before the morning and that sleep is the most precious of all gifts that the good god Morale has to give to soldiers.

I believe that traditionally those whose job it is to waken condemned men on the fatal morning are supposed to say: "Come, Mr. X, be brave; your time has come," or words to that effect.

I was woken by Hobman saying: "It's half-past three, sir, and beginning to rain."

I don't believe there is anything more terrible than having to wake up in war time – to have to face horrible reality when one's mind is still half-conscious and so ready to take refuge again in sleep. The agonizing seconds while everything seems to say: "Cling to illusion for just five minutes more, just five minutes' oblivion to blot out this monstrous world of discomfort and misery. You'll be finished once you get up, you can't help yourself then. Why not rest a little longer; why surrender yourself to everything you fear and detest when you can escape in sleep?" I never achieved the art of being "suddenly alert." It was always like a ghost being tortured for the umphty-umpth night, only on some new and slightly bewildering rack.

Steel helmet, belt and revolver, map case, binoculars; everything present. I made a rather dazed journey to the command post and found Michael Adeane there on duty. He became Second-in-Command when Bunty Stewart Brown was wounded, and as it was the general practice to leave the Second-in-Command behind during a battle he was a convenient person to saddle with the task of manoeuvring the command post while everyone else rested. He produced some Calvados, which he kindly offered me, as people do on these occasions. It brought tears to our eyes, as if to make up for our lack of emotion at such a time. Fortified, I felt eager to say something like:

"Nature I loved, and, next to Nature, Art;

I warmed both hands before the fire of life;

It sinks, and I am ready to depart."

But all I could remember was the last line, and I had an uneasy desire to change "sinks" to "stinks." There was nothing to be done but say: "Well, I must be going now; *au revoir*," and stumble out to marshal Battalion Headquarters together.

Outside I found Gerald Style, our Signals Officer, and together we checked up that everyone was present, then stood by the roadside watching the companies march by and waiting to slip into our place in the column. The long cavalcade went trudging past, section by section, platoon by platoon, all very heavily laden with the paraphernalia of war: men carrying Bren guns, men carrying wireless sets, stretcher-bearers, men carrying 2-inch mortars and ammunition, all barely distinguishable one from another in the darkness. The last platoon passed by and we followed along behind, down the road to Cagny. At the far end everyone spread out across the paddock in their appropriate places; the timing was perfect: there was hardly any time to wait for H Hour. I detached myself from Battalion Headquarters and found Colonel Sandy.

A few minutes to go. We consulted our watches and made comments about the light. The dawn had come up fast; it was going to be just about right with some mist to help things. A minute to go; the leading companies started to pick up their belongings and edge towards the start line. Then with a great rodomontade of noise the guns opened up and the first shells of our barrage went whistling overhead. We watched No. 2 Company scramble through the hedgerow along the start line and advance up the hill towards Frenouville, with No. 4 Company over on their right. As they came to the end of the first field a shell fell short, right in the middle of a section. The company slowly vanished into the mist, leaving the field suddenly bare and empty except for three bodies, the refuse of war. We waited anxiously, trying to distinguish the noise of enemy fire from the explosions of the barrage. There was no sound of small-arms fire; there didn't seem to be any enemy. We tried the wireless and soon got the news that the leading companies were all on their objectives – no, there had been no Germans, only a couple of snipers. It seemed almost an anti-climax: all that preparation, a full-scale barrage and no enemy. Well, they were there last night; perhaps they walked out as we walked in. At all events, we had had a walk-over, for which we were duly grateful.

The reserve companies were given the word to go and the S.P. antitank guns clattered off up the hill with a great deal of noise and smoke. We climbed aboard the scout car and followed.

In the village a few men were cautiously searching the empty houses with that anxious air people have when they expect something to go bang. Michael Willoughby's company, No. 2, were in the orchards to the left of the village and we found them digging in with the quiet preoccupation of people who have "got there." The Brigadier (George Johnson) drove up the main road, made a short survey of the scene, then retired and we went on to Billy Hartington's company, No. 4. An S.P. anti-tank gun manoeuvred its way across the road so as to get into a good firing position. Shortly afterwards it was hit by an 88 that had, so to speak, had the same idea first; and from then on the day developed into a series of rather similar events, with both sides hedging about and discovering more and more of the rather unpleasing propinquity of the two positions.

No. 4 Company was in front of Frenouville between the main road and a railway that ran on each side of the village more or less straight into the German lines, and south of the railway there was a rather confused jumble of orchard and houses occupied by No. 3 Company, commanded by Anthony Gibbs (at that moment a little uncertain as to whether they or an incoming party of Germans were in possession). In fact it was one of those situations best described as obscure, and as such we left it and drove back to Battalion Headquarters while things sorted themselves out.

Battalion Headquarters shared a field with the reserve company and we found them all digging in for dear life, urged on by occasional shells that began to fall here and there, forerunners of more serious trouble to come. Anxiously we watched little puffs of black smoke spring into life above the village – air bursts, used very probably to fix the ranges. Toby Graham, who commanded the Gunner battery supporting us, did some ranging too, and both sides settled down to knock hell out of each other.

After the first hour of digging everyone was about up to their knees; two hours later we were hardly any deeper down – we'd struck rock. It was all most aggravating; it was worse, it was very exhausting, and from the look of things we were going to need every inch of cover we could scrape up. Colonel Sandy and I found an ex-German position and settled ourselves into that, but it wasn't very satisfactory, as the German plan was to construct little hides more like rabbit holes than slit trenches. In fact, all they consisted of was some logs put crosswise over a ditch so as to give one overhead protection, and some straw at the bottom to keep out the mud. You had to crawl in like a snake, and once inside it was almost impossible to do anything but lie there ruminating on the inconvenience of things, added to which they smelt of the unpleasantly scented soap that the Germans all used, and were littered with spent cartridges and unused cartons of mortar ammunition.

As the day wore on the little dots of blue on my map representing the known enemy positions developed like an attack of measles, as also did the network of lines and blots denoting the places that had been registered by the guns as defensive fire tasks or harassing shoots. The field grew slowly more like a rabbit warren as slit trenches were expanded and elaborated for convenience or comfort. The route up from rear Battalion Headquarters became more and more of a quagmire until finally we could only get tracked vehicles to and fro. In Frenouville glass fell from the windows and tiles cascaded from the roofs under the constant explosions and vibrations of shell fire. The mayor's wife, the only inhabitant, was persuaded to give up the search for her husband and leave for a safer place. Back in the crater by the start line, which had become the R.A.P., Bob Tomlinson, the Padre, doled out cigarettes to the living and buried the dead. We searched the wood between Anthony Gibbs's company and Battalion Headquarters for snipers that weren't there. Another S.P. gun was knocked out. The Commanding Officer visited the companies and struggled with plans for patrols, plans to get up our food for the night, plans to discourage the enemy and plans to encourage ourselves. It was a very busy day.

Buster Luard was bothered by a goat which insisted on sharing his trench in all moments of crisis. Bob Thompson's jeep broke down on the fatal stretch of main road through Michael's company, and had to be hastily abandoned. Anthony's headquarters was attacked by a bull which decided to die almost on top of him much to his discomfort later on when it began to decompose. Michael lit his pipe, sat himself down behind a haystack at his company headquarters and listened to a wireless tuned a great deal closer to the blandishments of a dance band than the admonitions of Battalion Headquarters. It had been hot and sunny during the day, then suddenly it was dusk and growing very cold. The night was upon us.

For me the night became a sort of "Q" siege conducted by Charles Lambton (the Adjutant) over the wireless. Would I make this, that and the other arrangements for meeting the dinner meal when it arrived? What ammunition did we need? Would I arrange a guide to deal with the water truck? It was a bad system, with Charles reigning over operations at main Battalion Headquarters and myself trying to deal with the results up at the command post and carry out my ordinary jobs at the same time. "Q" problems have never been very near to my heart at any time and it's a matter of some wonder to me that we got everything done as well as we did under the circumstances. The final blow to my morale was the arrival of the rum ration. By this stage it was past midnight and my patience was becoming more than a little frayed. I can still see the portly figure of the R.Q.M.S. standing beside the packing cases saying:

"Well, there you are, sir, four jars – a tablespoon per man per company. You'll have to work it out on their ration strength." His voice was a sort of walking advertisement proclaiming, "Drink more beer."

"Well, couldn't we just divide it up into six and forget about the tablespoonful business?"

"Couldn't do that, sir; too much for the rifle companies – too little for Support Company."

"Oh! Anyway, it's going to be a little difficult with only four jars. What else have you got that we could put it in?"

"Haven't got nothing, sir."

I can't remember what flash of genius finally solved the matter, but it kept us busy for nearly an hour pouring rum from bottle to bottle like medieval alchemists trying to synthetize the philosophers' stone, and after that it came on to rain – not a shower, but a downpour. The R.Q.M.S. boarded his half-track and left me standing amid the wreckage feeling that indeed the world had forsaken me – there wasn't even a proper command post to sit in. Everyone had vanished to seek what shelter they could under groundsheets and tarpaulins. However, a faint humming and buzzing noise from the middle of the field proclaimed that Corporal Lyons was still faithful to the world of communications, so I found the trench and crawled under the tarpaulin.

It wasn't really a trench at all, it was so shallow; and sitting on the bottom you either had to bend completely double or support the weight of the tarpaulin with your head.

But for the rain I should have fallen asleep. It trickled down my back in rivulets, it accumulated underneath me in ponds, it became a Chinese torture that drummed upon the tarpaulin over our heads until we were driven into a sort of trance of discomfort. In the midst of all this we were suddenly subjected to an extremely unpleasant stonk.

"Weeeeeeeeeee, crump, crump, crump, CRUMP! Weeeeeee, crump, crump, CRRRUMP!" In the short intervals we contorted ourselves into positions reckoned to be less vulnerable and waited for the next salvo. Rumble, rumble, rumble went the distant guns; eeeeeeee, crrrump, ssst, rumpt, ssssstyrump! went the shells.

Fragments of metal sizzled overhead and little clods of earth clumped upon the tarpaulin. The violence of the explosions seemed to do you an almost physical injury, even though nothing had hit you.

"Very uncalled for, I'd say, sir."

"Most impolite."

Rumble, rumble, rumble, eeeeeeee, crump, CRUMP, crump, crump! It lasted for about a quarter of an hour before we could emerge into the acrid smoke-laden air.

A wounded man was calling out for stretcher-bearers and the field was alive with fumbling figures assessing the damage.

"Anyone hit?"

"You all right, Alf?"

"Cor, that was a bit of all right – woke me up proper, the b******s did!"

"This way, the stretcher-bearers; there's a man got a nasty one here."

Amid the general investigations I found Buster tending to the Commanding Officer, who'd been hit in both legs. Bob Thompson, our only relief for the wireless, was wounded too, but refused to be sent back, and we'd hardly got the wounded on to the carriers when the whole thing started all over again. It was the hell of a night and the morning when it came was not much better.

A melancholy, grey sky dripped upon us, as though it had sobbed itself out during the night and was now emotionally exhausted. We were rather exhausted too, but determined to get our own back, and we sat down to work out a plan of revenge with Toby.

"There's masses of ammunition," he said; and we used it, putting down stonks on every little pocket of Germans we knew of. This took up a great deal of the morning, as the shoots had to be observed by the companies, who were the only people with a good view of the targets, and the procedure for this involves a certain amount of teamwork.

First of all, the company has to get someone ready to observe the shots when they arrive.

"Hullo, Zebra Three. We're going to have a shot at that wood you mentioned. Say when you're ready. Zebra Three over."

"Hullo, Zebra Three. All set. Over."

"O.K., Zebra Three. Wait. Out"; then to Toby aboard his halftrack: "They're ready!" Then follows a great deal of Gunner mumbo-jumbo while Toby gives the orders to the guns, and when they are ready: "Fire!"

"Shot," comes the word from the guns.

"Shot," cries Toby to me.

"Hullo, Zebra Three. Shot. Over." Then there is a pause while the shells go whistling overhead, and everyone waits for the result. Back from Zebra Three comes an angry voice: "Blast you, that was practically on me. Up three hundred!"

"Up three hundred!" I yell to Toby, and we try again.

"Shot," says Toby.

"Hullo, Zebra Three. Shot. Over."

Eeeeeeeee goes the salvo; then umph, umph, umph, umph, as it lands at the other end; then a pause while we wait for the verdict.

"Hullo, Zebra Three. That was fine. I think it hit something, as we saw a lot of people running about afterwards. Can we have a good stonk there? Zebra Three, over."

Once on the target the real business begins and in moments of major importance all the guns of the regiment take up the fun, which is signalled by Toby as "Mike target, Mike target, Mike target!" It's all very good for one's morale, and by ten o'clock we felt we'd got some of our own back and adjourned for large quantities of hot tea and rum while the Germans thought out a return match. The hot tea and rum was our main source of nourishment for the next forty-eight hours and very necessary. We were all drenched through and getting a good deal wetter, as it started to rain again, besides which cooking was impossible.

Michael Adeane came up from Battalion Headquarters to take over command from Buster, after which we set out to do our tour round the companies in the scout car. As it turned out, this wasn't a very good idea, as its proper driver had been wounded in the night. However, Corporal Tremner, the wireless operator, assured us that he was intimately acquainted with how it went and we trusted his word. The situation was then further complicated by my making a slight mistake in the route, and before the matter could be put right we crested the hill by No. 2 Company into full view of the enemy.

"Stop," said I.

"Whoa," said Michael.

"Back!" we cried in chorus.

There was a very uncomfortable pause while we came all too slowly to a halt.

"Surely, Corporal Tremner, you know where the reverse is?"

Unhappily he didn't but fortunately no one took a shot at us, and after a few agonizing minutes we at last started to go backwards and hurriedly vanished below the skyline.

Anthony's company position was far from healthy. It was one of those places where orchards and copses stretch almost indefinitely one after the other so that eventually the hope of placing some good, wide field of fire between the Germans and the forward platoon had to be abandoned and an unpleasant jungle was left as the common playground of both sides. The key to all the ensuing hide-and-seek was the forward platoon, and we were duly painted a picture of unsurpassed drama by an extremely mud-plastered, breathless John Knatchbull. John was always on the point of being surrounded by the enemy or involved in some situation of unspeakable complication; not because he walked into this sort of thing or cultivated it, but because he was Irish and this is always the way with Irishmen. With whole battalions of Irishmen the results defy description. Still, it seems to work very well, and I believe they really rather enjoy the studied confusion and atmosphere of major crisis that surround them in war.

Dutifully we crawled about from hedgerow to hedgerow, and made ourselves as invisible as possible when told to do so; then decided it was time to hurry on.

When we reached Billy Hartington's company, No. 4, we found that he had temporarily taken up residence in one of the houses and was having an impromptu bath, but it suited the moment and we seated ourselves on what furniture we could find in one of the bedrooms while he completed his toilet, and the imperturbable Guardsman Ingles laid out hair-brushes, clean socks, etc., with infinite care, regardless of the total chaos and ruin in the rest of the room.

Would we like a glass of rum? We said we'd love a glass of rum.

"Ingles, some glasses!" Then, of course, we must take a look around the company position, and, most important, we must see "the gun." That would also be very interesting, we agreed.

Billy was a great enthusiast for showing people over his position; it was all done with the care and pride with which people take you round their houses and discuss the new decorations. "The gun," an 88-mm., eventually became the showpiece of the Battalion position, and people were taken to see it rather as one goes to see the lions fed at the Zoo. From a suitable viewpoint your attention was directed to a distant hedgerow; then after a long wait, if you were lucky, the thing fired and you could see a spurt of flame and a little puff of smoke through the hedge. Once you knew where it was you could actually pick out the outline of the gun mantle and the barrel – it was all very remarkable; and, stranger still, we never managed to eliminate it to the end of the chapter.

The next call we had to make was on Michael Willoughby's company, and after having to abandon the scout car in a slough of mud we eventually found Michael still sitting behind his haystack and listening to "Lilli Marlene," somewhat distorted by the endeavours of another company to renet. Michael's company was a fairly peaceful place, provided that you didn't try to cross over the main road, and as we were by now beginning to weary of doubling about behind hedgerows this was definitely decided against and the business of the day was conducted in a fairly peaceable way behind the haystack.

Back at Battalion Headquarters I found an enormous envelope marked "Top Secret" containing a message from

Corps Headquarters. It said: "Expect counter-attack by two or three battalions, 12th S.S. Division, sometime next twelve hours."

As the Intelligence Officer on the spot, I felt that it was a definite affront to receive such an unprepossessing piece of information about our own pet enemy from a corps headquarters, and hotly denied that any such event was going to take place. Michael Adeane was of the opinion that they always sent out that sort of message to new commanding officers just to try their nerve, and actually it was decided to ignore it. We were right; nothing happened.

The afternoon turned slowly into evening while we got muddier and muddier sitting in our trench. Perhaps "sitting in our trench" gives a wrong impression, for we actually sat on the edge, as the bottom was by now full of water into which we had to slither like sea-lions whenever we were shelled, added to which we were continually disturbed by the telephone ringing or messages coming in over the wireless so that our position was neither restful nor comfortable. We had to have both wireless and telephone going, as the lines were constantly broken by the shelling, and even with this double system of communication it wasn't always easy to keep in touch with everyone. Still further to aggravate our unhappiness, the visibility suddenly became greatly improved, and we discovered that we were in full view of a neighbouring hill occupied by the enemy, so that the rain of shells upon our position became even more intensive and accurate than before. Perhaps we ought to have moved elsewhere, but the labour and sweat involved in digging even the modest trenches that we had were more than anyone could face by this stage, and there was no other alternative but to sweat it out, aided by constant hot tea and rum. In the evening Derek Eastman came up to provide a relief, so that someone could go back and spend a quiet night at "A" Echelon, where Cecil Fielden had instituted "Fielden's Luxury Hotel." I was the first guest.

I couldn't have been more delighted by a magic carpet to the Ritz. It was about the pleasantest memory I have of Frenouville, though thinking of it now Cecil's hotel could only claim to have the most modest of luxuries.

"A" Echelon consisted of the bulk of the Battalion's vehicles parked some three miles back in what a cornfield had once been but had by now become acres and acres of thick, black mud. In the middle of it I discovered that the ever-faithful Hobman was waiting for me, and he led me to my suite – a T.C.L. Down the row of seats in the middle I found a large basin of hot water, dry socks, dry boots, my sleeping-bag and blankets – it was bliss indeed!

I had a very hasty meal, then retired to bed and slept and slept and slept. I was still very tired when I woke up the next morning to find it was already broad daylight and time to return to Frenouville as soon as I had breakfasted. Cecil had almost finished eating by the time I arrived, and sat opposite me on another packing case with that air one reserves for guests who over-estimate the assurance that "Breakfast is any time you feel like it," but it is ungrateful to complain, as his thoughtful arrangements did more to restore my sanity than anything else during the war, and for the joys of the "Hotel Cecil" I will always remain extremely thankful.

After breakfast Derek arrived to take over my suite and I prepared to go. Unfortunately, the peace and quiet of my visit were shatteringly destroyed at a most inconvenient moment by six Messerschmits. They came suddenly out of the sky straight at us with everything blazing at once, and for a moment I thought I was certainly dead, but, strange to relate, not a single thing was hit, as is so often the case. The light A.A. guns were as surprised as I was; however, they made up for it after the Messerschmits had gone by a very fine display of shooting into nothingness.

I was sorry to have to leave Cecil so soon and even sorrier to have to go back to Frenouville. In my mind's eye I could exactly visualize what the situation would be and how things would look; when I arrived there I found I was right.

It started to rain again and to rain hard. It poured, it dripped, it splashed and oozed. An eternal and all-embracing shower of wetness that turned the muddy paths and roads into even greater quagmires so that you no longer tried to pick your way or avoid the soggier bits; you just floundered. Where originally one vehicle had followed another, by now they had to fan out in an unending search for firm ground that turned whole fields into mud, and still things got stuck. Roads were engulfed by the spreading ooze and vanished in the mud.

At the command post the two half-tracks draped in their camouflage netting looked as forlorn as ever, and one of them had been hit for the second time. In the night the rear-link half-track had received an even more fatal hit than at Demouville, and Ginger, the wireless operator, was the only survivor this time. When they managed to extract him from the chaos inside he was still murmuring "Frequencies" and instructions on how to net in the new set, should one ever arrive, and though he was in great pain, he had to be forcibly persuaded from helping to get the replacement wireless going.

The rum jar had survived, owing to the great presence of mind of Derek, who took it with him when he crawled under the vehicle for protection as the trouble began, and he produced it proudly when I arrived. All around the ground was littered with the usual sordid remains of burnt paper, clothing, and the charred contents of the halftrack. Everyone looked a little tireder and had become a little stupider than when I last saw them, but morale was excellent; we were to be relieved the next night and go back to a rest area. But even when you are due for relief the seeming endlessness of war comes like a brake upon one's feelings, for there will always be the next attack and the next bloody place to defend and the next move to make. This time everything went well, this time is coming to an end, this time I have survived, but there will be another and another while fewer and fewer remain. What does it matter that the war must soon end when time has become so slow, that lives, whole ages of events, and centuries of discomfort have come to crowd themselves in so closely upon one another? Tonight is fifty years away, tomorrow may never come – but amid the dreariness and gloom there are sparks of comfort and pleasure that seemed like bonfires of hope, so that for everything that oppressed or wearied there were moments and times that heartened and uplifted one as never before. In fact, all the normal moods and circumstances of life as one knows it, only enormously heightened and quickened by the illusory nature of war.

So there I was back at Frenouville. There were another twelve hours to go that finally ended in a Calvary of weariness and exhaustion when we marched back to our rest area at Giberville, but it would serve no purpose to recount the rest in detail, or to describe any of the many other situations like Frenouville. It is best to leave that corner of unhappy memories as it is, with shells falling from time to time and the guns renewing the endless vendetta under the cold, grey sky. There are still many people who will be wounded in the next twelve hours and still some who will be killed, but that is one of the details, and when the twelve hours are over some will be the concern of the Graves Commission and some the concern of the N.A.A.F.I. – everything is accounted for in war – or at least almost everything. And what cannot be accounted for cannot be expressed.

NORMANDY CONTINUED

WHEN WE arrived at Giberville everyone was too tired and it was too dark to absorb any impressions of the place, and all I was aware of was that Hobman had put up my camp-bed in a little brick shack and that it was comfortable beyond my wildest expectations. All the wirelesses were closed down, there were no lines or telephones to anyone and nothing to be done but sleep until we could sleep no more.

It was eleven o'clock when I got up the next morning and in the night the weather had cleared – the sky was blue, the sun shone and summer was back again. The soothing effect of having slept so long and comfortably filled me with a sort of comatose contentment, as though I had taken some new and efficacious drug that was guaranteed to cure the ills of war. How pleasant it was to spend nearly an hour changing into clean clothes and washing and shaving in an enormous bowl of hot water! I was very hungry and Sergeant Westmacott was cooking some eggs for breakfast. The weather that had hung upon us like a malignant melancholia had changed and now it was summer again. Whole multitudes of unimportant trivialities suddenly joined together to make life extremely enjoyable, and on these occasions we nursed the precious moments for all that they could give, knowing all too well that they would soon vanish and everything would begin again, but the golden mood of the moment had its real and practical value even if it was perhaps only a relief from the anxiety and worry that one tried to pretend didn't exist by projecting it on to the day-to-day discomforts or circumstances that came first and most immediately to one's attention.

Superficially there is nothing good to be said about Giberville; it was a sordid and largely destroyed offshoot of Caen. Our area was about a mile from the factories and gasworks of the town itself, and the greater part consisted of a featureless field, but Battalion Headquarters was mixed up in the houses bordering the main road that divided us from another battalion, and we saw life through more urban eyes than the companies. The presence of a string of little ruined estaminets and villas of the ugliest type gave a certain character to the place that, in the first exuberance of happiness, seemed to add to our pleasures, just as later when we found we were still in gun range and came to loathe the place they became a symbol of our dislike.

The houses were too dilapidated to be of any use, but we investigated them with care and caution on the chance of finding some wine. Care and caution were necessary, as the area was heavily mined and we suspected booby-traps.

I can't remember at what precise moment we first discovered that we were in range of the German guns, but I recollect that in the morning, when I was innocently, as it were, surveying the property, there was a sudden warning sizzle and an air-burst exploded above my head sending a blast of concentrated heat and sulphurous smoke down my neck. More followed, and from then on we never again felt quite the same about the place.

Later we found out that our position had been specially chosen and with a purpose, but it didn't console us very much. At this time the Americans were preparing for their break-through and it was of paramount importance to keep all the German armoured divisions busily engaged on the British sector. The role of the Division at this particular juncture was to sun itself in full view of the German Army as a threat and decoy to the German Higher Command. It is true we were not in the line and were not under heavy bombardment or even battle conditions, but our presence was sufficiently close to be clearly visible to the enemy and act as constant invitation to 88's with nothing better to shoot at, so that we could never be sure that the apparent peace wouldn't be suddenly and shatteringly destroyed.

A rest area should be a rest area, we said; however, there was obviously something wrong with this one, and, mustering as much sang-froid as we could manage, we set to and dug pits for the protection of our vehicles, and trenches for the protection of ourselves. In the afternoon a Brigade conference was suddenly summoned, and Michael Adeane, accompanied by myself and Charles Lambton, had to go dashing off to attend it.

"Back to battle so soon?" we asked.

"Yes – so soon; probably tomorrow," they told us.

Apparently yet another attack was being launched to the south of Caen and we were earmarked to take part in support of a Canadian division.

Brigade Headquarters, apart from a mine which had blown up one of its vehicles, was very happily disposed in the usual orchard. While we waited for the "O" Group to begin everyone made light conversation to each in their best cocktail-party manner: "How were things in London now the flying bombs had started?" or the latest news of the

Camembert cheese market in Bayeux. Kenneth Harrington suddenly appeared as he has a way of doing and gave us the latest gossip of the 6th Brigade. Michael Rosse went by laden with maps and air photographs, most of which he deposited on me with intimations of more to come. Officers struggled in and out of the A.C.V. seeking the latest news and hoping to pick up some secret information about the future which no one else would know. L.Os. fussed to and fro inveigling people into the conference tent before the Brigadier arrived, and everything went "as merry as a marriage bell." It always did. Throughout every campaign Brigade Headquarters always managed to preserve an air suggesting that one was about to sit down to a Fortnum & Mason picnic lunch and that if it rained it would be quite simple to call the whole thing off and go home. It was all very wonderful, and if one arrived early there would probably be a very spruce Tom Dundas ready with gin and vermouth to sustain and

Colombelles, east of Caen, Escorting prisoners of war after Operation Goodwood.

heighten one's picnic spirits. Afterwards, everyone disperses to their cars with a feeling that the war is going very well, the higher staff are all tactical geniuses, and the war likely to be over very soon. It is only when one gets back to greet the Battalion "O" Group and is confronted by rows and rows of faces expressing patient, dumb suffering that somehow the magic wears off, to be replaced by the conviction that life is, despite all things, very uncertain and full of nothing but predictable discomfort and inconvenience.

In the evening I went over to Michael Willoughby's company to have a drink and found that Bob Tomlinson and John Ingram, our doctor, had had the same idea. We sat in a tent which Michael had put up as an officers' mess. In the middle there was a large pit into which the guests could precipitate themselves if necessary, and though no one mentioned the matter I seem to remember that as the evening drew on we all edged our chairs closer and closer to the trench and the conversation turned to sin and the wages thereof. Finally we felt unable any longer to ignore the increasingly insistent noises outside, and the party broke up, leaving Michael to contemplate the choice of sitting with dignity outside his trench, or, with safety, in it.

In the night there was an air raid; it was noisy, it is true, but I never allowed a London air raid to disturb my sleep and this was clearly an occasion for turning over and going to sleep again. It was not to be; something came down with a noise like an express train and before I could do anything the corrugated-iron roof of my shack vanished into space and was replaced by a canopy of flame. I behaved very much as scalded cats do, and very shortly found myself, clad in nothing but my pants, in a very water-logged trench. The air raid ended, but it spoilt my night and I never again felt the same peace of mind and confidence in my shack.

The next morning we found that the physiognomy of our back garden was quite visibly altered. Charles Lambton had been sealed up in his trench like Merlin in his rock and had to be dug out by the ever-faithful Jenkins. The wall on which our snails were still valiantly trying to finish a race begun the day before had been completely flattened, and most of the Officers' Mess furniture was reduced to matchwood.

All through the day our part in the battle to the south of us was postponed and postponed, then finally cancelled and this was followed by still better news: we were to move back to the delights of our old rest area near Bayeux.

We had only two days' rest back at our old area near Bayeux, but they were a pleasant interlude that gave us time to write letters home and have a bath, which may sound very trivial but is not. At times these things provided one with the only straws of sanity to which one could cling amid the nightmare of war that seemed to be sweeping away every

Derreck Plater in trench, reading the post from home. Normandy

vestige of familiar life and placing in its stead a chaos of shattering experiences that were only bearable because there was no alternative.

On these occasions, though, you could walk away by yourself with a pencil and a very grubby piece of paper, to a quiet corner of a hay-field where you could sit down on a bank in the sun and write:

"DEAR MUMMY,
We are having a bit of a rest now and so I have at last got time to write to you. Everything seems to be going very well and I do not expect the war can last much longer now. Please keep on sending the cigarettes, which make a lot of difference to me, etc ...

I don't think we ever really wrote what we were thinking; it would have been too difficult to put on paper, and, anyway, one didn't want to worry people or upset them, but after writing a letter home it was difficult not to be reminded of all the people who would no longer be writing letters home – already we had had over two hundred casualties, and it had been such a short time, a mere introduction to war, with months and months of battles to come. Perhaps at the same time one also had to think hard and write a letter to:

DEAR MRS. SO-AND-SO,
I cannot say how sorry I am about your husband's death. Everyone in the Company was fond of him. I know that I can say how much we all sympathize with you, and that we will never forget how much

he did for us all. I'm sure that you would like to know, etc ... ."

There was really very little that could be said to Mrs. So-and-so, but one said it with desperate sincerity, and I often wonder how much or how little it helped them. And then, after the letter writing, there was nothing to do but stretch oneself out on the turf and notice that the sky was very, very blue and how strange it was to be so struck by the fact – but one had grown a lot older very suddenly in the past few weeks and there was little then that didn't appear different from all that had been before, and if it was a jigsaw puzzle that couldn't be fitted together at least it was a realization that:

There are more things in Heaven and Earth, Horatio, Than are dreamt of in our philosophy."

And if that was an interesting thought to muse upon, even more inviting was the idyllic day and the pleasure of lying on one's back in the sun with nothing immediate to worry about; but two days is a short time, and it was gone almost before we had savoured it. Things were said to be loosening up. The whole Division was beginning to be on the move, whole corps and armies were on the move, for this was the prelude to Falaise, and over the whole Allied front our gathering strength was preparing for the "big push together" that was to achieve such decisive results in the near future. "Loosening," however is a relative term and before the Germans finally cracked there was a great deal of levering and wedging to be done, which gave us as much trouble and trial as any other part of the war, largely owing to the very difficult and hilly country we were fighting in and the stubborn resistance of the S.S. divisions.

We left our old familiar orchard on the 30th of July, and while the 15th (Scottish) Division and the 6th Guards Tank Brigade opened the offensive with a memorable attack through Caumont southwards to the famous Bois du Hommes, we trundled across the bridgehead so as to be suitably positioned when the moment was ripe for an armoured rush through the hole in the enemy's line that they were forcing. The plan was that ourselves and the 11th Armoured Division should break out and seize the hilly country around Le Beny Bocage so as to protect the American left flank as it wheeled round to the south. The "rush" part never quite came off, as there was never a hole through which we could rush, and despite the tremendous damage done to the enemy during the first few hard-fought days there was never a breakdown in the German defensive arrangements, and ideas of sweeping everything before us had to be modified. For though the original neat line of German divisions one beside another that we studied or amended so carefully upon our intelligence maps was steadily pushed back, and though from the casualty lists we were able to write off unit by unit as largely destroyed, something fresh always turned up to fill the gap.

The field divisions eventually became demoralized under the obvious threat that was hanging over their heads, but the S.S. divisions held on to every inch that they could, despite the Armageddon ahead. The less stubborn who panicked they shot, and every available piece of artillery or equipment that could be got hold of they seized for the last stand, so that while we were fighting them there were no easy victories or moments when we could relax, as their powers of counterattack were always kept up and no

opportunity of hitting back was let by, however unavailing
the final result might be. In the end it was decided to save
the S.S. at the expense of the divisions caught in the pocket,
and they finally made a general withdrawal from our front,
leaving us without an opposition, but by that time we had
finished our role and the story of Falaise belongs to others.

From our orchard near Bayeux we were moved up to
near Caumont and here we waited for our final orders with
that curious mixture of feelings that varies between "Well,
let's get it over as soon as possible" and "I wonder whether,
perhaps, we may not be needed in the end?" We were already
a little weary, and the heat grew more overpowering day by
day until in the end it was of itself enough to discourage
one from doing anything very energetic. This "moving up"
took thirty-six hours of dusty and uncomfortable driving
on roads that were a solid mass of transport. Vehicles were
moving practically head to tail to save road space. At the
periodic halts we snatched a few bites of food or sleep, or
when more occasionally there was time to move into a
harbour area off the road we cooked a meal and washed.
"O" Groups at short notice, probably just as one was about
to shave, hurried distributions of maps and all the thousand
and one details that have to be arranged and checked as
the battle looms up – all this was tiring, but it was a side-
line and it would be tedious to go into the details, however
important they were at the time.

In the end we had to push our way into battle right
at the end of the day, and we only managed to do this by
double-banking columns of other units' vehicles that were
blocking every inch of the road space all the way up to St.
Martin des Besaces, which lay just behind our start line. By
the time the attack on Point 238 went in it was beginning
to get dark, and we felt like a boxer who has to fight his

Operation Bluecoat. Under enemy fire at Saint-Martin-des-Besaces, on 31st July. 1944

way through the spectators to get to the ring. At first our attack was unopposed, and when in the complete darkness which enveloped the last stage Anthony Gibbs and Billy Hartington, whose companies were in the lead, reported that they were being fired on, we flatly accused them of firing at each other.

Point 238 was a huge lump of a hill, all hedgerows and banks, so that when very late that night we finally started to dig in, all that could be said with certainty was that Anthony and Billy were right, and that there was not much more than the width of a field between them and the enemy. Exactly where either they or the Germans were it was impossible to say until daylight arrived. The initial part of the attack, however, had been so completely successful that we were confident that everything could be quite easily dealt with in the morning. But it was not so. Ken Thornton's company, No. 1+, and the Mick Squadron[5] that attacked together in

---

5   We were formed into a composite group with the 2nd Armoured Irish and various supporting arms when we left our concentration area the day before.

the morning to clear up the situation had heavy casualties as soon as they started. Eight tanks were lost in almost as many minutes and the company lost about forty men; it soon became impossible for them to go on any farther. In fact, before we knew what was happening the German tanks which had been the chief cause of all the trouble started to advance themselves. They mounted a bigger gun and had more armour than the Sherman tanks, so that the odds were heavily against the Micks, who hardly had time to realize that they were being shot at before they were hit. For a time we were all very worried, as besides the other casualties Michael Adeane, who was commanding the Battalion, and Ken, the next senior officer with us, were both wounded. At one time the leading company was right back by the orchards around the command post, and there was not much that could have stopped the Germans from rushing the road back to St. Martin, or at any rate demolishing half of the Battalion position. However, in the end they held back and the situation was largely restored.

At this moment Brigadier Norman Gwatkin arrived, a highly coloured silk handkerchief around his neck and his jaws busily munching chewing-gum. He suddenly blew into the midst of our rather unhappy conclave at the command post and disposed of our doubts with a wave of his hand. "Oooooh …a company squadron group should be ample to deal with the situation. I'm quite sure we'll have no difficulty at all. Now I'm confident the way to do this is round by the left" – indicated with a great sweep across his map. "We've got lots of guns available and we'll put down some medium artillery fire in support. … "

I copied the fire plan off his very ill-marked map and came to the conclusion that No. 4 Company, who were to do the attack, were going to their almost certain death, but when the time came the plan worked perfectly and by the middle of the afternoon we were able to give the "all clear ahead," and the Motor Grenadiers passed through us in pursuit of the retreating enemy.

In the evening Buster Luard came up from "A" Echelon to take over command from Billy, and we all said "Tomorrow ... ah, now, tomorrow we really are going to make a big advance." Centre lines were marked up on our maps twenty miles ahead, but the next day wasn't really any different from the first two.

Early on the opposition stiffened so that, though we all got ready at 6 a.m., we didn't actually start until after midday, as the Grenadiers were still fighting their way up to the point at which our two routes diverged and there was no road for us to move on until this point was cleared.

We advanced as a mixed tank and infantry column. The first group with the infantry mounted on the tanks, then after that mixed groups of all arms, with the companies in T.C.Ls., which is a comfier way of travelling than on a tank but almost suicidally unpleasant when the column gets shot at, which it frequently was; and one of the features of that day that sticks most in my mind is the number of times everyone had to debuss, re-embuss, get off the tanks, get on them again, etc. It was all very irritating and at times very frightening. The heat and discomfort also remain a vivid memory. Just ahead of me there was always a tank grinding away in bottom gear so that the road trembled and vibrated, and the dancing dust was swept up into my face by the hot air from the exhaust. In the combined heat, dust and noise I was almost mummified by the din and dirt; and when every now and then we stopped and got off on to the roadside it felt as though one had been at sea in a bad storm, unused to the sudden feel of terra firma and the quiet.

St Charles de Percy, taking cover in a ditch.

It was a day of incidents: disconnected, disconcerting and very tiring so that in memory it all comes back to one in little kaleidoscopic scenes, like the stretch of the route just before St. Charles de Percy, where the road, after a steady climb up the hill, suddenly rolls over the crest before dropping down into a steep, wooded valley: It was an exposed place, and as Buster and I in the scout car drove by I took a particularly careful look at the hills on either side of us with my field-glasses. We were doing this, anyway, as of course they were a rather unknown factor, uncleared and unliberated, that gave the feeling of hundreds of German guns invisibly trained upon you from their secret covers; but there was nothing secret about what I saw on this occasion – across the valley there was a Mark IV as large as life. When I pointed it out to Buster he said he was too busy to pay any attention. We halted a couple of hundred yards farther on where the road takes a scoop out of the hillside, and before we had time to light a cigarette in the ditch a sudden fusillade of H.E. shots hit the bank above us – and that is how Buster was wounded. Most people will remember that stretch of the road, as the whole column eventually had to pass down it, and it was one of those places where, when the column halted, you notice that there seem to be curiously few people about. A couple of dead horses and a dead German were the only unmoved spectators of the situation, and they had been resting there a long while.

When I got to the wireless to send for Billy Hartington, "as Sunray has been wounded," the reaction was very nearly, "What again?" and it was at an even more difficult moment than the time before. Beyond the cross-roads at St. Charles de Percy the battle had begun that in one way or another lasted until the night came. Later in the afternoon it was attempted to turn the complicated and extended little series of battles into a co-ordinated blow, but it was a plan for "rushing in where angels fear to tread"; there was more against us than we had bargained for, and we couldn't pull it off. By nightfall we were out of touch with nearly all the companies and the situation seemed extremely serious. We knew from the tanks that Derek's company, No. 4, had been heavily engaged, but we'd heard nothing more from them and had only a vague idea where they were. Michael Willoughby's company when we last heard them on the wireless were advancing towards a rendezvous which no one was able to reach, and the situation was made still more complicated by the fact that we had ourselves been lost amid the maze of bocage for quite a time. Night came on. Billy and I spent two hours winding our way about unexplored lanes with James Willoughby's tank trying to find the lost companies. I sat on the turret of the tank with a map and a torch to read the way. It still rankles within me when I remember that as I complained of feeling rather unsafe there, all James did was to emerge out of the turret and hand me a Sten gun. I had to hold the map with one hand and the torch in the other, so it wouldn't have been much use; however, it was a hopeless search and we had to abandon it without finding anyone.

In the small hours of the morning we discovered one by one that the company were actually only a few hundred yards away from us all the time! The enemy had all withdrawn.

It was nine o'clock before we started off the next day, not because we overslept – on the contrary – but because we were having great difficulties with our supplies. Petrol for the tanks, ammunition, food and water were needed and until the small hours of the morning most of the Battalion had been virtually lost, so that it was not surprising that this caused a little delay and it still seems a miracle to me that the Adjutant ever managed to produce these things for us at all. The later part of the advance had all been across country, so that a way had to be found for our vehicles by completely unreconnoitred lanes in the pitch of darkness and considerable uncertainties as to whether they were free of enemy or not.

As to sleep, I don't think anyone got any that night, and I remember that when Corporal Tilshead, who drove the scout car, offered me some breakfast I fell asleep with the plate in my hand. Normally it is impossible to go to sleep just as and when one pleases and sometimes it even becomes impossible to sleep at all, but at that time we suffered from the exact reverse. There were moments when nothing but sheer physical effort kept one's eyes open, and even to sit down seemed unwise, as you would have immediately been overcome with sleep. Had it been possible to snatch even two hours' rest this wouldn't have happened, but at the time we were too short-handed to manage reliefs on the wireless or to spare anyone from their job during the night, and when the day came we were on the move. Eventually one lapsed into a state of drowsy numbness, neither fully awake nor fully asleep, but jerked from one to the other like a marionette. The spasmodic moments of dreaming semi-consciousness seemed as vivid as the reality that one tried to hang on to, and one's wakening intervals seen through swollen eyes assumed that feverish unreality that the world presents when one is very ill.

I was still in this state of fevered sleeplessness when we resumed the advance towards Estry, and I think everyone else was the same.

All the companies were mounted on tanks this time, as that was practically the only type of vehicle that could manage the cross-country going, and Billy and I in the scout

St Charles de Percy, Billy Hartington in the jeep, took temporary command of the Battalion following the wounding of the Commanding Officer.

car were rather like children on Shetland ponies following a hunt, only there was no fun in this hunt and far fewer gates than one might reasonably hope to find.

For the men mounted on the tanks it was a nightmare day, as in the confined bocage countryside you were liable to be shot at with no warning at almost any time. There is nothing that feels so exposed as sitting on a tank, and generally it was impossible to see more than a field ahead. At each hedgerow there was no alternative but to take it blindfold and as the tank approached the three-foot bank you could see everyone craning forward; then, with any luck, the nose tilts up, the tracks grip, and over she goes through six feet of hedge like a ship cresting the wave. Sometimes the banks were too high or too steep, and several tanks got stuck; as for the scout car, when there were no gates it had to be dragged over by a tank or lifted by squads of helpers.

From an infantry point of view there was very little that could be done at this stage. The company wireless sets bumping along on the tanks over a very wide area were soon put off net and, anyway, where we went was entirely up to the armour. It was a case of clinging on and hoping for the best. Late in the morning the cavalcade began swarming over the ridge which lies in front of the Estry feature, and as the tanks started to climb the slope opposite the trouble began and a battle developed.

I remember very well sitting in a ditch with Billy having lunch. We agreed that the weather was perfect, the bocage was looking at its loveliest, and if it hadn't been for the war one would have been very happy. Little wisps of cloud sat motionless in the sky, the natural counterparts to the straggly poplar trees that lined the hedgerows like ill-used feather brooms. We shared a tin of sardines, plastering them between biscuits with a pen-knife, and washing it all down with very muddy compo tea.

It was an odd situation because just over the brow of the hill No. 3 Company were under heavy fire and a lot of Mick tanks had been knocked out, but there was nothing we could do about it at that moment and we were surprisingly cheerful.

A Frenchwoman appeared cautiously out of a little farm cottage and asked us:

"Est-ce qu'il y a de danger?"

"Ah … mais non, pas de danger," we said.

It was hardly the truth, and about an hour later Dick Lomer was winning an M.C. only four hundred yards away. This time we were up against a strong defensive position that nothing but a staged attack would shift, and as we were now completely isolated with no one within several miles of us, orders were given out that we were to halt the advance, take up a position on the ridge in front of La Marvindiere and wait until there was something up on either flank.

It was a great relief. We had become unbelievably tired, though our defensive position was hardly a rest, and we were soon being harried from all sides.

The Micks had lost a third of their tanks in the past twenty-four hours, and since the beginning we had by now lost over three hundred casualties, which included the six senior officers. All the companies were beginning to be very short and every life had become doubly precious. It was a bad time for the Battalion, and if I had been writing this then I would never have said "three hundred casualties," for that is a figure only and makes nonsense of all that we felt. You cannot say: "Mark Howard, Bunty Stuart Brown – write down two killed"; and yet there seems to be no way in which one can express the meaning of our losses in the human terms in which they occurred. For three years we had worked and trained and lived together until there was something more than a battalion – there was a community of spirit and feeling that made the Battalion as much a part of oneself as one was a tiny fraction of the whole. And now, when the evening light began to turn the tall hedges into long, black shadows across the bocage meadows, one felt suddenly as though the darkness that was beginning to separate trench from trench and each man from his neighbour was like the loneliness that was coming upon the Battalion as the friends one had had diminished one by one, killed or wounded.

We were beginning to be a little uncertain of ourselves, and the forty-eight hours that followed were anything but reassuring. In the darkness of the night German half-tracks could be heard moving to and fro in the country round about us. The German artillery was beginning to size up our defences and their guns were getting to know the ranges. When the morning came it was discovered that we were virtually cut off by the enemy tanks which were able to rove the countryside behind us more or less at will, and it was impossible to get anything in to or out of the position. The wounded couldn't be evacuated, we ran out of food, and if it hadn't been for the supplies that the Micks were carrying on their tanks we should have gone hungry for two days.

The position was not alarming, as we would have been fully capable of holding our own against anything that attacked us, but at the same time it was distinctly unpleasant to have to fight a battle on all four fronts at once, and we were sadly short of sleep. A great many factors combined together to bring this state of affairs to an end, but from the Battalion's point of view the chief event was the arrival of a new Commanding Officer. By this time I had lost my steel helmet, gaiters, collar and tie, and my battledress was coated in mud and dust; in any circumstances other than a battlefield I think I would have been arrested as an undesirable tramp, and yet no one was very much better and I would never have noticed anything amiss if it hadn't been for the arrival of Colonel Roddy Hill. He seemed the very epitome of smart turn-out; it was a revelation to us, and curiously enough neither the circumstances nor the trials of the succeeding months ever altered this.

He made a detailed tour of introduction round the Battalion with Billy and one's first impression was of slow, carefully measured sentences, and a trick of emphasis that made words suddenly appear as though they had been underlined with a pencil. There was about him an air of unhurried disregard for the immediate alarums of the moment that was wonderful to see – we felt we'd never seen such imperturbability, and the effect on everyone was miraculous. Everything was going to be "quite all right," which was just as well, because the next day we were ordered to attack Le Busq, a little village across the valley on the same ridge as Estry.

During the past twelve hours the ground to our right had been captured and as a result of extensive patrolling it became clear that we were now in a position to make the next move forward. By the morning we were able to walk about in the forward company areas quite openly, but it was a luxury we had no time to sit and enjoy; preparations had to be made for the attack on Le Busq. The Commanding Officer took the company commanders off on a reconnaissance of the start line, though in practice it turned out to be more of a patrol than a reconnaissance. A quarter of an hour's walk down a narrow, dusty road brought us to the area occupied by the 11th Armoured Division on our right, and from here we struck out into a terra incognita by way of a deep, sunken lane that ran off to the left, parallel to our own front but across the valley. We knew, of course, that this side of the hill was unoccupied, but over the brow lay Le Busq and there was no guarantee against meeting a German patrol, so that we had to move rather cautiously with everything

ready, just in case.

On either side of us the hedges were so high and the brambles so thick that it was impossible to see anything, and the lane was more of a tunnel through the

Lt Colonel Roddy Hill DSO, who took over command of the Battalion. 4th August 1944.

The Commanding Officer at Battalion Command Post at Le Busq.

undergrowth than anything else. We talked in low voices and peered round corners with drawn revolvers rather as people in training films do, and I felt that if we suddenly did come face to face with a German he would be much more likely to say "Boo!" than to shoot. It seems a slightly opera bouffe affair now, but it was serious enough at the time and, like all events in war, it is often only a very narrow margin that separates tragedy from comedy.

Half-way down the lane we came upon one of the Mick tanks that had been knocked out two days before as they tried to capture the ridge. One of the crew had escaped alive, so we knew which tank it was and who was in it, but otherwise nothing but their identity discs could have shown who they were. Always, always it seemed to be the same: "The paths of glory lead but to the grave"; that, one might accept, but, "Oh, God, is this the grave?" Day after day the same sight – the huddled bundles in the ditch; the corpse-like attitude; the rotting uniform for a shroud; bodies curiously shrunken and frozen, gesturing like a tailor's dummy; the waxen face that knows no more surprises; and then in the heat – skin turned parchment, blackening; a hideous caricature of man, a mockery of life. Familiarity and time bring no inoculation against the horrible revulsion that one feels, and over all the sickly, inescapable stench of putrefaction until there comes a time when death is not so much a state as a smell, and the last honours that can be paid to one's fellow-men become a repulsive nightmare. That carcass almost too frightful to look at that was once a friend who walked and talked as we still do – what lies between to make such a Satanic gibe at life? How many people will ever know what agony it cost to bury them? There are no answers to questions like these; one can only say that the task was never shirked.

We didn't linger once the start line was chosen; we found that the lie of the land made it impossible to see anything of the ground we would have to attack over; and in confirmation of our suspicions we met a French farmer who told us that only a few moments before a German patrol had been scouting around the area, so there was little but the prospect of a most unwelcome encounter to keep us there and we made our way back to La Marvindiere for the "O" Group.

I have never known a leisurely prelude to an attack – however much time has been left for giving orders and making all one's preparations, there is always a feeling that you will never have time to get everything done, and that some important detail will be forgotten in the rush; but this is probably a merciful circumstance. Nothing is so damaging to one's spirits as those painful pauses before an attack when everything that can be done has been done and you are left a victim of the fancies of imagination and the natural forebodings of the moment. A carefully timed scramble is the best of beginnings, so that as soon as the last item has been mentally ticked off it is time to be going.

In this case there was plenty to keep us busy right up to the last minute, as only half an hour before we were due to start the artillery programme that was to have supported the attack had to be cancelled through lack of ammunition, and this made several modifications to our plan, though in the end it turned out that there was no need for a barrage, which would only have made the attack more complicated.

The Brigadier (Douglas Greenacre) came to see us off. Charles Lambton and I had a hurried consultation on the future command post and one by one the minutes raced away. The two signallers arrived with our wireless set and began calling up the companies to test the net. It was going to be very hot, a shimmer of heat-waves pulsated above the parched earth, and I would have liked to leave my coat behind, but I needed all the things that were stowed in its many pockets.

The leading company marched through the orchard behind us on their way up to the road.

We consulted our watches – it was time to go.

To get to the start line we merely had to follow the same route that we took earlier in the day, so there were no worries about finding the way and we knew exactly how long it would take – ten minutes down the road and there were the outposts of the 11th Armoured Division; left turn down a path through a small wood and we came to the cluster of farm buildings where the R.A.P. was to be established; still going left through the barns and out-houses, we found the entrance to the sunken lane; and then after another ten minutes we reached the big gap in the hedge and the track that was to mark the inter-company boundary; here

Digging in, trenches at Le Busq.

we halted. A tangle of hazel and brambles topped the banks on either side, filling the lane with dark shadows and cool patches where the grass was still quite moist with dew despite the heat of the day. The whole length of the lane was full of men, taking up positions by the gaps so that they could scramble out into the fields beyond when the time came, and having a last cigarette in the few moments of quiet that remained. Michael Willoughby, whose company was to attack on the right, and Francis Brown, who had taken over No. 1 Company on the left, came down to our command post in the centre to have a last word before the "off." Quietness lay over the whole scene like a blanket, as oppressive as the stifling heat – not a gun fired, nothing marked the steady progress of the minutes, then suddenly the mortars in the field behind us began to fire. It was the opening signal and everyone began to scramble out of the lane into the fields beyond.

"Bang, bang, bang, bang, bang."

"Well, here we go – what a long time they take to come down!"

"Crump, crump, crump, crump."

"Any news on the wireless yet? No? Of course not; there couldn't be yet."

"Bang, bang, bang, bang, bang," went the mortar bombs; they seem to get caught up in the clouds.

"Crump, crump, crump."

We stepped out of the lane, through an orchard and then down the side of a large cornfield. In the shadows of the lane one had become unaccustomed to the glare – it felt like stepping out on to a stage.

I walked along with Colonel Roddy. We were a lonely little party, about six of us, and no one in sight anywhere, but then, of course, there couldn't be, as we were the only people going by that route and there were too many hedges and orchards for us to see anything on either side.

The Commanding Officer said: "We ought to have had some sort of escort to protect us – we'll look silly if we run into some enemy." The idea hadn't entered my head until then, and after that I felt miserable and became a prey to calculations about whether you ever heard the one that hit you or not.

Beyond the cornfield was the main road moving along the top of the ridge just as we had expected, and then down the far slope a couple of tiny meadows and another sunken lane that led one across the hill towards where we knew Francis's company would be. By now the companies were getting down to the stream at the bottom of the valley which had been given as the final objective, and we made our way down the lane to our left where it runs into an orchard and a small farmhouse that seemed suitable for Battalion Headquarters. Farther down in the valley we could hear Bren guns firing, and there had already been reports of engagements with snipers and outposts, but otherwise very little trouble. As we came to the end of the lane the situation suddenly changed.

Brrrrrrr ah brrrrrrr ah – there was no mistaking it, and soon it was not one Spandau firing; it had become a battle.

We could hear German mortar bombs coming over – Eeeeeeeeeee.

"No, not us."

Crrrrrrrumph, crrrumph, crump – it was down in the valley where the right-hand company was.

Then again the German mortars fired – umph, umph, umph, umph in the distance.

Eeeeeeee, crrrump, crump, crump, crrrrump. As the shells came down it was a little closer, so that one began instinctively to measure the distance to the nearest ditch.

Brrrrrrrr ah, brrrrrrrr ah – there was the hell of a battle going on just below us. Things began to spatter and whiz through the branches above us, and I remember eyeing a little plaster-coated cottage a few yards farther on as a suitable shelter.

"Another cigarette is essential – extraordinary how dry one's mouth becomes on these occasions; it must be smoking too much."

Zzzit'ang, eeeeeeeeee, crrrrump, ssssssstrump. Something exploded in the wood beside us, filling the air with smoke and the smell of cordite.

"I think we'll move the wireless up beside that house. … " I was quite determined to sit behind something, however inadequate, and it served its purpose. The wireless was working wonderfully; we could speak to everyone, but there was no need of a wireless to know what was happening – we were all spread out on the exposed side of the hill in full view of the German defences, open to their fire in exactly the way they must have expected, and in the big fields below us, where the corn stood high ready for the harvest, life was becoming increasingly tenuous under the growing weight of fire that the Germans were putting down.

Brrrrrr ah brrrrrr ah. Leaves and twigs were snapped off and fluttered on the ground about us. Mortar shells were bursting in the lane, sending up showers of earth and leaving the air full of smoke and sound. We shifted about against the yellow-plaster wall wondering whether there was anywhere better to sit and what was coming next.

The little things immediately all around me still remain as vivid as at the time. The bakelite microphone growing damp and moist in my sweaty hand, the nettles and grass that grew more luxuriantly just where we sat at the juncture between the yellow-plaster wall and the ground, earth sticking to the talc on my map, and the UMPH iiiiiiiii-ing of whatever it was that was much too close just then.

"Hullo, Baker Two. Yes, that is quite clear; I will tell Sunray … . Wait out."

The companies were having heavier and heavier casualties and the Commanding Officer decided to pull back and hold the reverse side of the slope; our present position was untenable. Michael always said that in all the war he never received a more welcome order.

Meanwhile there was a lot to be done: we wanted our guns in action to help us back over the hill; there were all the details of our new positions to be fixed; and a great deal else. I was more than a little worried because during all these deliberations while the companies withdrew the command post still sitting by the cottage had become by now one of the foremost posts of the Battalion.

Eeeeeeeee, crrrrrrump.

"No, not right here!"

CRRRRUMP, crump, crrrrrump.

"The bloody something somethings."

"Noisy, isn't it?"

"It's a bit rough, sir. Have a cigarette?"

"Ah, yes, the very thing; thank you. Blast! – what was it they said? I couldn't catch it."

"Only got the first part, sir."

"Hullo, Baker Niner. Say again last message, Baker Nine. Over." "Hullo, Baker Niner. I'm in position now where you said and have contacted Sunray hard friends. Are there any orders for him? Over." "Hullo, Baker Niner. Willco. No, no orders yet. Hold on to him and Sunray will be round to see you soon … .

Baker Niner, out … . The carriers are O.K., sir and … hullo, one zero; no, wait out … and the squadron's up there too.

What about the tanks?" And so it goes on – but all I wanted to do was to move elsewhere, and it was a great relief when at last the time came.

"Well, Jocelyn, I think I've got everything arranged with Toby now and I shall go over to see Francis's position; you go back to that cornfield just over the hill – do you know the one I mean?"

"Yes, sir."

"Right; that's where we'll have the command post. You go back and get that arranged and I'll join you later on."

I was delighted and started back as fast as I could. In the lane I found No. 2 Company and some wounded who were being helped back up the hill.

"Do you know where the R.A.P. is? … Good, well done … . Any idea how we can get out of this lane?"

Eventually we found a gap that we could get through and I made my way back up the hill to the cornfield behind the main road.

There was a short lull when we got back on to the ridge so that suddenly it seemed one was again able to reflect and consider, as opposed to merely registering the impact of events. It had all been most unpleasant, very much more unpleasant than I had expected. Was it only two hours since the attack started? It seemed almost as though it must have been a different day when we first walked down the lane. Something had happened since then so that I almost felt like a different person, tireder, not quite so self-possessed, or, to be honest, I had been very frightened. Now after the immediate crisis was over the sensation was one of intense satisfaction. We've done it; of course there was never any doubt about that, but it's nice to be sure. Come what may, we're the master of the situation now. We've captured Le Busq – probably no one else cares, but that doesn't matter very much; we've discovered an immense secret, wholly inexplicable but good to have. How many casualties have we had? Probably not many of poor Nick Coles's platoon got back. Oh, yes, one knows the cost of war now … . Lest we forget … lest we forget … . Can one ever forget?

And while all this strange jumble of thoughts was going through one's mind, half an understanding that was clear and certain and half incomprehension, all the time there were endless problems to be dealt with as the machinery of our defensive position fitted itself together piece by piece into one co-ordinated whole. Ben Blower came up and put the anti-tank guns into their positions, the mortars registered new tasks, Toby got out a defensive-fire plan for the guns, and the Pioneers started to dig the command post. Signallers began to lay lines out to the companies, the command post vehicles arrived in the field behind us, messages had to be sent back to Brigade Headquarters and orders received. No. 4 Company were digging in in the field beside us, and beyond this No. 2 Company were already in position astride the road. A message came back from No. 1 Company to say that Sunray was on his way back and would like a cup of tea. Toby in his tank was registering the new fire tasks. Slowly the shape of the world in which we were to live for the next two days was taking shape.

The lull turned out to be only a short one and soon we heard an old familiar sound ... Erwerp, erwerp, erwerp, erwerp ... (nebelwerfer) ... .

"No hurry yet; they'll be a long time arriving ... ."

Weeeeeeeeee ...

"Yes, it's our way this time. Don't dither; get in the trench ... ."

eeeEEEEE ... WOOMPH ... !

Six of them all at once – a huge mushroom of smoke rose up from the corner of Derek's field where they landed and then out of that a mass of flame and a pall of black smoke that went pillaring up into the sky growing and expanding as it went. One of the shells by a million to one chance had gone straight into the open turret of a tank, completely overturning it so that now all that remained was an inferno of heat – a self-consuming furnace. Even when you had seen it happen it seemed incredible that such a cataclysmic piece of destruction could occur.

There were three or four batteries of nebelwerfers in action and for a time the noise was almost continuous. The houses behind us were hit and the thatched roofs caught fire so that soon they were all aflame. Beams fell from the roof, sending up showers of sparks. It was a complete tinder-box and no sooner did the fire die down in one place than it caught on again somewhere else with a crackle and roar of revived energy. And then almost before we had had time to complete all our arrangements the night was upon us, cold, curiously quiet, and very dark, with nothing but the still-smouldering hulks of the houses showing up through the hedge to lighten the scene. Routine and order descended upon the command post; the steady hum and cackle of the wireless, the last swig of Calvados and a cigarette before curling up in a blanket for some sleep, a subdued conversation, earth falling off the sides of the trench and trickling down one's neck ... .

"Well ... that was that. How long is a night?"

Once you have become familiar with a new field, a new hill, or a new wood, after that everything that follows is a question of pattern – a gradual ageing that wears the countryside down to the ever-repeated pattern of war. The winding festoons of signal cable in the hedgerows grow in number and complexity, the cornfields become trodden in by countless pathways or flattened and pock-marked by shelling; shell splinters lop boughs off the trees and the bark becomes seared and scarred by hits; paths are turned into lanes, lanes are turned into roads, and everywhere the dust begins to rise, powdering the hedges, growing, endlessly multiplying, until it alters the whole landscape. The turfed bank, the tree beside one's trench, everything takes on an air of permanence and individuality so that at times it seems almost as much a part of you as anything that one has ever known.

Perhaps all this may give the impression that we, too, were no more than passive entities weathering the storm like the Rock of Gibraltar. Nothing could be farther from the truth; we had to feel out all round us to discover what the enemy were doing and keep up a constant anti-nebelwerfer warfare. With infinite ingenuity and care Sergeant Dales and his patrol were established at the bottom of the valley within a few hundred yards of the Germans and connected up to the command post by telephone. It was a Cyclops, an eye right in their midst that proved a gold mine of information. And when at Corps and Army Headquarters the higher Acorns*[6] mark up the map with such an assured and well-informed air, I often wonder if they ever knew upon how few and upon what a tenuous circumstance their information rested.

Patrols; shellreps (we were determined to get the better of the nebelwerfer), adjustments, reports on this and that; all the time we were assimilating and adding to our hold upon things. And over and above there was the eternal and ever-difficult problem of maintaining our existence, cooking, feeding, water, ammunition, sleep, casualties, petrol, communications, batteries, maps, an endless series. Long-awaited dawns, and then perhaps at stand-to a visit to a neighbouring company to chat on this or that and free one's mouth from the tyranny of heavy smoking and little sleep.

Everything at first dark and hidden, the hedges and trees mere shapes on a familiar and oft-repeated path.

"Do you know where Major Mackean is ?"

"Just over by that truck, sir."

Is it? Yes.it is.

"Ah, my dear George! Good-morning, good-morning. How goes the world?"

"Pretty grim. What's the news?"

"Oooh – all quiet on the Western Front. What did you expect?" "Well, you ought to know. What's the bigger picture?"

It all helped to while away the tedium, and I liked to watch Guardsmen Melks cooking George's breakfast. Then from Support Company it was only a question of walking

---

6   Intelligence officers.

on through a couple of cornfields and you came to No. 2 Company and could resume the same sort of nonsensical conversation. An inexplicable instinct seemed to urge one to keep touching things just to make sure they were still there. And so the days began; but, they were not days or nights on a conventional pattern: we slept as and when we could, and it was not so much a routine of night and day as an unending story with a background of alternate light and darkness. And then when it was time to stand-down, back down the road past the burnt-out tank, left turn through the gap in the hedge and there was the old familiar cornfield, by now no longer a world of silhouettes, for colour is creeping back into the tall line of trees behind the command post, and in the middle of the four-square trenches the pile of earth is changing from a shape into a mound of brown and yellow earth. Through the trees the ruined remains of the cottages have become grey, stone walls, and above the sky is turquoise blue.

We held the position at Le Busq for three days, from the 6th until the 9th of August, and the duel between ourselves and the nebel- werfers was a constant feature. Certain hours of the day were more likely to be noisy than others, and in time one discovered that some places were more frequently stonked than others, but there was never any guarantee, and at times it required a tremendous effort to leave the comparative safety of one's trench. If you walked across to a company it was always done with one ear ready and listening for the warning sound of a coming shell, and one eye open to the possibilities of sheltering in the nearest ditch. One had to steel one's nerve for even the simple demands of a daily necessity; nothing was entirely without anxiety or uncertainty, so that even the few hours of sleep that one managed to snatch were constantly liable to be shattered by the thunderous detonations of a stonk. With sleep came escape; it was the most wonderful tonic of all; but then, just as you lay down and closed your eyes there would be: "What was that?" "Erwerp, erwerp, erwerp."

"Oh, hell, here they come again!"

EeeeeeeEEEEEE, sssst ERUMPH, UMPH, UMPH, UMPH, UMPH.

And then, of course, you have to get up and see if everything is all right.

How to sleep when all the time you are listening and thinking; it isn't easy. We didn't sleep very well. Besides all this, we were frequently shelled by our own side. Estry that we had tried to capture with a company attack three days before was now the centre of bitter resistance, and less than a mile down the road to our left a whole division was battling away to capture it and the overs from their attack all landed on us. It took many attempts before it was finally captured, but at any rate we felt that our reputation was redeemed " since a division failed where we had failed with a company.

We were never able to have a company in reserve, as No. 3 Company couldn't be relieved when we moved from La Marvindiere, and when finally another battalion did take over that position our commitments were still further extended so that we were permanently a thin red line along the crest of the hill and isolated, with both flanks open, it was a worrying time. But amid all these difficulties we were growing more and more confident and more and more sure that we were a rock about which the storm might rage in vain.

It was far quieter when we left Le Busq; still, we were glad to go, and though we had to march down the ridge and take over a position behind Le Bas Perrier it was at least a reserve position, even though it was liable to be shelled, and it gave us some opportunity to get organized. To be exact, it gave us forty-eight hours, and the locality was not a very desirable one. The fields were full of dead cows all swollen and distended into monstrous attitudes, with their feet sticking woodenly into the air like overturned rocking-horses. Everywhere smelt of death: the bodies grew more and more putrid. Whole horrible cycles of maggot life multiplied and thrived upon the feast, and the sickening stench was so strong that even after you moved somewhere else it clung and haunted one's every moment.

It would be a great injustice to say that we rested there; we were still having occasional casualties from the shelling, and on the 10th we prepared to attack the village of Chenedolle. We were in action until the 18th, but the next six days must be unrecorded; they were a repetition of the previous toil and torment, and on balance the focus must remain on Le Busq, though in its way Chenedolle too was a very triumphant attack. But war is an endless story, so perhaps for that very reason this account should end at the cross-roads by Point 210 that we marched past early the next morning to begin the attack on Chenedolle.

The cross-roads were on the summit of a ridge and in front you could see a deep valley, its multiple hedges and cornfields all bleached by the sun and whitened by the dust, with a wood and the village of Bas Perrier, where the Welsh Guards were on the hill opposite. The white road shows up clearly as it dives down the near side of the valley, then crawls slantwise up the opposite side, and all the way along you can pick out the marching column growing smaller and smaller until the string of figures merges into one in the distance.

The surface of the road had become ground down into a fine powder, so that even the tramp of feet raised a haze of dust, and the valley was being shelled nearly all the time. It was not a very inviting prospect that lay ahead.

"Come on, close up, close up. Don't leave a gap there."

It makes a lot of difference to the timing. The barrage for the attack is to come down on Chenedolle in an hour's time and it can't be stopped if we're late.

The long column of marching men goes trudging on. "Good-morning, Julian."

"Good-morning, Sergeant Townsend."

"Well, there they go."

"The men who march through Picardy,
Through Picardy to hell ... ."

And by the road there stood a large wooden crucifix, and notices that read "Go slow. Dust brings shells. Dust means death." Perhaps it was a sign and a comfort to some who never reached Bas Perrier; it was about the last thing they ever saw.

BRUSSELS

WHILE WE were at Le Busq the Germans made one last trial to save the situation in Normandy, and four S.S. divisions attacked the Americans at Mortain in the hope of driving through to the sea-coast and cutting off the spearhead of the American drive to the south. Our air superiority broke up the attack the day it started, but catastrophically Hitler decided to continue the battle despite this and the growing danger of his forces being cut off at Falaise. When the Battalion captured Chenedolle on the 11th of August the suicidal effort was still being pressed on, and we found ourselves still engaged with S.S. troops, who were holding on to each position as firmly as ever; then on the 12th von Kluge gave the order to withdraw to the Seine, and as at this stage our position was needlessly isolated in view of the changed circumstances we too withdrew, but on a more modest scale and for different reasons! From a position back by Presles we kept a watch on the German withdrawal by constant patrolling, but after two days even this became unnecessary; our sector had been completely evacuated and we were left in a state of peaceful isolation while the tide of battle swept eastwards towards Falaise.

If the decision to counter-attack at Mortain had not been made, or even if the attack had been called off two days earlier, it is probable that our drive to Brussels would have been a rather different story, but as it was the bulk of the German Seventh Army were caught in the trap and only remnants of the S.S. divisions managed to extricate themselves. Portions of the German Fifteenth Army were rushed up to bolster the defences of the Seine and some sort of a stand was made; however, nothing could have retrieved a catastrophe of such dimensions, and within ten days of the last shot being fired at Falaise armoured divisions were sweeping across the whole of Northern France in a blitzkrieg that has never been equalled in its speed and scope.

But while the prelude to this advance was being fought some thirty miles to the east of us, we settled down to our first rest after over three weeks of continuous fighting, and we were not in the least sorry to lapse into a state of "chinagraph warfare." On ever larger and grander maps Sergeant Ayres marked up the moves of whole armies and groups of armies; everyone became amateur generals, and we watched the tide of battle with a critical enthusiasm that only detachment can bring. This was the lighter side of our activities, as immediately we were out of contact with the enemy the urgent and essential job of reorganizing and re-equipping the Battalion had to be set about with all speed in preparation for the next offensive which had already begun, and we knew that it would not be long before we were called forward again.

The Battalion had been reduced to three companies by the end of Operation "Bluecoat," and most of the senior officers had become casualties, so that a new company had to be formed and a large draft of reinforcements absorbed into our depleted ranks. Vehicles with their precious loads of stores and equipment had been destroyed, and our boots and battledresses needed repairs and replacements and among other things it was now over three weeks since anyone had had a bath. Sidney Cooper's stores were turned into a sort of military Woolworths where you could get anything and everything, only free and in wonderful profusion. One had never known the Quartermaster ask so few questions; he was a man with a cornucopia and all the time it bubbled over with new socks, new boots, new shirts, and the bewildering catalogue of oddments that make up the "necessaries" of a fighting man's kit.

On the 24th we moved on to a big hill beside the road from Flers to Conde-sur-Noireau: that too was like a new issue; the fields were green and unfought over, wonderfully refreshing after the worn and decimated landscape we had been living in. The trees were no longer scarecrows shorn of half their branches; they were luxuriantly green and undismembered. There were no putrefying cows or corpses to poison the air, everything was as clean and sparkling as the waters of the River Odin, where we went for our baths. I can still vividly remember the riverside site of the mobile baths – it would have provided a most suitable setting for the frilled and laced beauties that Fragonard liked to paint as they picnicked among the glades of Fontainebleau, but we disported ourselves by the river bank no less gaily if with less grace. And whenever there was an opportunity we explored the countryside for miles around: Domfront, La Ferte Mace, Rennes, Mont St Michel, Chartres; and some very nearly reached Paris. We brought back wine, butter and cheeses; though Charles rather spoilt the innocence of our fun by bringing back a nude from Dinant. We dined by the hedgerow on compo stew washed down by an indifferent bottle of St. Emilion and talked and talked and talked

Rest area at Flers, before the advance on Brussels, officers of both 1st and 5th Battalions relaxing together, pictured are Lt -Rt: Nico Collins, Bill Anstruther-Gray, Col Roddy, Jimmy Priestley, Bill Blackett. August 1944

until it became too dark to see. Latterly we began to ask ourselves, when all had been swept away up to the banks of the Seine, why were we, an armoured division, still sitting in a field in Normandy? But it had all been worked out. On the afternoon of the 28th I visited Michael Rosse at 32nd Brigade Headquarters. He was sitting in a tent of his own design, very much like a crystal-gazer's booth at a fair, and I found <u>him</u> trying to disentangle the remains of the Seventh Army's order of battle.

"Well – how goes the war ?"

"Ah," came the reply, "the very person I wanted to see! I've got some maps for you; we're moving."

There were two thousand, and in less than half an hour I had to get the right ones on the Commanding Officer's map board and return to an "O" Group with him. The tempo of the events then moved faster and faster; we got back to Battalion Headquarters and two hours later left with a small advance party for the village of Gourney, near L'Aigle, some sixty miles away, which we reached very late that night. The Battalion moved up through Falaise to join us, slept for a few hours and then on we went again at two o'clock in the morning, through Bretteville, Evreux, Gallion and to Vernon. The weather broke and as we drove through the town and over the River Seine rain spattered against the windscreens in a steady torrent and went coursing down the gutters. The Seine seemed unexpectedly small; it was a distinct disappointment, but all that mattered now was that we were in a new and different world with quite a new future before us. Normandy already had become a memory of the past as remote as the shores of England, and everything before us was full of promise and good omens.

At about midday we joined the 5th Brigade on a hill above the river close to the little village of Haricourt, and here we halted for a few hours while the vehicles refuelled

Flers, from Left to right, Brigadier George Johnson, Commander 32nd Brigade, General Dick O'Connor, Colonel Roddy Hill

and the final orders for the advance from the bridgehead were given out.

We felt rather ruefully that everyone else had got an unfair start on us. The 11th Armoured Division on our left were already away, the 8th Armoured Brigade had reached Gisors, and an American armoured division, accused of "bumping and boring," had overflowed on to one of our centre lines. We spent two hours at Haricourt, which was just time enough to get bogged in a very muddy field and see the sun come out again. Then we set off at the tail end of the 5th Brigade column, and reached Gisors as darkness was coming on.

The Brigade had by now passed through the 8th Armoured, but some enemy held up the leading troops and we had to halt for the night. Towards midnight there was an "O" Group that was remarkable if only for the fact that we were all somehow or other crammed into Brigadier Norman Gwatkin's caravan.

"Tomorrow," he said, "we will cross the Somme." (Come, come; you must be joking, I thought.) "Start point cross-roads 564 320. We'll start at 0200 hrs. and aim to be through Beauvais by first light." Colonel Eddie Goulburn protested that his leading company was in contact with the enemy who were still holding the cross-roads that was to be our start point.

"Very well; we must go round it somehow."

When we started in the small hours of the morning there was no moon to dispel the darkness of the night and we moved along hardly faster than at walking pace, keeping close to the vehicle in front so as not to lose sight of it. Often there were long halts and it was difficult to keep awake when the column stopped for any length of time, so that the journey was punctuated by fitful snatches of sleep and sudden awakenings as everything wound on again. We seemed to make hardly any progress at all and the day came with equal hesitation. Then at last the silhouette of the woods beside the road grew slightly firmer, and the outline of the hedges more distinct: it might almost have been imagination. Over to the east the sky became faintly luminous, grey, but growing lighter every minute, and then suddenly it was dawn, a cold, shiver-making morning with a clear, blue sky and every promise of fine weather. Soon afterwards there was a long halt and we discovered everything at a standstill for over a mile ahead of us. However, it was a very convenient time for this to happen, as we were all beginning to feel hungry and this gave us an opportunity to cook some breakfast and wash.

The people of the village were just getting up; one by one they emerged from their houses to stare at us as we shaved by the roadside, and then, having thought very deeply on the matter, they asked for our soap, which was an inconvenient request, but everything was amicably arranged and we ended up with eggs for breakfast. The happy, friendly peasantry is one side to the picture; unfortunately, there is another, so that it is as well that I have forgotten the name of the village, as we were witness to an inexcusable parade of wanton savagery against a collaborateur, and if I were Solomon I should pass judgment on the matter; as it was, I left the village feeling very disgusted and couldn't forget about the matter.

After this long pause everything went much faster. We passed through Beauvais at top speed, and there were practically no more halts until we reached the high ground just before the Somme Valley soon after midday. Here we heard that the Grenadiers were across the river and in firm possession of the far bank; apparently the F.F.I. had prevented the Germans from blowing up the bridges, and there had been no opposition on the far side except from a couple of anti-tank guns. The whole crossing was won at the cost of only two tanks. It was all wonderful; we were across the Somme with no big rivers ahead for hundreds of miles, and there did not seem to be any enemy to worry about at all. Actually there were quite a lot, but they all took to the woods, and later in the day surrendered to the F.F.I. by the hundred. Morale had collapsed to zero. We knew for certain now that this was the big moment we had been waiting for so long. There was nothing that could stop us now and we drove down into Corbie to take over the Grenadier positions feeling that it was going to be roses, roses all the way, and if possible fine weather too.

"The Somme – good gracious me! To think that this really is the Somme!" I had to keep saying it to myself to make sure that it wasn't all a dream, and doubly so because the river itself was yet another surprise. I never discovered to the end which actually was the Somme, as there were about six rivers running through the town, none of them much bigger than a stream, and all looking equally unimportant.

We had to guard the bridges and hold the slopes of the hill opposite which turned out a peaceful affair with no suggestion of anyone attacking us, and about our only task was to receive the streams of stragglers who came in to surrender. They were the Wehrmacht's very lowest: Turkistans, Mongolian Hilfswilligen, remnants of Bau battalions, and Todt units, a complete riff-raff of all nations and every circumstance. Still, a quiet night was what we most of all needed, as we had had practically no sleep for two nights and the next day we had been given Arras as our objective.

The Welsh Guards were to go ahead of us and capture Albert before branching off to the right, and at daybreak their tanks went rumbling through our position on the first leg of the advance, but Albert turned out to be a surprise: it was strongly defended and showed no signs of surrendering, so while they went into action around the town we were ordered to bypass it on a route to the west by Hedeauville, Yette and Beaumetz.

"We" had by this time become the Coldstream Group and from then until the end of the war the 1st Battalion and ourselves fought most actions hand in hand as one joint force of infantry and armour under the command of Colonel Roddy Hill, though "command" is not exactly the right word, as it was more of a co-operative arrangement that depended upon whether the armour or the infantry were playing the chief part as to who made the chief decisions. It was a remarkably successful combination, and the first two days together were crowned with success. Later on we always advanced with the two battalions mingled into one and organized as a series of joint company/squadron groups, which we achieved by a manoeuvre known as "marrying-up" whereby the two battalion columns met at the start of the advance and the prearranged groups of tanks and soft vehicles were knit into one column, but during the advance to Brussels there was so little opposition that it was more convenient and quicker to move with all the tanks in front and ourselves following behind.

The advance up to Arras gave us very little trouble, and when we were mortared going through one little village it seemed more of an impertinence than an aggression.

All the way along we kept passing cemeteries of the last war, with their ordered array of neat, white crosses, and it was almost as though we were trespassing upon the dead to be fighting once more over the fields of Flanders. On our maps we read St. Pol, Albert, Arras, St. Quentin, the Somme; everywhere the names echoed the past and filled one with a perplexity of feelings. What an inscrutable twist of destiny that we should find ourselves here in the land of trench warfare where our fathers' blood was shed to end all wars, and where for five years the mud had lain so deep; our wheels but stirred the sleeping dust and woke a monstrous comment on our times. But such a collision of the past and present was too violent for either to be comprehensible; besides, we had no time to stop and stare and the column raced on towards Arras; already the tanks were far ahead of us.

A town the size of Arras was a quite new problem to us, and the Commanding Officer was of the opinion that if we met any really serious opposition it would be impossible by ourselves to do more than invest the city, but the tanks were already entering the outskirts and meeting very little trouble, so it was decided to take a chance and the armour drove straight in. For us, however, the possibility of being involved in street fighting while still in our vehicles was a rather different question, so while the Battalion debussed just outside the town Colonel Roddy and I drove on in the scout car to see what was happening. We found the main street leading to the Place de la Gare packed with tanks and the citizens of Arras running in and out of their houses in a state of frenzied excitement while the leading tanks engaged an anti-tank gun in the square beyond. Every time the tank fired a burst of Besa or anything fired back, all the faces at the windows vanished; then as soon as there was a pause everyone reappeared more excited than ever and bubbling over with spurious information and advice. A man with a newsreel camera filmed the proceedings with methodical care, and I had a feeling that any moment he was going to ask us to "smile, please," but the hold-up came to a sudden end before he had a chance. The twenty to thirty tanks in the streets started up their engines together with a thunderous roar that nearly rattled the glass from the windows and shook the pavement like a jelly, then we rumbled on, making for the station, which was to be the rendezvous for Battalion Headquarters, while the squadrons went on to their allotted objectives. Ten minutes later the companies came marching in down the streets, now emptied of tanks, and in a short while we were able to report that we were firmly in possession of Arras.

It was a psychological victory, for, though the Germans were not properly armed or equipped to make much of a defence, there were well over a thousand in the town and they could have imposed a considerable delay on the operation if they had chosen to fight, but a rapid and calculated show of force proved the right technique for the situation and we had little trouble. In fact, we soon had so many prisoners that they were an embarrassment to us: it was hard to find a large enough space to collect them in or sufficient guards, and the populace, who had by now emerged into the streets eager to take part in anything that might be going on, were the greatest embarrassment of all. The group of command vehicles outside the station was besieged and overrun so that the Commanding Officer was kissed on both cheeks by a bearded Frenchman and everything was held up while we sang the "Marseillaise" three times over. It was all very overwhelming and the order to move on up to the high ground beyond the town came as rather a relief. We fled, leaving No. 3 Company, now commanded by Billy Hartington, to cope with things. Sergeant Todd, whom I left to organize the F.F.I. into a

Mike Bendix shaving.

guard on the prisoners, got involved in a civic reception by the mayor and a battle in a Gestapo headquarters; I don't know how he managed to get anything done at all, but this sort of thing was his metier and it was not the first time he had saved the situation.

It was a remarkable day and we had by now made such a big advance that it was impossible to record it on our usual map board; in fact, we had at this moment run completely out of maps, and I remember that when we met General Allan Adair on his rounds we found that he had been reduced to explaining the situation on a silk handkerchief map, such as you may find in an atlas, which was the only suitable thing for the occasion.

We wandered about on top of the hill feeling flushed with success, wishing that all warfare could be like this, and the only trouble we had was from two Spitfires which shot-up the road most effectively and destroyed the Welsh Guards' petrol lorries. They probably reported back "Enemy petrol installations destroyed"; it certainly looked like it, and I've seldom seen such a high column of smoke as rose up from the remains.

By now we were level with the 11th Armoured Division, and in the late afternoon we stole the lead when the Irish Guards and No. 3 Company went on to Douai. Douai wasn't such an easy affair as Arras and they had one of those sudden engagements that may always at any time occur in this type of warfare. It cost us several casualties. Unexpectedly and almost out of the blue every now and then there would be a clash; we were never likely to forget this, but time has obscured it when it should still be remembered – it wasn't all roses; bouquets and grenades were occasionally mixed.

The next day we had to have a pause for maintenance, as tanks are not like private cars, capable of running until they drop. They have to be constantly tinkered with and nursed or they very soon break down. The tracks begin to stretch and links have to be removed to tighten them up again; all sorts of adjustments have to be made and the crews cannot stand up to the strain of driving indefinitely without a rest, added to which we were getting an immense distance ahead of our supplies without which the advance couldn't go on, and for every mile that we drove the R.A.S.C. had to drive double to get things up.

We got up late the next morning to find that it was raining and blowing hard. The Canadian war memorial on Vimy Ridge that we had seen quite plainly the day before was hidden in mist and cloud, but it didn't matter very much, as all that we had to do that morning was to drive up to a little village near Douai and prepare for the next day.

In the evening Brigadier Norman held an "O" Group in one of the buildings on Douai aerodrome and the objective for the next day was announced – it was Brussels. It's a long way from Douai to Brussels, but we already knew that this was our final objective, and the only thing that came as a surprise was the decision to make it in one hop which would constitute by far the longest advance we had ever made in one day. It would be one of the longest advances ever made by anyone, and the matter required some careful consideration. Two centre lines were now available to the Division, and so the 32nd Brigade was given the main route with the prospect of meeting the most opposition and the 5th Brigade, which we were in, was given the wiggly route which would probably be less strongly held but was much longer and liable to break down under the heavy burden of traffic. It was a fairly even-money bet as to who would get there first. To ensure the capture of the more vital places on the route, the Airborne Division, after a heavy bombing programme, were to seize various points on the road ahead of us, but with this went the snag that we wouldn't be able to cross the Belgian frontier until eight o'clock, as otherwise we ran the risk of being caught by our own bombers. However, the air programme depended upon weather conditions and in the end a strong wind began to blow so that airborne landings were out of the question and we were left to our own devices. It was much better that way, and we were able to start two hours earlier.

The morning of the 3rd of September was cold but dry, and even though we were late starters it was still dark when we passed the start point and we had been up since 2 a.m. First to go were the Household Cavalry in their armoured cars, then the Grenadier Group, then ourselves. We felt that we could count upon an interesting day, not overburdened by anxiety, and for once we were right.

One of the most crowded areas in Europe sprawls across the countryside between France and Belgium, and for the first few hours we passed through an almost continuous string of mining villages and drab industrialism that spreads out from nearby Lille and Roubaix for miles in every direction. Lining the routes there were acres and acres of soulless little streets whose houses are more fitted for displaying the endless advertisements for "Bock Artois" or "Byrrh Vin Genereux de quinquina" than for living in, but despite this the welcoming crowds by the roadside, which had been growing more and more numerous since we left the Seine, were as enthusiastic as ever, and they all brought their gifts: apples not quite so ripe and plums not quite so luscious as in the countryside; still, the spirit was there, stronger and more vociferous than ever before.

Pont-a-Marq was the first real check, and a full-scale battle developed there that held us up for two hours until an alternative route was opened. It seemed like waiting for two days, and I remember thinking, "Of course, it will be very disappointing if we don't reach Brussels tonight, but after the loss of two hours our chances are very slight by now."

It was a Sunday, and as we sat by the roadside just short of Pont-a- Marq clusters of people all clasping their prayer-books and dressed in their Sunday-best made their way past us towards the church at the end of the road. I wonder if they prayed for us? And while I was thinking of this, loud hooting and shouts of warning proclaimed the arrival of a carload of F.F.I. grossly overloaded, with its passengers extruding out of every window like a packing case that has burst its sides. They whizzed by, scattering the churchgoers and the sightseers on either side as though the whole issue of the war depended upon their urgent business. I suppose they enjoyed themselves, but I very much doubt whether they ever fired a shot at anyone.

We edged slowly forward while the battle overflowed on to the centre line, involving Support Company in a slight skirmish, and the C.S.M. was misdirected into Pont-a-Marq, where he became a prisoner for some days. I wonder how many lives were lost during the war owing to misreading a map? I can think of about twenty without hesitation, and there were three men killed with the C.S.M. It probably ranks among the three easiest ways of losing one's life.

Pont-a-Marq was one of the 2nd Battalion billets in 1940, and for many of the Battalion the fields and woods we passed through were as familiar to-them as Big Ben. Could they ever have dreamt of such a return as this? But, then, it's always the most extravagant of fancies that turn to fact, and with Brussels as our objective the whole day seemed fabulous.

We crossed the frontier munching sandwiches, for it was lunch time, but it was on such an insignificant little road; there were no Douane or striped and coloured sentry-boxes to mark the change of country, only some obsolete pillboxes unfitted for any period of the war, which stood uselessly along the frontier boundary. At the first village, however, there was a brave display of the Belgian colours, and flags hanging from every window. The girls were all dressed in black and yellow and red costumes, and whatever they may be shouting now they cried "Vive les allies! Vive le roi! Vive la liberation!"

Tournai was swarming with people; the entire town had turned out to welcome us, and at every stop they crowded round shouting with glee and begging for souvenirs. Little children were lifted up so as to shake hands with a liberator or present a bunch of flowers, and under the stress of the moment I gave away half my stock of cigarettes, which I never ceased to regret, but, then, the whole day was a tornado of rejoicing and celebration, so that it is really very surprising that we were sane and sober at the end of it all. Kings may drive through the streets in triumphant procession, but what king has ever done it from six in the morning until twelve at night ?

It didn't take long to get through Tournai, and we went on at full speed to Frasnes, where there was another long halt while a battle took place in the next village ahead. I remember Frasnes well because we stopped opposite an inn whose owners had been sheltering an escaped British prisoner and were quite overcome by the importance of the situation.

"Bill a demeure a Aldershot – ah, un soldat magnifique – un vrai gentilhomme."

"Vraiment – vous connaissez Aldershot – mais ca c'est remarquable !"

They must have thought a great deal of Bill, I think, for they were far too grand to shout "Vive" anything; and in celebration of the occasion we were given some hot, fizzy beer. Then they told us all about the parachutists who had landed. If the weather had been different and the landings had taken place they would have been quite correct – the information was common knowledge along most of the route.

We smiled in a distant sort of way and said: "Mais vous etes certain?"

"A oui, nous les avons vus!"

"Tiens – c'est extraordinaire."

With so much that one heard or was told it was always the same: a grain of truth surrounded by clouds of error, and at least twenty people to swear: " ... but I saw it with my own eyes! hurt surprise and indignation welling up at the least suggestion of doubt.

After Frasnes came a long run of country, an unchanging panorama of gentle hills that runs from Flanders to the flatness of the Flemish Plain. Not hills in the commonest sense with well-defined valleys and contours, but an ocean swell of rising and falling land, hedgeless and covered with a patchwork quilt of careful cultivation. Squares of green and stripes of brown in every shade and size imaginable. Plough, stubble, cabbages, potatoes, beet: a chessboard of agriculture with hardly a tree or wood to break the endless skyline, but the monotony has a charm of its own and under a blue sky it was as pleasant as one could wish. How well one knows those endless pave roads with their line of straggly trees on either side and the dead-straight miles ahead that seem to stretch out into infinity with undeviating aim. Endless generations of Englishmen must have passed down them with very much the same feeling as us, only they were unlucky and had to walk.

At Lessines we left John Knatchbull and his platoon behind to guard the bridges, as there were a number of German units still in the district and we didn't want to risk a debacle taking place behind us. As a result of the recent battle the whole town was still a little uncertain about leaving their cellars and sometimes in their faces you could catch that expression people get who look suddenly and unexpectedly upon war and see the head of Medusa. They were short of food in Belgium, though by no means starving as we had expected, but meat was non-existent in some places and in a street where two German transport horses had been killed I saw about twenty people scrambling over each other to get meat off the carcasses.

While we were in Lessines we heard that the leading troops of the 32nd Brigade were about to enter Brussels. The race was theirs, but we felt no envy or disappointment over the matter, as Brussels was everybody's prize and big enough to welcome us all. It was the fruit of the countless costly battles of Normandy, the endless weariness and strife of the past months, and even the years of training before that had paved the way to this crowning success, and as to who got there first was a small point. Brussels was a divisional triumph.

We left the town and took the road to Ninove. It's a long day that starts at two in the morning, and I was beginning to feel that I had eaten too many plums and pears – yes, it had definitely become a surfeit; the back of the scout car looked like a greengrocer's shelf and still everywhere along the road we were showered with fruit. It wasn't a case of being handed anything; as, if the column happened to be on the move, the Belgians merely lobbed their gifts in through the windows of the trucks and if you were exposed without a windscreen as I was you had to keep a very sharp look-out for incoming fruit or you were liable to receive a ripe plum in the eye.

The fronts of the vehicles were all draped in flowers and garlands, giving a rakish air of carnival to our war paint, and on the side of every truck a whole host of chalk inscriptions had been scribbled, ranging from "Vive notres liberateurs" to "Good luck, Tommy," or even "Ninette loves you" or "Fifi loves the R.A.F.," which was scarcely fair.

Sometimes the road was little more than a lane, and where on the corners the tank tracks had ground up the surface into indiscriminate heaps of earth squads of men appeared with spades and shovels to fill in the ruts. It was about the most valuable task they could perform.

Occasionally the road became almost impassable and several vehicles got stuck in some of the worst places, but we managed to struggle along, and slowly the light faded into darkness.

At about ten o'clock we began to reach the suburbs. By then the night was completely black and all that one could gather was that from the increasing number of big, dark shapes on each side we were about to enter the city – yes, it was unmistakable. We checked our position with care, and halted just outside to make a plan. It was all very dark and difficult, so that everyone had to crowd round the headlights of the Commanding Officer's car to see their maps, and even then were not much the wiser, as we only had ordinary maps, which showed a maze of streets on such a crowded scale that it was hard to be sure that we would ever find the right positions.

We had been given a sector of the city to hold, and by guarding various bridges could manage to keep some control over it from a military point of view, but this seemed almost superfluous and all we knew for certain was that

Brussels was in chaos, chaos and celebration absolute and without limit.

The column started up again and then slowly drove down the wide spaciousness of the Chausee Ninove towards the centre of the storm. There was a complete black-out in the city and the only visible light came from a line of masked street lights hung down the centre of the road like a green necklace suspended in the sky. At first the pavements were thinly lined, but soon the crowds were five, ten, twenty deep; and they cheered and sang and waved endlessly – a sea of faces that surged forward whenever there was a pause and clambered on to any vehicle they could get on to so that we were kissed and embraced and half- suffocated every ten minutes.

They were deliriously happy and we were happy too; it seemed that there had never been so much happiness: nothing like this had ever happened before or could ever happen again.

Tanks of the first battalion parade with guardsmen of the fifth battalion aboard during the joyful liberation of Brussels, an experience long remembered afterwards by those who took part.

Little groups collected together in the open spaces to dance hand in hand and sing:

"We're going to hang out the washing,

Sur le ligne Siegfried ..." or

"It's a long way to Tipperary,

It's a long way to go ..."

We might have sung with them, but we were too tired and it was very hard to be sure whether they were singing in French or English – it was all so mixed, a wonderful confusion of joyful noise.

Every now and then the door of a cafe would burst open, sending a great shaft of light across the pavement while people struggled in and out followed by great gales of laughter and mirth from inside. The night air smelt of cheap scent and cigars, but at the time it was like incense – it was Brussels.

I don't know how we avoided running over anybody in such a crowd, but somehow we managed to squeeze our way down to the end of the Chausee Ninove, then over the Canal du Charleroi and into a little square on the right called Place du Metz. We were there. All around us was Brussels, liberated Brussels, Brussels crazy with delight – for Brussels the war had ended, and I thought how nice it will be if our war ends this way, too, but it didn't; life is not so simple.

Throughout the night the celebration went on undiminished; the fount-head of gaiety seemed to be inexhaustible, and over all the revels and the singing the great dome of the Palais de Justice, a huge and solitary fire, burnt like a flambeau lighting up the darkness.

The next day the crowds seemed to be even bigger than before, and when I set off with the Commanding Officer to drive to 5th Brigade Headquarters by the Royal Gardens we were so mobbed on the journey that it took us nearly an hour. In the end we didn't even dare to stop and ask the way, as the only time we tried this about ten people immediately climbed on board the jeep to act as guides while twenty more crowded in front, making any further progress impossible. Eventually we got there and received orders to guard a series of roads on the outskirts so as to prevent any stray enemy columns from escaping through the northern quarter of the city. It seemed almost as much a measure for our self-protection as of military significance, and we drove out to our new home near the site of the Brussels Exhibition early in the afternoon. It was much quieter, and by exercising great diplomatic skill Bill Blackett found us some comfortable billets where we could escape from the turmoil and confusion in the streets to a degree of luxury that I had almost forgotten existed. It was nearly three months since we had last seen the inside of a house, and I found that I had become quite unaccustomed to sitting in a chair; it seemed much more natural to sit on the floor. As for the plumbing, if there had been the time we would have been happy pulling plugs and turning taps all day – just for the fun of it. But one way and another we were still kept very busy, and whenever there was a quiet moment someone was sure to arrive who claimed to be the chief of the underground movement or the head of the British Espionage Service. I've never known so many aspirants to cloak-and-dagger fame; everyone seemed to have gone spy-mad. Then on the second day they went peace-mad.

"Didn't you know? Why, yes, of course, the war is over – it was broadcast on the wireless – absolutely official – not a doubt about it."

Everyone in Brussels believed the rumour, and the celebrations began all over again with redoubled vigour. I spent the afternoon sitting in the command post, which was a schoolroom decorated with little charts giving the Flemish and the French names for various species of local fauna and flora. By the evening I could have made myself quite useful on a Flemish farm, but it's all gone now; only one line of thought was really engraving itself on my mind, and that went rather like this; "Surely the war must be over. This is such a very good moment for it to end; it's only right that it should do so. The whole picture fits; obviously nothing can keep it going for much longer, and this is the perfect situation for the finish. Besides, I can't believe that every single person in Brussels is mad. It seems much more likely that we are, and, anyway, I don't think I can compete with any more war. There's only one possible answer – it must be true; the war must be over."

It was wishful thinking on an enormous scale, but Brussels encourages dreams and when we wished for champagne, we got it in vast, unlimited quantities, a present from the Armde Blanch. We could have as much as we could carry away and we did, though our "vehicle loading scales" were hardly designed for this sort of thing.

On the 6th all our wishful thinking came to an end. Brussels had just been a festive interlude, a wonderful and unforgettable experience, and we all vowed that if ever it were possible we would come back, but it was still only an interlude and we took the road towards the north-east very early in the morning, feeling as one often does after a party.

Despite the early hour there was still quite a crowd to see us off and they stood in groups on the pavement waving and shouting:

"Good-bye, Tommy! … Good luck, Tommy!"

Good luck. That was very important, I felt.

BELGIUM

THE STORY of our advance from Brussels is a story of canal crossings and bridgehead fighting; and the backcloth to these actions is a vast stretch of unbelievably drab countryside that stretches from Diest up to the Dutch frontier. It's the type of land that appears to be dear to people who grow cabbages, live in mean, ugly houses with every convenience, and seem to have no other relaxation than to go on a bicycle from one characterless little estaminet to another. And interspersed with this are huge tracts of wilderness that at times become too inhospitable even for fir trees and degenerate into acres and acres of sandy waste that seem to have no use except to act as parking grounds for broken-down vehicles that are beyond human aid or interest.

We only spent ten days there and afterwards it became the land of dumps – ordnance dumps, R.E.M.E. dumps, R.E. dumps, and a home for anyone who had anything dumpable. It was as though Providence had designed and guarded the land through all time for this one glorious realization of its only practical use. Its titular capital, Bourg Leopold, once the Aldershot of the Belgian Army, became in later days a transit camp where the B.L.A. used to clamber on to cold, often windowless trains to go on leave during the depressing winter of 1945.

But to return to the tactical situation. After the wholly unsuccessful effort to try to hold us up on the Somme, the Germans were, so to speak, "getting to hell out of it," and after Brussels, the country being increasingly flat and featureless as it approaches Holland, there were only two lines on which the Germans could reasonably hope to hold us up for any length of time, and both of them were used; firstly, the Albert Canal and, secondly, the Escaut Canal, which run like twin ditches some ten miles apart and closely parallel to the Dutch frontier.

We left Brussels in the best of good spirits. The canal bridges would no doubt be blown, but the German Army appeared to have so little fight left in it we felt that at the most we would probably only be faced with rather desultory scrapping on the pattern of the last few days, and that the only serious delays ahead would be the time taken up by bridge building. I don't think the Higher Command held quite such an optimistic view, but at all events that was how it appeared to us. We felt like a champion boxer preparing to give the coup de grace to an opponent just tottering to his feet after being down for a count of eight. It's curious how often even the seemingly predictable turns out to be the exact reverse of what one expects. Certainly this was so in the case of the fighting on the Albert and Escaut Canals, and what we had forecast as a comparatively easy operation turned out to be, for us, one of the most hard-fought episodes in the whole campaign.

The Division advanced from Brussels on two centre lines. The main one ran through Louvain, already in our hands, via Diest to the crossing over the Albert Canal at Beeringen. We were then with the 5th Brigade and following a minor route just north of the main road which reached the canal some seven miles above Beeringen. It didn't take long to cover the odd thirty miles from Brussels up to the Albert Canal and by the early afternoon the forward troops had had time to investigate the possible crossing points and report them all blown except for the bridge at Beeringen, which was reported breached rather than blown, and accordingly this was chosen as the site for the Divisional bridgehead and the centre line which we were on was abandoned.

While the 32nd Brigade did the assault crossing at Beeringen we settled down for the night in the village of Tessenderloo, about half a mile back from the canal. We were shelled during the night and lost some vehicles, but personally I slept soundly throughout. It was all very straightforward. The next day for a start was also very straightforward. A German panzer division was thought to be advancing up the road from Liege towards Diest and in the middle of the morning we had to say a hurried good-bye to Tessenderloo and rush south to block the Diest road. The inhabitants were very alarmed to see us go, as after our departure there was no one to defend the village except the local resistance people. I armed them with all the captured German weapons that we had, but this was not enough, as later the Germans recrossed the canal and recaptured the village. It's strange how coldly one can record this now. There were disaster, panic and reprisals when the Germans came back, and I suspect that in the story of Tessenderloo there is as much of hope and fear and tragedy as anyone could wish for to fill a whole book, and yet it was a very small incident, not even recorded in the war diary.

We said, "What – the Germans back in Tessenderloo? Well, well. They'll have to take the flags down again." And that was that.

Diest is one of those towns that appear to have been maliciously and intentionally planned as a maze so that not even their inhabitants are always very sure of the way, and we had some difficulty in shepherding the Battalion column through its narrow and confusing streets, added to which there were by now an enormous number of other convoys making their way up towards the canal and producing the inevitable crop of traffic jams. It was well into the middle of the afternoon by the time we had finally got ourselves into position south-west of the town, and we were all very hungry, tired and rather cold. The summer was coming to an end amid periodic squalls of rain and fitful bursts of sunshine that were never quite long enough to dry one's clothes after the previous shower, and, besides the weather, the countryside was also beginning to take on the signs of autumn. In the orchard where we parked Battalion Headquarters just by the big road junction where the Liege and Louvain roads meet, the trees were all bowed down with the harvest of apples and pears. Backing our vehicles into the orchard produced a perfect downpour of fruit which was not altogether unintentional, as, though it was against all the rules to pick anything from the trees, fruit on the ground was regarded as fair game, and we were all very hungry.

At about four o'clock Brigadier Norman Gwatkin arrived and we received orders to move off as soon as possible to Beeringen so as to be ready to put in an attack at first light the next morning. Across the canal the bridgehead battle was apparently developing along the all- too-familiar line that the B.B.C. would no doubt refer to as "growing opposition." At first the opposition had been very slight. The Welsh had captured Beeringen on the far side and had passed on and got, with little difficulty, as far as Hechtel. By now, however, the Germans had got their counter-measures into action and numerous fresh identifications showed that they were doing everything in their power to contain the bridgehead we had so far formed, and would no doubt try to push us back across the canal. At first there had only been a rather unreliable infantry regiment against us, but since then a parachute battalion had arrived and Hechtel was found to be stoutly held by S.S. troops. The plan for the next day was that the Welsh Guards should attack Hechtel, some five miles to the east of Beeringen, while we pushed down the road to Bourg Leopold, about the same distance to the north. This would form a sizeable perimeter from which the Division could break out when everything was ready for the move up to the Escaut, and the two objectives were chosen because they sat astride the only main roads available. We were warned that the bridge and Beeringen were both being very accurately shelled, as the Germans could overlook the whole area from a huge slag-heap just outside the town; however, the Irish Guards were to capture this before our attack, so that we hoped for a fairly unhindered move up to our start line when the time came. But before anything else could be considered the Commanding Officer realized that we were going to have to make some very fast moves in order to take a look at the ground over which we were to attack the next day, and settle ourselves in by the canal before the light failed, and as it turned out we were unable to do any of these things: darkness won the race.

There was just time to eat a few mouthfuls of the usual bully beef and Maconochie stew and then the "O" Group was piled into an assortment of jeeps and we drove off at top speed to find the Irish Guards Headquarters in Beeringen while the Battalion was left to pack up as hurriedly as possible and follow us as soon as they could.

By the time we got there, however, it was too dark to go and reconnoitre the start line and there was nothing the Commanding Officer could do but exchange a few notes with the Irish Guards and give them the rough outline of our intentions for the morrow. I wasn't sorry to spend such a short while in Beeringen. It had been knocked about a good deal by German shelling and everyone was obviously expecting more trouble to come. They moved uneasily about the streets with that tired, strained look that people get after a heavy day's fighting. And though they probably say, "Oh, it's not going too badly," if you are rested yourself you can read behind the mask they wear almost exactly how the day has been – how many casualties they have had, how tired they are. The nervous strain seems to write things on people's faces so that the situation is not just a state of affairs to be studied on the map; you can feel it and see it in everyone you meet.

And then you go away almost guilty of your own easy composure and with the nasty reflection that next day you will yourself be in the land of the harassed and unhappy.

We just had time to earmark a field behind the canal as a harbour area for the night before it got completely dark and then we had to rush back to warn the Battalion of the arrangements that had been made. We were in touch with them on the wireless, so we knew roughly how far they had got, but with the roads so full of traffic it was difficult to be sure of intercepting the right part of the column in the pitch darkness, but fortunately we hit it off exactly, and while Bill Blackett was left to marshal the hundred-odd vehicles into our field the Commanding Officer and myself went off to arrange the plan of attack at the 32nd Brigade Headquarters. It was one of the darkest nights I can remember. A few lights had been put out to illuminate the prisoners' cage, a little dannert-wire enclosure with about two hundred Germans in it expressing dumb resignation and desolate despondency. It seemed incredible that such a congregation of unkempt and shadowy scarecrows could have been fighting troops a few hours ago and yet it's always the same, and we were cheered by the sight of so many Huns already eliminated from the battle. Beyond the lights one could see nothing at all. We asked: "Where is the A.C.V.[7]?"

"Oh, just over there in the corner of the field."

As we couldn't even see the person we were talking to this wasn't very helpful, but we got there somehow or other, and settled down inside to confer about the battle.

The chief decision was that the attack would have to be split up into four phases – two companies to do the first attack and then the remaining two to pass through them on to the next objective and so on down the road to Bourg Leopold. The Brigadier was of the opinion that we wouldn't complete the operation in one day, but we were to start as early as possible in the morning and get as far down the road as we could. We had our old friends the 55th Field Regiment to support the attack and the tanks of the 1st Battalion. When there was nothing more to be arranged they said good-night to us and good luck, and all the other things that people are given to saying before a battle. We stumbled back through the darkness to the scout car, and

I climbed on board feeling that it was more like a hearse than anything else.

There is always a slight gap between the impersonal stage of marking things up on a map, planning what is to be done, and the realization that the whole affair is something very deeply affecting oneself. While you are sitting in an

---

7   Armoured Command Vehicle.

A.C.V. listening to the Brigadier discussing objectives with the Commanding Officer everything is airily and pleasantly unimpassioned, a problem to be worked out with mathematical nicety according to the rules of war: then when the decisions have once been made it all suddenly becomes an inexorable snowball of events bearing you forward to who knows not what. It's no longer a question of "Shall it be this or that?" It is: "5th Battalion will attack...." ; and this like a sort of echo will be repeated by hundreds of people passing on their particular part of the plan for the attack until probably in the cold, dark hours of the next morning the section commander is saying to his men as they prepare to move forward: "No. 12 Section will attack ... etc." And wider and beyond the circle of men waiting for the start there will be hundreds and hundreds of others fitting their own special contribution into the march of events from the gunners waiting by their 25-pounders for the command to fire, down to the ambulances waiting to carry back the wounded. You come almost unconsciously to sense and feel all this until it is as though the "O" Group were like pressing a button to start up the engines of a battleship, and it is only when you hear the purr and feel the vibration as everything springs to life that you remember what it is really all about. And as far as battles are concerned the jolt always makes me feel a little hollow in the stomach.

Back by the canal bank we held a late conference on what was to happen the next day and the Commanding Officer gave out his orders in the back parlour of a very ramshackle cottage that we took over as a headquarters. Like most "O" Groups, it was a very crowded affair, with everyone squatting on the floor and squeezed together round two candles which were the only form of light available. We had some difficulty with the owner, an old witch of a woman who understood no known language but seemed unnaturally eager to listen in to everything that went on. Guns fired in the distance and now and then we could hear the crump of German shells falling on Beeringen. It was after midnight by the time everything was arranged and we were to have "Reveille" at four o'clock in the morning so as to have time for a hot breakfast before we left. I managed to snatch a few hours sleep, lying all bundled up like a sack of potatoes on a very draughty stone floor. Then we were woken up and ate some bacon and beans, washed down by quantities of tea. I didn't really want to eat anything, but it would very likely be the only hot meal going that day and for sustenance during the rest of the time we would have to "make do" with a haversack ration – mouthfuls of bread and bully and cheese, to be gulped down whenever the opportunity arose.

We left at five o'clock so as to have a generous margin of time in case of any hitches in the darkness and to give time for a reconnaissance of the start line before we formed up for the attack. By the time we got to the Irish Guards' outposts in front of the slag-heap it was daylight and we found ourselves on a very long stretch of straight road with a gasworks crammed with sinister-looking installations that straggled along the right-hand side, and an assortment of hideously variegated suburbia on the other. I took the scout car up to the top end of the road to wait for Colonel Roddy. There was a troop of Irish Guards' tanks there, parked outside what appeared to be the entrance to the gasworks, and some 15-cwt. trucks that had been bringing up rations. We had to sit and wait on the road, as there was a big iron fence down one side and trees on the other that made it impossible to turn off. Everything seemed to be very peaceful – then suddenly there wasssssssssst – bang! When

Forcing the canal lines at Beringen. Billy Hartington is stood on the left with Cecil Feilden and John Chandos-Pole just before the attack on Beverloo. On that day John Chandos-Pole was wounded and three platoon commanders were killed. Billy Hartington was killed the following day leading an attack in the next village of Heppen on 9th September.

The start line at Beringen where several tanks and vehicles were hit before the attack had begun.

I re-emerged from the depths of the scout car I saw smoke pouring out of one of the tanks and the others began to start up their engines and pull back into the entrance way, but almost before they had begun to move another one was hit and that also burst into flames. I saw two of the crew come tumbling out of the turret. They rolled over the back of the tank and flopped on to the ground almost as though they were rag dolls; then a truck tried to make a dash for safety, but it was caught right in the middle of the road with the back wheels knocked off and the engine on fire. Obviously the same would happen to the scout car if we tried to turn back down the road. The gun was now firing straight down the length of it and hitting some of our own transport about half a mile back. Fortunately we were more or less hidden by the knocked-out vehicles in front, but I had a nasty feeling that it was only a matter of time before we were hit and there was no immediate way out of things. I remember looking at the wireless set screwed on to the seat beside me and thinking that I must try to exactly memorize what all

128

the complicated array of dials and switches looked like, as perhaps at any moment I would suddenly never see anything else again. Normally I was either too busy or too frightened to think like that in moments of crisis, but on this occasion there was nothing that I could do and I even got rather a kick out of the matter-of-factness of my ideas. Eventually the whole road became hidden in smoke from the burning tanks and we made a dash for safety with success.

It was practically zero hour when I got back to the command post. I found a rather better parking place than the last one, then waited, watching the minutes going by and listening for the start of the barrage. But the barrage was a disaster; just before the start of the attack we were told that something had gone wrong and that there would be no supporting fire from the artillery. This was a bad setback and it made the first attack which we had hoped would be fairly straightforward particularly hazardous. No. 3 Company was on the right of the road and had to attack through an area largely covered by houses, and No. 1 Company was on the left with a big stretch of thickly grown fir plantation to clear. It was all slow going and very soon after the start we could hear the Bren guns firing and the distinctive bmrnr-ah brrrrrrr-ah of the German machine guns. We waited anxiously, listening in on the wireless for news.

Ben Blower came up. He had been wounded in the arm when the German anti-tank gun shot-up the road and hit his carrier. His face was slowly going through all the changes from white to grey, as happens with people who have been hit, but he kept on assuring me that he was quite all right and that he wouldn't dream of going back to the R.A.P. I wasn't being sympathetic; in my heart of hearts I was extremely envious, my mind full of visions of Ben going back to England on a hospital train and Ben enjoying London with his arm in a sling while I was still sitting in a wood being shot at – I couldn't think of anything in the world that I wanted so much as to be wounded like that.

It was a very hard fight to clear the Germans out of their first positions and by ten o'clock, though Billy Harrington had got his company up to their objective on the right of the road No. 1 Company were still heavily engaged and unable to capture some huts that the Germans were occupying and which made it impossible for them to reach their objective. They had had a lot of casualties in trying to do this, and the Commanding Officer decided to use another company and attack round the left of the trouble area. No. 4 Company were waiting close by so as to be ready for the next phase of the battle and so they were ordered to do the attack. It was a difficult decision because if anything went wrong all our plans would be almost irrevocably put out of gear, and as it was No. 4 Company would have to do two attacks running, but it was the only way to straighten things out, and it worked.

It took them an hour to complete this manoeuvre and they had to do some very close fighting with grenades before the enemy finally gave way, but it all went according to plan and soon afterwards we heard Cecil Feilden report on the wireless that they were no longer held up and that No. 1 Company were now on their objective.

We had captured about a mile of ground and ahead lay a more open stretch of country with the village of Beverloo some thousand yards on down the road where it makes a sharp turn to the right and there is a long village street which ends up calling itself Den Hoek as the road turns left and goes on to Heppen. The whole length of the twin villages was held by the Germans, and the companies as they came on to their objectives and reached the end of the wooded country were heavily fired at from the houses. It was the obvious place that the Germans would hold, but from our point of view it was a much better proposition than the last attack. We had our guns in action, we could see much more clearly where the enemy were, and this time we would be able to use a squadron of tanks.

Beverloo had already been decided upon as the objective for the next attack, and the Commanding Officer had already given out the basis of it, which was for No. 2 Company to capture the left-hand half of the village and No. 3 Company the right, with the squadron of tanks in support, so that only the details remained to be worked out, and the second attack of the day was timed to start at a quarter-past twelve. I wouldn't have remembered the time except for the fact that I had to take down notes for the war diary. I cannot think of a more timeless day: it was as though we were living in an eternity with minutes and hours but no morning, afternoon or evening – one long day going on and on and then suddenly and unexpectedly ending. We had already been in action for five hours and by the time the second attack started the companies had had casualties except No. 2 Company, which was comparatively fresh, or as fresh as one can be after starting at four in the morning.

For the start of the attack the guns fired smoke, and we also had a medium regiment to support us, which was just as well, as the village turned out to be strongly held and the Germans had a lot of anti-tank guns to stiffen their defences. But despite everything the attack was a complete success. Back in the fir plantation by the command post we counted over a hundred prisoners and three of the enemy anti-tank guns were also captured. The prisoners were perhaps the most heartening thing of all, as we had ourselves had a lot of casualties, but the German losses must have been far heavier, as besides the prisoners there were plenty of dead about the place and the total damage to the enemy could probably be calculated by making an estimate of dead and wounded and doubling it.

However, despite the encouragement we could get from all this, things were still very difficult and showed no signs of easing. Michael Willoughby reported that his company in the eastern edge of the village were under fire from anti-tank guns in the country beyond and all the time the Germans were continually firing on the more exposed parts of our position. There was never a moment when we could be said to be out of contact with them, as each step back was fought all the way, whatever the cost. Accordingly, the Commanding Officer decided to modify our system of attacks and do the next phase more gradually with a company going down the road as far as the railway station and then another company covering the last stretch up to the village of Heppen as soon as the first company was successful.

No. 1 Company, with the squadron, started out up the road at three o'clock and got to the station quite quickly, but the station itself was occupied by a Panther tank which they couldn't dislodge, and though the company had been able to get up to the station fairly easily by way of the thick woods on the left of the road, the squadron could only go by the open ground to the right and they had a very difficult task to do this, as all the way they were engaged by anti-tank guns and S.P. guns, which covered the road from the right. Two of the enemy S.Ps. were knocked out, but the cost was heavy and seven of our other company tanks were disabled. But this check was a matter of detail rather than a complete hold-up, and there was still time to put in yet another attack, so at four o'clock No. 4 Company were ordered to capture Heppen village and they made their attack through the thick woodland to the left of the station. They came under heavy fire almost as soon as they crossed the railway line, and though they managed to get one platoon into the village they had heavy casualties and were soon involved with very large numbers of enemy who couldn't be dislodged from the houses by the roadside and who made the company's position extremely precarious. A squadron of tanks went to their assistance and managed to make contact, but they lost two tanks in doing this and soon it became too dark for the tanks to be of any more help, so they had to withdraw, and meanwhile our wireless communications to the company broke down.

It wasn't a very good end to the day. True, we had cost the enemy a very heavy toll of casualties and were making steady progress down the road, but at the same time our own losses had been serious and No. 4 Company were still in a very uncertain position. Usually one ends the day with some feeling of elation – to have succeeded, to be still alive, whatever the cost; there is something that keeps up one's spirits, however tired one is. That evening as we dug our trenches in the field behind Beverloo we were in no mood to feel anything but grim and exhausted, and the fate of No. 4 Company was to us still a quite unknown situation. We knew that they had lost two platoon commanders and that John Chandos Pole, the company commander, had been wounded; we also knew from the reports of the tanks how things were going as the light faded, but beyond that was a question of conjecture. The Commanding Officer decided that they should be withdrawn back to Beverloo for the night and Derek Eastman, the company second-in-command, set out late in the evening in a carrier to locate the company and bring them back. In the complete darkness, with no preknowledge of the way and little exact information as to where the company were, it was not an easy mission, but he successfully got the company together and withdrew them back to Beverloo, for which he was awarded an M.C.

It was nearly midnight before the company got back; fortunately the night was quiet enough, with very little shelling by either side and not much to suggest how hard-fought the day had been.

The nights were noticeably colder and darker than before, so that in the command post I was glad to have a greatcoat to keep me warm through the long hours of waiting on the telephone. The 1st Battalion moved up their headquarters to join us in our field, which relieved us of some of our work, as they were able to provide an officer to work the rear link back to Brigade Headquarters and do duty during the night. They used to sleep in pits dug underneath their tanks, which is a good, safe sort of place to be, I imagine, but personally I would have felt more as though I were in a tomb than ever, and that night I don't believe that even a hundred-gun barrage would have woken me.

As soon as the next morning came the plan of advance was resumed and by a quarter to nine everything was ready for the attack on Heppen. We had more artillery available now and the advance was supported by the heaviest fire plan we had seen put into action for a long while.

No. 3 Company were to capture the east end of the village and No. 2 Company the west end. Heppen was another of those long, straggling, indefinite sort of villages that are so common in Belgium, and the last jump before Bourg Leopold itself. I didn't see the start of the attack, as we couldn't move up the command post owing to blocks that the Germans had made down our one and only road. They felled trees across it most of the way up and, though we had a bulldozer available, it couldn't be put to work, as the German anti-tank guns still covered the road and would have finished it off in a very short while.

The supporting fire for the attack was all that was promised; the guns made a tremendous din when everything started up, but even so the German anti-tank guns fired away with all the vigour they had shown the day before and Michael Willoughby's company lost several men as they advanced out of Beverloo. It was a quick attack and the whole thing was over in not much more than half an hour, but it was again costly and we were by now very much reduced in strength.

It's curious what a quietness sometimes sets in after a battle. It's not in the least a lull in activity, as in some ways there is even more to be done as soon as the attack is over than there is during the actual advance, but there is a psychological lull that comes with the silence of the guns, and the sensing that "We're there; we've made it."

The attack on Heppen was only just over when we heard firing and explosions going on in the distance some way behind us. To the south of us in roughly the direction of Beeringen we saw great pillars of black smoke rising up into the sky. It was definitely something "not in the programme" and in a very short while a frantic message arrived to say that the Germans were attacking along the canal bank and had got up to our "F" Echelon (our vehicle park). It might have been very serious; as it turned out, the M.T. drivers, the cooks, and a great many others rose to the occasion and held their own. As an example of a counter-attack it was not very impressive. We had been attacked at our most vulnerable point, and though we lost a few vehicles a completely impromptu defence had been quite sufficient to deal with the situation.

The capture of Heppen brought in another large batch of prisoners and they had an interesting story to tell. During No. 4 Company's attack the day before, the Germans also abandoned Heppen, but were ordered to recapture it without fail the next morning. By a million to one freak of war their attack reached the village about ten minutes before ours, with the result that they were hit by the full weight of our artillery before they were able to dig in or organize themselves against our attack. It finished them. When I had interrogated the prisoners I went to the command post. Colonel Roddy was back with the full story of the Heppen attack.

No. 3 Company had no officers left. C.S.M. Cowley had got the company through the last stage of the attack, for which he was awarded the D.C.M. I was going to ask, and then the Commanding Officer said, "Billy Hartington has been killed."

I said, "Oh." '

There is nothing else one can say. I thought: "So in war the infantry just go on and on and in the end it's almost inevitable. If you are lucky you are hit; if you are unlucky you are killed. How few people know what it costs to live like that? Already there are other generations with lives to live. This must never happen to them. Oh, God, watch over us and keep us, and whatever is to be the end it must not be in vain. Most people will forget because they have never known or understood, but if we who know the cost, if we survive, what hope will there be when we forget?" In my heart I knew I would forget as we all have – not the facts, but the misery and sacrifice which alone can give them meaning. I remember thinking almost exactly as I have written and, though one's feeling cannot survive the rub of time, I know that I was right.

At midday there was a very half-hearted counter-attack. The Germans debouched from Bourg Leopold with a troop of tanks and some infantry. By now we had a very considerable weight of artillery at our call and the attack never even looked particularly dangerous. It made no ground at all. The Germans had that day planned to push us back from the whole bridgehead. As it was, the possibility of a large setback seemed extremely remote to us, however costly our progress was. Still, if the desultory scrapping along the canal bank, the undetected attack on Heppen and the final effort had all been added into one we would have been very differently placed. Perhaps Heppen did far greater damage than we ever knew; at all events, it is hard to believe that the enemy planned to eliminate the bridgehead with anything so ineffectual as the actual counter-attacks appeared to us.

After Heppen our advance was stopped. I believe we could have captured Bourg Leopold, but at a price that would have far outweighed its value, and it was decided that we should be relieved that evening at dusk. Bourg Leopold and its opposite number, Hechtel, were both still in German hands, but the bridgehead was now of a sufficient size for a cross-country break-out to the Escaut, and our fight had achieved its object in practice if not in name. Most of us had to wait many months before we actually saw Bourg Leopold, with which our lives had been so closely connected. We were very bitter that evening when the B.B.C. announced its capture, but that was a minor crime. No one had been up to see, so how could they know? And in general the B.B.C. were paragons of accuracy compared with some sections of the Press; they could never have known what we said or felt about their report.

In the evening the 15th / 19th Hussars arrived and took over Heppen and Beverloo so as to give us time to get back to the Divisional concentration area near Beeringen and be ready to join in the advance the next day up to the Escaut Canal.

Our two-day battle for Bourg Leopold had cost us ninety-five casualties, twenty-six of them killed. No. 3 Company were by now short of five officers and sixty other ranks, and some of the other companies were also very reduced, so that in the end we again had to reorganize the Battalion into three rifle companies.

It was not a spectacular battle and yet at the same time we all knew that but for our efforts the fate of the bridgehead might have been very different, and against our own losses the damage done to the Germans was incomparably greater. The G.O.C. sent a special message of thanks in recognition of what we had done, and the Commanding Officer was awarded the D.S.O.

When we drove off that night down the road to Beeringen I thought, "Well, that is one place I shall never wish to see again," and yet most of us did see it again many, many more times, as our road later became one of the main routes back to Brussels during the fighting in Holland that winter. We used to drive past the station where Cecil had his encounter with the Panther tank, and then through Beverloo, where they were repairing the holes in its ugly Gothic church, and on past the field on the left which had been our headquarters. The trenches were all caving in and half-grown-over by grass, while in the ditches you could still see the rusting jerricans and debris of our short residence. And then memories would come rushing back so fast that one almost expected to see faint ghosts of tanks and vehicles and men, for, though it is all past and done, in another sense those fields and villages are now part of a story that will go on long after everyone has forgotten what took place there.

We woke up on the morning of the 10th to find that there had been a frost during the night, and I found that all the top layer of my bedroll had become as though crisply starched. It was a most unpleasant discovery – the cold and frosty morning which seems to make everyone so jovial in open-air treatises is a very different affair if you happen to have slept the night in a hedgerow, particularly when you expect to go on doing so with the weather growing from bad to worse. Even living in a house the chances of rain or sun seem to play a large part in one's life; living in the woods and fields it becomes an obsession, and the first frost of the year was to us an event of major importance. I remember the cold and discomfort of that morning more clearly than anything else that happened that day. We were in reserve and saw very little of the enemy, for which we were extremely grateful. Most of the time was spent in trailing down tracks through fir woods or over sandy wastes and heaths following in the tracks of the battalion ahead of us. As Bourg Leopold and Hechtel were still in the hands of the enemy the whole advance had to be made in this way, and at times the cross-country going was very difficult, as the sandy lanes had all been ploughed up into unrecognizable mire by the tanks that had been down there before. Sometimes we looked out across the miles of barren wilderness towards Bourg Leopold and wondered a little anxiously whether the column would be spotted and shelled, but it wasn't. The whole advance was not much more than ten miles; however, the difficulties of the ground slowed things down to a snail's pace and the leading troops had to contend with a lot of 88's and S.P. guns, which all took time to eliminate and often had to be attacked by very roundabout ways. At the frequent halts we got out of our vehicles and lay on the ground fast asleep in a few minutes.

We badly needed rest: it is about the only cure not only for lack of sleep but for nerves that get frayed and reactions that get overworked in battle. Now that the Battalion was all gathered together again as a column of vehicles, our losses were all the more apparent. All losses in a battalion are personal losses and everything that happened that day seemed to remind us of the gaps in our ranks. At the "O" Groups we felt: "How few of us are still here! How few will ever come through to the end!"

Late in the day the Irish Guards managed to seize the bridge over the Escaut at De Groote Barrier intact. It was a great coup, as the site was bristling with 88's and stubbornly defended. We settled down for the night in peace, only to be rudely disturbed in the small hours of the morning by orders to move up to the Canal as soon as possible. The column was on the move by four o'clock and we parked ourselves on a vast open heath about a mile back from the canal just before daylight – too late to go to sleep again and too early to wash and shave or start breakfasts. That day Nos. 1 and 2 Companies were sent off to hold a portion of the bridgehead. We had completely to disband No. 3 Company, and the remainder of the Battalion was used to provide patrols along our side of the canal bank. At first the fighting around the Escaut bridgehead was almost the complete reverse of the situation on the Albert Canal and most of the trouble occurred on the home side. As all the bridges had been blown except the one at De Groote, large numbers of Germans got cut off between the two canals, and some of the S.P. guns attempted unsuccessfully to rush the bridge from the south side. It was an incredibly bold venture – in fact, too bold – but they did quite a lot of damage before being knocked out; among other things, Colonel Joe Vandeleur's staff car was reduced to scrap.

The next day the defences of the bridgehead were reorganized and the Battalion was ordered to take over the northern half of the perimeter. The geography of the place is very simple. Once over the canal the road runs as straight as a line drawn with a ruler all the way to Valkenswaard, about ten miles to the north and in Holland. To the east of the road there is a fringe of woodland, but it soon becomes a maze of dykes and marsh that forms an automatic barrier from that side. On the west there is a large, square wood that was held by the Irish Guards, then comes La Colonie, a one-street-one-church village at right angles to the road, and finally more woods and the Dutch frontier. "Finally" is not quite the right word, as there were a number of small houses on the road by the frontier that constituted one of those perennial bugbears of defence – an unending string of potential enemy strongholds on the doorstep.

Originally the woods just north of La Colonie had been chosen as the front edge of the perimeter, but in the night patrols had found the frontier post unoccupied, and as the bridgehead was now being formed into its final lay-out we were told to hold the road up to that point.

The De Groote Barrier was seized by the Irish Guards in a surprise attack on the 10th September, later known as Joe's Bridge after their eponymous commander Lt Colonel J.O E. Vandeleur. It was from here that advance for operation Market Garden was launched.

The road position by the frontier was to be the responsibility of No. 1 Company, and as we moved up to La Colonie late that morning we discovered with unpleasant surprise that the Germans had got there first, or, to be exact, were getting there first – the two columns on foot met each other face to face. Fortunately we had some machine guns already in position and they immediately shot-up the German column, which went to ground more or less where No. 1 Company was intended to be. A small attack had to be put in, and with the aid of the tanks the company pushed on up the road to where a couple of striped sentry-boxes marked the end of Belgium and there was a little cluster of buildings with a modernist pub and a house marked "Douane." A few hundred yards farther on a notice proclaimed Zoll, first sight of Holland. When confronted by ill-mannered and officious Customs officials I often remember that scene. The frontiers of Europe are curiously inconsequential in war time. It is a pity that the damage was confined to knocked-down sentry-boxes and broken windows; I should have liked to have seen hundreds and hundreds of forms going up in flames.

We had only two wounded as a result of the attack; one of them was Cecil Feilden, which was a very serious matter, as he was the third company commander lost during the past four days, and by the end of the next day No. 1 Company was left with only one officer.

The attack brought a long spell of quiet and peace during which we knew and saw nothing of the enemy at all, so the Commanding Officer decided to send out two patrols that night to investigate the situation on the left of the road. I got hold of two local Dutchmen to act as guides. One of them was a smuggler and the other wanted to see his wife, who lived in a little village that one of the patrols was to go to. In the evening I gave them each a rifle and strict instructions not to try to fire them except in the gravest emergency; I had a sinking feeling that over-eager patriots might prove to be the greatest danger of all, but they were as docile as tailors' dummies and when the time came we set off together to No. 4 Company to meet the patrols. When we got there I found Derek Plater and Neville Acheson Grey, who were to be the patrol commanders, and with the aid of an interpreter they discussed the plan of action. The map was discreetly blank about the piece of ground we were to go over, but the two guides were brimming over with confidence – just say where it was we wanted to get to, then leave it all to them. We did so, and set off at about ten o'clock in inky darkness. The first discovery was that the blank on the map was actually honeycombed with drainage ditches that varied in size from small rivulets to large dykes, and in the darkness we managed to fall into them with almost unfailing regularity. I kept on looking back in the hope of memorizing the silhouette of the woods behind me, but it was no good and after about half an hour I had no idea where we had got to or how far we still had to go. We stopped to see if the guides were still on the route, but they assured us that they knew exactly where we were, so we went on and soon they pointed out some wooden posts which they assured us marked the frontier, which seemed reassuring enough. My own presence was due to little more than a childish desire to be among the first troops into Holland, and I decided that as soon as we came to the point where the two patrols were to part I would set out for home with the interpreter. We went on for about another quarter of an hour until finally the guides halted and said that they had been a bit lost but now knew where they were and that we were at the end of the marshes. At this point I said good-bye and followed by the interpreter set out manfully into space. It seemed an eternity of stumbling into ditches before we eventually came upon a large stretch of water.

"Die Dommel," murmured the interpreter. I was not much-put out by this, as I knew that here was a marshy river running to the east of us, and it seemed that all we had to do was to go a bit more to the right, but somehow the river made circles around us, as we met huge stretches of water wherever we went. After the interpreter had murmured "Die Dommel" to me for the tenth time, my patience gave out – we sat down and smoked a cigarette. We had long past given up any ideas of running into a German patrol – a genie of the marshes was about the most likely thing to meet in such a wilderness, and I had almost given up hope of finding the way when we heard a long burst of machine-gun fire. Our machine-gun section had been scheduled to fire a harassing programme up the road to Valkenswaard at midnight and the stream of tracer solved our problem, as it gave us the exact lie of the main road. From then on all was well and we got back easily, but my enthusiasm for crossing frontiers had been effectively damped. The patrols had an even worse time than we did, as the guides never to the end discovered exactly where they were and we got little out of our wanderings except the certainty that whatever else the Germans did they were unlikely to attack us from that direction.

The next morning was again quiet enough with very little evidence of any Germans until about eleven o'clock, when a whole company was seen walking down the side of the road towards No. 1 Company in single file. The machine guns caught them completely unawares and they were bowled over like ninepins before they could disperse into the cover on either side of the road. Almost immediately after this five S.P. guns came up across the heathland to the left of the road. We had a 17-pounder by the roadside and it fired but missed and was knocked out before it could fire again. We didn't take the arrival of the infantry too seriously, as we had already met with files of Germans ambling down the roadside, but the arrival of the S.P. guns definitely heralded a counter-attack and the squadron of the 15th/19th Hussars supporting us went off to engage them.

At the same time as this was happening, heavy firing broke out over on the left where the Irish Guards were, and for a short while the enemy had a weapon aligned to fire straight down the main street of La Colonie, but we were not much worried by this, as to attack us the Germans would have to pass straight across the front of the Irish Guards, which was what they tried to do. In front of No. 1 Company the situation was much more serious, as the infantry, despite their first setback, continued to come on and got to within a hundred yards of the forward sectors, where they were forced to ground but went on firing enormous quantities of ammunition. They also set up mortars and began to pound the wood behind us, though this was not much use, as there was no one there.

The tanks were fully able to compete with the S.P. guns and knocked out two, while our own anti-tank guns knocked out two more, and with the loss of the S.P. guns the situation became well in hand. Over on the left over a hundred Germans surrendered to the Irish Guards, and after a very ineffectual attempt to get up to No. 4 Company the whole attack petered out.

The attack was made by a battalion of parachutists and a penal battalion. In retrospect it was an incredibly incompetent affair that played into our hands in every way imaginable. In military terms they did what is called "drifting into battle," and despite expending enormous quantities of ammunition the total casualties that we sustained were two killed and two wounded.

I questioned some of the prisoners whom we had captured and found them all very dismayed and indignant about what had happened. They had been assured that recapturing the bridge was to be a virtual walk-over, as they were only opposed by one weak and demoralized Guards battalion. We may have been rather low in numbers, but we were certainly not demoralized. After this we felt on top of the world.

After the counter-attack it became clear that the Germans, even if they could not eliminate our bridgehead, probably had sufficient forces to make a break-out a difficult business, and they now had some artillery supporting them. In the evening they shelled the village, not very heavily but with considerable luck, as one shell made a direct hit on an ammunition truck just in front of the command post. It caught fire almost immediately and at the same time we realized suddenly that parked right beside it was our second ammunition truck. Everything happened so fast that it was impossible to put the flames out. The R.S.M., Dusty Smith, said: "Shall I try and move the other lorry?" "No, certainly not," said the Commanding Officer, but by that time the R.S.M. was half-way there and he boarded the second truck just as the whole canopy of the burning wreck caught in the blaze and the ammunition started to explode. I often wonder what his thoughts were as he pressed the self-starter; it was only a matter of seconds before the whole area was engulfed in flames and exploding ammunition. He drove off amid showers of sparks and metal, but it saved the second truck and at the same time prevented a lot more of our transport from becoming involved.

Within half a minute there was a great column of smoke over a hundred feet high and the light given out by the white-hot blaze of the burning vehicle illuminated the night sky for miles around so that people several miles back thought that a complete ammunition dump must be on fire. Under fifty yards away in the command post we were imprisoned in our trench by the hail of bits that the bursting mortar bombs sent out, and sometimes large blobs of burning phosphorus were flung into the air so that we were hard put to prevent ourselves or the two command vehicles from catching alight. It was impossible to go even from trench to trench for about a quarter of an hour, and after that all that remained was a heap of red-hot metal that still continued to detonate occasional rounds until late on in the night. Two well-loved original members of the Battalion, Drill Sergeant Reason and C.S.M. Griffiths, were killed in the disaster – but for the R.S.M. it might have been far worse, and he was awarded the D.C.M.

Shortly before this, two gentlemen of the Mr. X variety were sent up to us. I don't think I've ever seen two people register such fright and alarm as they did when we were shelled, and yet they were both unquestionably gallant and had come to risk their lives in a way that very few choose to follow. When I saw them sheltering in the trench I thought that their nerve would fail them for ever. It's strange but true that nothing makes one feel so confident as the sight of somebody obviously more frightened than oneself, and I was preparing to be horribly patronizing, but it wasn't necessary because they were soon under control again. Ian Liddell was taking out that night's patrol and by the time we had the whole party mustered together it was one of the strangest collections of people that have ever set out on such a mission. Anyone other than Ian would have quailed at the prospect of leading such a team, but I think the novelty of the situation only spurred him on; he had a genius for the improbable. What with the two agents, a Dutch police guide and others, it was a fourteen-man international gathering that eventually set out.

Loosing off the spies was the first problem, but they successfully managed this despite the rather belated discovery after they had gone about three miles that one of them had a wooden leg! Their chief task was to investigate a bridge and if possible shoot-up anyone they found defending it, and this they also managed to do most successfully. In his description of the attack Ian wrote:

"When we arrived within fifteen yards of the bridge I could see about six Germans standing there with their hands in their greatcoat pockets in the approved fashion. The patrol lined the bank of the first stream, then I threw two grenades right amongst the Germans. One passed some remark when the bombs landed, but they remained standing until they exploded; then we opened up with our automatic weapons and shot-up the whole area. Directly we stopped, more Germans came running in from a field and stood looking at the bodies. We waited until there was a good bunch there, then repeated the performance. As we were in a very exposed position on the bank, we then withdrew, leaving the Germans shooting at each other, which they continued to do with great verve for quite ten minutes after our departure. Our only casualty was 'Willy' (the guide), whose curiosity overcame his caution when I threw the first grenade, and thereby got his chin nicked by a fragment."

It was an outstandingly successful patrol, as they had to find their way across about eight miles of country which in that flat and benighted land was no easy task. The next day we continued to make more discoveries about the German dispositions, and they were a good deal more active than usual, presumably getting ready for the inevitable break-out down the road to Valkenswaard.

In the evening we were relieved by a battalion of the Devonshires (50th Division) and moved back across the canal. It's always a big event when the time comes to hand over to another battalion and move off to the safety and comfort farther back. We could look forward to whole nights of undisturbed sleep with a roof over our head, and a hundred and one comforts that cannot be managed in the line. Days which didn't start before sunrise, and meals that were not dependent upon the chance of events. Perhaps it would even be possible to have a bath and a change of clothes. I thought of all this as the Battalion column went rumbling back down the long, tree-lined road to the canal and over the bridge where the knocked-out 88's gaped uselessly at the blackness of the sky. We knew the way too well to have to pay much attention; even in the darkness the shape of a familiar cottage was almost as good as a signpost, and once back across the bridge everywhere by the roadside one passed the well-known lanterns marking the turnings to the various headquarters and administrative units behind us – the sixty on green of the 32nd Brigade, the sixty-four of the Support Company or the ninety-eight of the field ambulance.

And because in battle everything looms a little larger than life, one's contentment was also of a deeper kind that it is now not easy to recall. You can never know true comfort until you have known discomfort; you can never know happiness until you have known misery – it's a question of experience, and experience is largely a matter of experiencing the things one would not wish to, which you may find out by growing old or going to war.

Jocelyn Pereira.

Dick Lomer MC.

David Kennard MC.

Mike Bendix.

Gerald Style.

Charles Lawrie and Ben Blower.

HOLLAND

THE FEVERISH optimism that surrounded the capture of Brussels had been cooled by our experiences on the Albert Canal and the days that followed, but we still felt that there might be an end to the war just around the corner, though when we got the details of Operation "Market Garden" we put a strong curb on our wishful thinking. None the less, it was a venture that fired the imagination with renewed hopes and expectations. The plan itself was of the boldest and most ambitious sort which seemed to promise a thousand possibilities if it came off and at the time we had very few doubts but that it would. It was to be an Army offensive right across Holland, with XXX Corps at the head of the advance, and for our Division the orders were to break out of the bridgehead across the Escaut Canal and head for Nunspert, a little village on the Zuider Zee about a hundred miles away, thus splitting the country into two and cutting off the German Fifteenth Army from Germany altogether with the V-weapon sites and much else besides. To ensure a rapid advance over the boundless waterways of Holland three airborne divisions were to be dropped along the route ahead of us, forming an airborne carpet all the way to Arnhem and seizing the bridges before the Division arrived.

At first there would be only one road for us to go on so that our front would be no wider than its width, or if you look on it from a different point of view it was liable to become the length of either flank, twice the distance we advanced. But in due course there would be a corps pushing up on either side, turning the narrow, one-tank front into a salient and securing our communications from either side.

Three to four days we hoped would see us safely on the banks of the Zuider Zee, after which, of course, there would have to be a pause, as it was not much over a month since the break-out from Normandy and our supplies were still coming in via the "Mulberry" harbour at Arromanches, now beginning to break up as the weather worsened, but Channel ports were urgently being got into action, and once in possession of Holland the future would be revolutionized even if there had to be a pause. No Siegfried Line or Rhine would then bar our way and we would be all set for an attack into the heart of Germany by way of her most vulnerable frontier. We got out our atlases and decided that perhaps there was still a chance of ending the war before the winter; the possibilities and probabilities for the future seemed to be unbounded.

We were briefed with the details of the operation at a little village called Linden, where we had been resting for the past twenty-four hours after being relieved at La Colonie, and we felt more than usually speculative, as the break-out and the lead during the advance were to be done by the 5th Brigade, and we were now back with the 32nd Brigade. In addition to that, we were also in reserve, definitely a spectators' role.

At noon the next day, as the barrage blasting the way ahead of the Micks began, we heard the distant drumfire of the big artillery barrage and almost at the same time the first flights of aircraft carrying the airborne troops passed overhead. We waved them good luck and then waited anxiously for reports on how the battle was going. It went very hard. The Micks succeeded in forcing their way out of the bridgehead and down the road as far as Valkenswaard, but the opposition had been very determined and their progress costly.

For us that evening was one of irritations and boredom which ended up with us peering across the canal from the little village of Neerpelt, where No. 4 Company were put to guard against a possible counterattack, and were unpleasantly mortared for their trouble. The rest of us sat in Overpelt farther back – or at least we were all in Overpelt until about midnight, when there was suddenly another alarum and No. 2 Company had to rush off in the blackness of the night to guard Divisional Headquarters, which had somehow become involved in a battle. It was an irrelevant day and the only incident that sticks clearly in my mind is dining with the ex-stationmaster and being made to admire a very ugly clock given to him on his retirement by a grateful if unimaginative railway company. Once more "the Coldstream Group," the next day we moved up to Valkenswaard, and the day afterwards continued to follow along behind the 5th Brigade through Eindhoven.

This was the famous "club route," and in the months to come as we passed up and down countless times on various moves it became so engraved on our minds that we could recite the names of the villages along it almost like a litany; it became as familiar as the Strand and at times there seemed to be just as much traffic on it. The advance to Nijmegen from our point of view was a liberation excursion all over again; only isolated, small-scale actions took place after the initial break-out and then once more the way was lined with

The Liberation of Eindhoven 18th September 1944.

the familiar welcoming crowds with all the exuberance and enthusiasm of the French and Belgians. Dutch flags hung from every window, everyone was ribboned and bedecked in orange, and all the way along we found the same scenes of celebration.

The Dutch, we had been told in a pompous little handbook distributed beforehand, are a very clean people. Alas, they had no soap, but their houses were startlingly spick and span. It looked as though someone with a modernist and slightly cosmopolitan view of life had taken Welwyn Garden City very seriously to heart, then applied an improved version to a whole country. The result is not very lovely, but at least it is better than many another nation has achieved. We had also been told that there would be a lot of windmills and we did see some, though not so many as imagination had pictured, but, still, the scenery was definitely Dutch in its boundless expanse of flat farmlands as green as the fields of England, and with every spire and steeple visible for miles, so that even the multiple spans of the great steel bridge across the Maas at Grave showed up long before we reached them. And here among the dykes and huge banks that cut up the water meadows on either side of the river we saw the litter of an airborne landing with all its familiar scenic apparatus. The gliders had come down all around this area and in every field there were masses of them – with their disproportionately long wing span and the daubs of camouflage paint they looked like a plague of giant locusts come down to browse on the cabbages. Parachutes lay around everywhere, on the roadside, dangling from trees, or collected together in mounds of green and white and orange; and the wonder seemed that such a profusion of aerial impedimenta produced so few airborne troops. Of course most of them had moved on to different objectives, but even so there were not many to hold the huge tract of country that they had captured which formed a vast triangle from Nijmegen down to the German frontier by Groesbeek across to the Maas at Grave, then in little blobs all the way back down the centre line to Eindhoven. To the two airborne divisions there was now added our armoured division and other troops were due to follow, but it made things a little thin on the ground" for the moment, and complications were developing ahead of us. South-east of Nijmegen the waters of the Rhine split into the Waal, which flows past the north of the town and is crossed by one of the largest bridges in Europe, and the Nederrijn, which flows just south of Arnhem and is crossed by a less imposing affair; in between these two lies a tract of land known as "The Island," and at this moment it was very much an island: it was the barrier between ourselves and the 1st Airborne Division, for though we held both Nijmegen and Arnhem we held neither of the bridges on to the Island.

Still, it was only the third day of the operation and when the Battalion arrived that evening at Valenburg there seemed to be no great anxiety as to the final outcome.

The next day we were put under the command of the famous American 82nd Airborne Division and joined them south of Nijmegen, where two long, dark hills covered in forest and heather glower at each other across the Dutch-German frontier. The Americans held the home forest while from the Reichswald opposite a series of patrols and attacks were made to try to dislodge them from their positions. For us the three days which followed were a constant move from one end of the hill to the other according to which portion of the long perimeter was being most heavily attacked, though we were actually never properly in action, as somehow the situation was always retrieved without our being committed. The 1st Battalion, however, fought one or two engagements and our anti-tank guns fired a few rounds in the Battle of Mook; we also sent some carriers with a reconnaissance tank patrol which crossed the frontier and added yet another claim to the long list of people who say they were the first British troops into Germany. But although we were never committed to battle, the constant shifting about gave us little rest and the entire seventy-two hours remain in my mind as an almost ceaseless drive down forest tracks and clearings in search of "Conquor Main" and "Chestnut Red," or whatever was the name of the particular American headquarters in question.

On the Island things were very much more unpleasant. The Grenadiers, together with some of the 82nd Airborne Division, captured the Nijmegen bridge late on the evening of D + 3, but the next day, when the tanks started to advance down the road to Arnhem, they found themselves on an embanked road that was completely dominated by anti-tank guns, and as the country on either side was impassable they could make very little progress. The next day also produced few results, and when on D + 6 the 43rd Division finally managed to link up with the besieged airborne troops in Arnhem the possibility of successfully continuing the advance up to the Zuider Zee was out of the question; in fact, the heavy casualties of the Airborne Division made it necessary to withdraw from across the Nederrijn altogether back to a little bridgehead over the Waal in front of Nijmegen. And though this was a bitter disappointment it was unavoidably necessary and for more than one reason, as besides the situation at Arnhem the progress of the troops on our flanks had been slow and difficult, so that the centre line remained a single road held by nothing but posts and the convoys which happened to be driving down it. By now the whole sixty miles of road was one continuous stream of supply vehicles bringing up nourishment for the pulsating heart at Nijmegen and at all-too-frequent intervals the vital artery was severed. Somewhere along the miles of sparsely protected route there would be an attack followed by a massacre of transport vehicles, and after that the road was cut and nothing more could get up it until the way was cleared by a counter-attack. During the first ten days at Nijmegen the road was only usable for five of them.

On the 22nd of September a serious break was made and in the afternoon, as we were about to move for the umpty-umpth time, orders suddenly arrived that we were to rejoin the 32nd Brigade and follow the Grenadier Group hot-foot back down the centre line to clear Vechel, which had been recaptured by the Germans.

"When do we move?"

"We move *now*."

It is bad enough when you have to move "in one hour's time," or "be ready to move at fifteen minutes' notice," but to "move now" can be preposterously annoying, especially when you are about to begin eating a meal, or have just off-loaded one of the trucks, but it is things like this that constitute so large a part of the trials of war, and as a soldier in an armoured division, besides the more obvious martial qualities you must develop powers of infinite patience and stoicism.

We "moved now" and, among other things, parted with Michael Willoughby's company, No. 2, which was sent to guard a town called Oss. "Among other things" is less than justice, however, as Oss was a place of fable and renown with a food dump of prodigious size that supplied all XXX Corps for many days, and as at that time we couldn't supply ourselves its importance can hardly be exaggerated.

It was too late to clear the centre line that night, but in the morning we set out early to discover how the land lay and operations began soon after ten o'clock, with ourselves advancing towards Vokel to the east of the centre line and the Grenadiers going down the main road towards Vechel, where the 50th Division were, just south of the cut. Since the heavy casualties we had had on the Albert Canal we were still without reinforcements and the Battalion mustered only three weak companies, which with Michael's back at Oss, left us with only two for the attack, so while one squadron went down the road No. 1 Company, under David Long, mounted on another squadron, followed behind ready to put in an attack as soon as we bumped any trouble, which left another company/squadron group still in hand.

We met trouble where we had expected to, just outside Vokel, and soon after midday, while the leading squadron engaged the enemy down the road, David and another squadron attacked through the woods to the right of it; two hours later we were in possession of the village. It was typical of so many of the actions of that kind that we fought during the war. On our side one company and two squadrons were involved; holding Vokel there were probably about two companies of German infantry, not so well armed but with the advantages that always lie with the defence. It was not a very spectacular or decisive attack, but it had to be done, and it was – exactly according to plan. And because so often these things are merely recorded as "a most successful little attack," it should be remembered in capital letters that IT ALWAYS COSTS LIVES, and the company suffered casualties that included David Long killed and Basil Whitehorn, the only other officer left in the company, who was wounded. C.S.M. Farnhill, who took over during the attack, was awarded a D.C.M.

And that was not the end of the story of Vokel. There was a great deal of exploiting, patrolling and concomitant activity, but the details would be as long and tedious as they were at the time. Eventually we were relieved and moved back to near Oss, which was just as well, as the operation was now reaching a state where mobile warfare ceases and every little village and every road has to be held as the enemy redeployment against the results of the advance takes place and gradually a front develops. We knew that fairly considerable enemy forces in the area of Hertogenbosch were moving eastward against the flank of the salient and with Michael's company alone and isolated at Oss we were not too happy; in fact, one evening when Oss was attacked we were extremely anxious, but they held it off and in time we were able to strengthen the garrison with tanks.

The end of September was a colourless, depressing period. Our dreams of the Zuider Zee had ended in the tragedy of Arnhem and it was now plain that there was no hope of the war ending before the winter; indeed, gradually and inevitably it was slipping back into the old familiar pattern with nothing but the usual "blood, sweat and tears," made all the more gloomy by the prospects of the weather ahead. Five dreary days were spent in and around Oss; then suddenly we were switched back to Mook in expectation of another attack, but it didn't happen, and in anticipation of a rest we moved once more, but that didn't happen either, and we moved yet again as a result of an attack which had happened: we moved on to the Island. And our stay on the Island deserves rather special treatment, as it was a rather noteworthy place.

It was explained to us with great tact when we arrived at 5th Brigade Headquarters that life on the Island at that time was far from comfortable. The 9th S.S. and the 9th Panzer Divisions were both present and had been counter-attacking during the day; there was a quite unusual amount of artillery supporting them, and the Micks had been attacked with

Driving over Nijmegen Bridge on the way to the 'Island' close to the village of Amm where the battalion was to spend an uncomfortable few days. 3rd October 1944.

flame-throwers. We were recommended to take only a minimum of transport up to the position, as the Micks had lost a lot of vehicles that way; their casualties had also been heavy and they were by now getting very tired, so that it was essential to bring them out of the line for a short rest. All this was told to us in a most good-natured way, but somehow nothing could soften the blow, and every way one looked at it we were obviously in for a very nasty time. As if to emphasize this, a battery of field guns positioned in the orchards all around us kept up a continuous shoot that was deafeningly loud at such close quarters. You become unaccustomed to gunfire in a very short while, but I found that for the first half-hour I jumped every time that they fired; after that I found that my eyes blinked with equal uncontrollability, which is almost as annoying; and then in the end you become noise-proof and nothing has any effect except that you feel as though the whole affair is a personal assault upon your own peace and quiet, for which a thousand curses on their heads.

As we drove up into Elst and turned right towards the Mick position all our suspicions were confirmed – the tileless roofs and the holes in the walls, all of it was obviously quite recent damage. There was an overturned signpost that read "17 Km to Arnhem," and over everything hung that indefinable smell that heavy shelling produces in a street. The position was centred around a place called Amm, but it was really only a hamlet with not more than a dozen very scattered houses tucked away in orchards and none of it looked much better than Elst.

Earlier in the morning Battalion Headquarters had been quite a fine farmhouse with a cream-coloured stucco front, but by the time we saw it nearly all the top floor had been destroyed and gutted by fire, while outside on what had once been the front lawn there was nothing but a pile of charred wreckage and the burnt-out hulks of some Mick wireless trucks. We picked our way through the debris in the hall and surveyed our future home with a critical eye – it had been christened "Stonk Hall," and everything went to show that the name was very apt. There was only one good thing about the place, and that was the cellar, which was divided into two large halves big enough to take in the command post and reckoned to be proof against anything, the only trouble being that at that moment besides its regular inhabitants the "O" Group was also crowded in, and the result was like the beach at Blackpool. There were people talking on the wireless, telephone bells ringing, officers eating a meal or trying to go to sleep, and on the heap of coal in command of the situation sat Colonel Joe Vandeleur giving out orders. It was always said that Colonel Joe was never happy until some portion of his headquarters had been knocked flat or burned to the ground, and I believe it was true; he certainly seemed to rise to the destruction and havoc all around as though they were almost a stimulant, and when the Micks departed after dark we felt rather as though we had been giving a party with too small a room for so many guests. Most of the time while we were taking over it was fortunately quite quiet and by the time the first heavy stonk arrived we were all prepared, which was just as well because it was a really heavy programme shoot with a continuous fall of shells for a quarter of an hour or more, and the only pauses were between the salvos, when you could hear the German guns rumbling away before the next lot of shells arrived. Not for a long while had anything on that scale been happening and it was all very ominous.

Despite the enormous sameness of war, despite the endlessly repeated features such as fear and boredom and exhaustion, no one position is ever quite like another and no amount of advice or information will ever entirely prepare you for the actualities of the situation; there are always so many factors changing and subtly different from what they were a moment ago, so that there is only one solution: you must come to find out the "form" for yourself, and the important thing is that you don't take too long to find it out. Before stand-to the next morning, with all its dismal ritual of tramping to and fro in the cold greyness of the morning long before the petrol burners cooking our breakfasts had begun to hiss and roar in the knocked-down shacks and ruins of the company areas, before all these activities began to usher in a new day we had already come to a number of conclusions about the Island that set the tempo for the next four days. The most important feature was that the land was so flat that almost every portion of our area could be observed by the enemy, and as we knew they had a great deal of artillery there was only one thing to be done and that was to be as invisible as possible while it was day time and keep all the moving to and fro to the hours of twilight or darkness. But however much everyone keeps to their own area and the well-known coverts where they know they can't be seen, there is inevitably a certain amount of coming and going between companies that cannot be avoided and just as inevitably there is some shelling, though here in most cases it was counter-shelling. The Germans were remarkably casual about concealing their own movements and we came to know a great deal about their dispositions after a few days of careful watching, so that from our O.Ps. eventually we only had to watch certain areas and particular orchards, as we knew these were company positions, and every time anyone was seen we would shell them, but it had the disadvantage that we were usually shelled in return and as often as not

"Stonk Hall" was the target. It was to a large extent gunner warfare, with the usual searching after enemy gun positions for our mediums to engage, and ever-growing and more intricate fire plans and harassing programmes. All of this was more than usually tricky, as our maps were inaccurate, which made it exceptionally difficult to give exact map references for anything that we could see happening.

The country, anyway, made this hard, as it was so flat and lacking in any distinct definite features to relate one little copse or line of dyke to another that all one could see at a first glance was a maze of intersecting hedges and banks and ditches that were as confusing as the layout of a crazy pavement. In the beginning we were even at a loss as to the geography of our own position because wherever you went everything looked much the same: orchards all very like each other, meandering muddy paths that seemed to be without purpose or direction, and numberless, half-demolished cottages, each a seeming image of the last one one had looked at. Now that familiarity and a map have robbed the maze of half its secrets it is perfectly easy to describe the basis of our layout with a simplicity that overlooks the jumble of the actual terrain.

Since the days at Oss the Battalion had been reinforced by a large draft which included a lot of people who had been with the Battalion before and had come back after being wounded in the days of Normandy, and as a result there had been several changes in company commanders. Michael Adeane came back as Second-in-Command and Bill Blackett took over the newly formed No. 3 Company. Jack Hamilton returned and took over No. 4 Company which Derek had been in command of, and we had had a general reorganization throughout before coming on to the Island.

As a rule, Colonel Roddy went round the Battalion each day at stand-to, and then in the evening Michael Adeane would make the grand tour of the companies. These two circuits were one of the main means of passing on all the news or orders that were too lengthy or complicated to pass over the telephone, so that they constituted a series of little conferences and were an important part of the day's routine. The mornings and the evenings were, in fact, the two chief moments for going round to see people and for fixing things up, as in the half-light you could go anywhere without fear of bringing down a stonk, and, besides this, these times were convenient for making arrangements both for the coming night and the next day. You could visit a company by day, but it was in many cases an unpopular thing to do, as it is generally not the visitor whose indiscreet wanderings bring on the stonk who gets hit, but the unhappy people who have to remain in the position after he has gone.

And now in the growing darkness you might as well take a reminiscent walk round the company areas as I saw them one evening going round with Michael Adeane. You wouldn't want to go round; it would be your very last wish, as, quite apart from the fact that it was a long and tiring walk lasting for about two hours and covering every conceivable type of rough going, you would, unless endowed with unheard-of foolhardiness, have been very apprehensive about leaving the comparative comfort and safety of what was unquestionably "the better 'ole" for the uncertainty of the open. There used to be a Kate Greenaway jingle which ran:

"Oh, the night has come and I daren't go down,

For the bells ring strangely in London Town."

Poor girl, she had an age-old terror, hauntingly related, but what can one say of the guns on the Island? It was a big area thickly covered by artillery on both sides and so there were as often as not the rumble and detonation of someone stonking or being stonked, and though it was only occasionally that it intimately concerned ourselves, none the less one was always subconsciously listening and expecting in a way that it is hard to describe now. To say that so many hundred shells fell on the position each day, or that we were shelled at such- and-such a time, entirely fails to convey the sense of continual uneasiness one felt, with a perpetual Father Time and his scythe walking along in one's footsteps.

We must go: the first call can be made in daylight, and we don't want to be too late back.

"Corporal ! A pox upon him – where's he got to? … Ah, there you are!"

We set out towards No. 2 Company down the road that ran from Elst northwards, past "Stonk Hall." This was only a short ten-minute walk down a very muddy road with a convenient embankment on the left that hid one from view. The embankment had been built to carry a road over a huge, uncompleted autobahn that we called "The Hitler Highway"; it came to an end in Michael's position and over it there was a useless concrete bridge spanning the gap in the twenty-foot bank. Still, it had its uses. The levelled fairway that was to have been the main road ran for about a mile straight through our position to the German position opposite and the bank carrying the by-road over it made an excellent O.P. from which we could see practically everything we wanted to. The roadway was covered by both sides so that in daylight one generally had to run across it to avoid being shot at, but in the failing light there was no great danger and you could saunter over to the O.P. on the far side with complete confidence.

When we got there the light was not good enough to see much, but Michael Willoughby pointed out some of the places where the main events of the day had occurred and then we went back down the road and turned right up another muddier and still smaller road towards Jack Hamilton's company, No. 4. It was really only a farm road and, like so many in Holland, had huge drainage ditches four feet deep on either side so that in the mud and darkness vehicles often slipped off the narrow crown of the road and became hopelessly jammed if not overturned; but they also were useful, as in the day time many stretches were under observation, and you could walk along the culverts unseen and safe from shells. Except by night it was practically impossible to visit Jack, as the route eventually involved recrossing the Hitler Highway much too close to the enemy for safety; in the evening, however, we were not troubled by this and we found Jack sitting in a trench dug into the ditch a few hundred yards farther on.

This was one of the most constantly shelled places in the position, and my only wish was that our visit should be as short as possible; already there had been an unpleasant crump on the road farther back and things appeared to be working up for further trouble. I can't remember the exact layout of Jack's position, but one thing that struck me was a curious and inexplicable procedure that always seemed to be gone through on the way to Michael Wall's platoon. You had to go through a straggly house now reduced to nothing but a shell, and every time I went Jack always used to show the way along a paved path and through the tangle of ruin in a sort of mimic sequence of what happened before the bombardment – had there been any doors they would have been dutifully opened and shut; the garden gate always was. Michael Wall's position was a most unpleasant place.

On a map it does not show up very much, but when one's there the sensations of the forward section of the forward company of a forward battalion are plainly imaginable – it's a very considerable strain for any length of time, and particularly so when the enemy are active and under four hundred yards away.

By the time we started back towards No. 1 Company's position in an orchard on the other side of the road it was already night and we bumped into the sentries on the road.

"Halt! Who goes there?"

"Friend."

"Advance one and be recognized."

I was always a little anxious about sentries at night. If you falter or make a mistake, which has been known to happen, it's nobody's fault but your own if you get shot. A lot of people's lives depend on sentries so that they cannot afford to make mistakes, and eventually you come to develop a technique of carrying on a rather self-conscious conversation as you approach the place where you expect them to be. On no account should they be subjected to sudden and unexpected surprises!

We found David Kennard preparing a patrol that was due to go up the road and investigate a house that had been causing some trouble. When the Irish Guards were counter-attacked they had had to withdraw one of the forward companies, with the result that the next bridge up the Hitler Highway from Jack and a small orchard about four hundred yards down the road were taken over by the German outposts. They used to use a cottage just opposite the orchard as a sniper's post, and they had made several attempts to remove a knocked-out Mick carrier from the roadway beside it; altogether, they were too close in on us to be allowed to stay in peace. The first night we raided the bridge and captured four prisoners, and tonight after the guns had shot-up the roadside cottage another patrol was to raid that. We discussed the prospects with David, then hurried on towards No. 3 Company. We knew that the raid was almost certain to bring back something on our heads and we were anxious to reach a good trench before the trouble began. We got to Bill Blackett's headquarters just in time and dived down into his cellar as a salvo of shells landed plumb on the company area. It was not a very concentrated stonk, but it went on for half an hour with something arriving every minute or so, and each time we decided, "Well, that seems to be the end," and started to go, there would be a renewed umph, umph, umph,umph.

Eeeeeeeeeeeeeeeeeeeee.

Crrrrrrrump, crrrrrrrump, **CRRRUMP,** crump.

We said, "Let's give it another ten minutes," but every time it was the same. The house was hit, and even in the cellar we began to feel a little uncomfortable. Bill went out to investigate the damage and soon afterwards Corporal Henry appeared with someone who had been wounded; he laid him on the straw piled over the cellar floor and dressed his wounds by the light of a candle, while outside everyone searched for the company cook, who had vanished after the explosion. No one could find him anywhere; they were all certain that he had been asleep in the room that was hit; in the end he was discovered still asleep but in another room. There was only one casualty as a result of half an hour's shelling; it's remarkable how often a heavy stonk does no damage at all and then unexpectedly a single shell will catch five or six people when nothing else has fallen in the area for several hours.

It was after ten o'clock by the time we set out on the short trip back to "Stonk Hall," and it was beginning to rain. Occasionally the horizon would flicker with light as a distant battery fired, but most of the time it was pitch dark and we squelched along, keeping well to the middle of the waterlogged road so as to avoid falling over signal cables or slipping into the ditch. When I got back I expected a sympathetic welcome. Perhaps someone would say how worried they had been when we didn't come back for such a long time, and no doubt someone else would have got a meal ready and reserved a corner of the cellar for me to sleep in; but, alas! it was quite the reverse. Charles Lambton was perfectly convinced that "Stonk Hall" had borne the whole brunt of the bombardment; he was much more eager to tell me what they had been going through than to listen to an account of how Bill's headquarters had been hit, and Otto Plymouth, now Signals Officer, was in an unforgiving mood because I was late in taking over from him on the wireless. Nothing, however, really disturbed the calm and good will of Battalion Headquarters – we had been living together much too long to let that happen, but it often seems to me a remarkable thing that we managed to keep so perpetually good-natured under the conditions we lived in. We slept, we ate, we worked; everything we did happened in the cellar, and except for occasional journeys back to Brigade Headquarters or the daily round of the companies we spent the greater part of every twenty-four hours living down there until in the end we used to amuse ourselves by chalking up fictitious situation reports on the conditions above ground – visibility, broad daylight; weather, raining hard; stonking, not too bad at present; etc. Counting the gunner communications, there were often three wirelesses and two telephones all in use at once, and with only three officers to do turn and turn about we seldom managed to get more than five hours' sleep in twenty-four and even then one was constantly disturbed, so that day by day we grew more and more tired. It was not the type of exhaustion that comes over one after several days of attacking, but a cumulative weariness that made everything one did seem increasingly tiring and every day a greater burden. But this was probably one of the best command posts that we ever had, and we had no cause to complain if we compared our condition with most of the companies: they had in many cases little or no shelter, so that through the endless hours of light and dark, rain and fine, there were no comforts against the weather or the cramping misery of a trench and little but the endless routine that revolves around eating, washing, being sentry, digging new trenches, or changing over with another company, to relieve the endless monotony.

On the third day a big attack was launched over to our right which straightened out the line and made our position much easier to defend than it had been before, as it removed the danger of our being attacked from that direction, but, as always, our commitments were extended so that No. 3 Company had to move from their area and take over the new position. Although by this time the Island no longer held for us the importance that it had a few weeks ago, it was still a vital part of the front and there were larger German forces concentrated here and by the Reichswald than almost anywhere at that time, so that its defence was by no means confined to digging in and holding on to what we had. Before it assumed the unchanging irrelevance that it did later in the winter there were numerous attacks, counterattacks and alterations to the general layout, and for a long while the Germans were sufficiently strong to have made a big attack there. I wonder what it was like during the winter? Someone visited it a few months afterwards and found

"Stonk Hall" practically razed to the ground. It must have become inconceivably dismal; perhaps it was submerged by the floods, or was it a battalion headquarters right through to the end? We were only there for four days, but when the great day arrived and we were promised a relief it seemed as though half our lives had been lived there. Agonies of disappointment came over us as throughout the day the arrangements for the take-over were continually altered and changed; we almost despaired of getting away that night, but in the end a battalion of the 43rd Division arrived to relieve us and we tiptoed out of the place at one o'clock in the morning. A take-over under these circumstances can be a very costly business; if the enemy hear a lot of tracked vehicles creaking about in the night and shell the position heavily while the companies are marching out casualties are inevitable, but we managed to extricate all the carriers and vehicles by covering up the noise with continual gunfire and then the Battalion marched away, hardly daring to speak – everything was so silent. Still, the stage management worked perfectly and during the anxious hour while we were changing over not a single shell was fired at us. Only one man was killed and fifteen wounded during the time we were there, which was a surprisingly small figure when one considers how heavily we were shelled at times, and probably the chief reason for this was that we kept ourselves out of sight and underground as much as possible.

Between us and our rest area only one anxious moment still remained, and that was the crossing over the Waal at Nijmegen, which was always a case of running the gauntlet. The great road bridge across the river shows up clearly for miles around and most of the time the Germans had a good enough view of it to see the convoys of vehicles as they went over it, so that it was shelled at all hours of the day and night. Few things are so harrowing as being showered with air bursts when you are going across a bridge in a very slow-moving convoy, and I never made the journey without feeling miserable. To deceive the Germans into thinking that we were building up our forces, by day the bridge was only open to one-way traffic, which all went streaming over it on to the Island, then at night the convoys used to creep back, using the pontoon bridge downstream which couldn't be seen in the dark.

When we reached the river we were confronted by an almost breath-taking sight. The huge, single span of the great road bridge was completely floodlit by searchlights; everything else was hidden in darkness, but the gigantic arch, with its tracery of steel girders, was so caught in the light as to look almost as if it were made of neon lights. It was so lovely it hardly seemed necessary to ask for an explanation; actually the searchlights were there for its protection, to stop any further attempts by "duck men" to demolish it as they had very nearly succeeded in doing a few nights previously. I doubt whether any other bridge in the war has ever been the cause of so much exhaustive ingenuity on the one side to destroy it and on the other to preserve it; every imaginable device was launched against it, and in the end it was the way to little more than acres of floodland. Tremendous glamour surrounded it in those days, and though it eventually rather lost its importance, at any rate it is still standing and a very fine bridge.

After our stay on the Island we had our first real rest since the day that we left Normandy; we were very ready for it, and though we didn't stay long in our original area, when we got to Hatert we were there for three weeks of quiet and peace. Hatert was so close to Nijmegen that it was hard to be sure where one ended and the other began, and it was to Nijmegen that we usually went whenever we wanted to have a bath, see a cinema, or had nothing better to do. It was a remarkable town, with an individuality all of its own, and I suppose it must have seen almost as much of the British Army as Bayeux or Brussels. In peace time guide books sometimes suggested that it bore a resemblance to Oxford; it had been heavily bombed by the time we saw it, so one speaks only on surmise, but I suspect that it was quiet, suburban and rather snobbish – in fact, not at all the sort of town that one would expect to find cast for an heroic role; none the less, it unhesitatingly qualifies as a very remarkable front-line town. The inhabitants looked pale, thin and perpetually worried, but despite this everyone always carried on with complete disregard for the war that was going on all round them and every day you would find the streets thronged with people going about their daily business when the front line was never more than three or four miles away for over six months. You could read the war in their faces or see it in their clothes, for as well as the usual shabbiness almost every other person wore some garment made of parachute silk scrounged at the time of the air landings. Silk scarves, silk blouses, even whole dresses of it; the mottled green and brown was almost a local uniform, and I expect they were justly proud of it.

Almost anything might happen to you if you spent the day in Nijmegen. The possibilities were endless – frequently it was shelled by the German guns on the Island; almost every day a couple of Focke-Wulfes would burst out of the clouds and shoot-up the streets with a hail of bullets, and then there were our own long-range and heavy guns, which fired over it from every possible angle and direction. No wonder the citizens became nervous wrecks! Besides this, it seemed to be a great centre for the cloak-and-dagger world, spies and spy catchers, hidden wireless sets and I presume a good quota of false mustachios. I never saw any, but I was told all this and it certainly fits the picture.

The countryside around was dull and uninteresting; occasionally if the light was right you might catch a hint that this was the land of Ruisdale and Hobbema, but most of the time I felt oppressed by the flat sameness which held no attraction or beauty, whether it went under an exotic name all "i's" and "j's" or not. Mostly we went out into the country to barter cigarettes for eggs, and though no one spoke any Dutch the procedure was so simple that this was unnecessary. The first thing to do was to approach a farmer and murmur "Eyer." He then probably vanishes and returns soon afterwards with a couple of eggs, at which point you produce a couple of cigarettes. If he knows the current barter prices he will shake his head and say, "Ne, ne." You then go on producing cigarettes until the eggs are handed over, by which time you've had the worst of the bargain.

But all this probably gives an unduly rosy picture of our life; it was actually a depressing and gloomy period of the war. Antwerp was now the key to everything and it could only be used as a port after the long, costly battles of the Schelde Estuary had freed the entrance to the harbour; everywhere else the front was becoming more and more static as the winter came on, and though we were glad enough to be out of it all for a little while we knew that it wouldn't be for ever. The days of great achievement seemed to be over and every prospect ahead was uninviting; besides which there was probably another reason for feeling rather flat; during any long rest you inevitably become geared down from a highly strung state of existence to the level norm of routine life, and there is no longer any call upon motive power that has kept you going in the past, so that unconsciously one is like a drowning man who has been trying to hold his breath for a very long time and when you can suddenly breathe freely once more the sensation is strangely unexpected. It's a pity to carry an analogy too far, but broadly speaking we were able to see with new eyes how unpleasant it had been in the water, and to be sorry about having to jump back into the flood. And though there had been long weeks of blue skies and brilliant sunshine, now the leaves of red and gold were beginning to fall from the trees, and a cold, unfriendly wind began to blow them about streets that were coming to look ugly and dismal.

More and more I found that I had begun to dread the day when I should have to break myself in once more to the tempo of war. It was going to be much worse than starting off in Normandy – we had learned such a lot of inside information since then and now the year was dying fast, getting darker every morning and evening.

We did a lot of useful training, N.C.Os.' courses, drill courses, lectures, etc. I can still see the schoolrooms at Hatert and the huge sliding blackboard with the neatly chalked-up regimental battle honours. We sat at desks like school children, only we hadn't long years ahead in which to grow up 'and forget about the lessons of history; we only had a few more days and perhaps there would be another Waterloo next week. There would certainly be more battles and you don't get put to the bottom of the map-reading class – you get shot.

And then one morning I was called by Guardsman England, who had taken over as my servant from Hobman, and I noticed that something was wrong. It was very wrong: for one thing it was four o'clock in the morning, and for another my kit had been packed. I was half-asleep, which deadened the blow of awakening consciousness, and my memory was able to filter back through the haze of slumber by gradual degrees. "Yes, of course we're leaving; we're going off to take over a position in the Maas pocket. I must be ready to leave with the Commanding Officer at five-thirty. Ah, well, here we go again; given half a chance I wouldn't go at all. Wonder if I told the scout car where to meet us? I suppose everyone feels as miserable as I do. I might forget all this in five minutes' more sleep. No, that would be fatal; I must get up, I must get up" – and then I used to repeat as though it was some miraculous formula:

> Awake! for morning in the bowl of
> night Has flung the stone that puts
> the stars to flight ...

This, always, as I actually got up: it had come to possess a sort of hypnotic significance so that I almost automatically stepped out of bed as I said the words. All around me the four papered walls harshly lit by the unshaded ceiling light seemed homelike and inviting; it was a little box of a room with only such furniture as was unfitted for anywhere else, and yet now I was looking on the last I should see of such comfort or privacy for many days. I thought to myself, "I have been through all this so often before." The secret is just to become a robot and have no thoughts at all, and then as I shaved it occurred to me that the next thing to do would be to have breakfast and on top of this a nauseous wave of ideas about war went flooding through my mind and I was nearly sick. I've seldom started a day feeling so miserable; I was almost drowned in self-pity, and when I got outside it was dark and idly cold, much colder than ever before – it was November. The winter had come. It was not only the season that changed during our rest at Hatert; the whole nature of operations had become altered. While the main centre of interest was the Schelde battle, which was to open the way to Antwerp, a smaller and less spectacular operation was in progress to push the Germans across the Maas and clear the western bank, but what it was hoped would prove a comparatively easy affair met extremely stubborn opposition; in fact, the enemy managed to retain a large bridgehead across the river from just north of Venlo down as far as Roermond, which was called "the Maas pocket"; they not only held on to this but reinforced their troops across the river and counter-attacked towards Eindhoven.

This attack petered out during the last days of October, but our troops holding the line had been without rest since the original attacks began, and on the 3rd of November our Brigade was ordered down to a sector near Venray to relieve a portion of the extremely weary 11th Armoured Division. We were not taking part in any particular operation; it was to be a routine relief for a brigade holding the line.

I don't know if anyone sang:
"We don't want to leave you,
But we think we ought to go."

It would have summarized our feelings on leaving Hatert and we felt still more sorry about leaving when we drove up to 34th Brigade Headquarters to receive our orders. Everywhere there were the signs of heavy fighting and with the bad weather the roads had all become coated with layers of mud like a thick, brown sauce. Mud was spattered all over the leafless, war-scarred trees; it coated the soiled minefield tapes by the roadside; it clung like toffee to the signal wires draped along the telegraph poles; it seemed to have been sprayed over everything like a coat of paint; and the whole dismal landscape of waterlogged heaths was of the same dreary colour. When we left the headquarters and drove down the big main road that ran behind our position, intermittent gunfire rumbled away to the south of us; it was quite a long way away, almost like a distant thunderstorm, but as I looked out across the acres of flatness I saw a little cluster of houses being shelled. Puffs of black smoke were spurting up all around them and towards the centre of the target, merging into one dark-grey cloud that hung over the village as an ugly omen of what we were to expect in the future. I checked it on the map and as far as I could see it was our future headquarters, but, then, at the time I was bumping about on the back of the scout car and it may just as well have been Leunen or Veulen – whichever it was it looked nasty, and everything we saw was equally depressing. The turning down to our command post was marked by a very battered Calvary and a row of graves, some of them marked by wooden crosses but mostly just a mound of earth with a rifle dug into the ground at the head and a steel helmet on the top of it. A sort of forlorn resignation hung over the place, as though it had been set aside from the world as a showground for desolation, for endless days of dismal, grey weather and for every mood of gloom. When we went round the company positions there was that curious absence of anyone very much "about" that brings such a sinister and accurate warning of shelling to come, and everything we were told about the place confirmed our impressions: "It was a pretty bloody position; they were very glad to be getting out of it and hoped we wouldn't fare too badly."

It was a large sector for a battalion and there was no means of arranging for a company in reserve, but besides ourselves two battalions of tanks and two batteries of anti-tank guns remained behind with us after we took over from the Rifle Brigade battalion, so that though things were a little thin on the ground there was no lack of fire power.

If you looked at our positions marked up on the set of air photographs that we had you saw the countryside shaped rather like a giant horseshoe, the horseshoe part being a confused jumble of hamlets and orchards that at one tip merged together into the village of Leunen, where No. 1 Company was, and at the other into a cluster of farm buildings, where No. 3 Company was. In the middle was a huge, black area of nothingness known as the Leunscheveld, which was ringed on our side with a minefield. It was too open and exposed to play any part in the battle during the day, but during the nights it was an important piece of ground in the numerous patrols and skirmishes that were to follow.

The most inconvenient thing about the lie of the land was that the tips of the horseshoe didn't come to an abrupt end, but straggled on into the enemy lines opposite the two forward companies, so that besides the unknown ground on either side of them they also had to keep a very close watch on the strings of orchards and copses that ran all the way up to the front of their positions. Sometimes a cottage or a wood that had been held by the Germans one night would the next night be held by us or vice versa; it all had to be very carefully watched. As well as the systematic reconnaissance and vigilance of our night patrols, there was also the ceaseless day-time watch kept up by our O.Ps., and here again the process was mutual, as there were plenty of church steeples and Windmills available to both sides which, though constantly shot at, could never be completely put out of action. Both the foremost companies could be observed on a good day so that you always had to be careful how you moved about there in the daylight or otherwise there was sure to be trouble in the form of a heavy and accurate stonk. And if one refers to the days as troublesome the nights must

No 2 Company, Autumn 1944, Gdsm Clements, L/Sgt Dobbinson, CSM Skells, CQMS Ayres.

be classified as very near to hell, though neither term does much to reproduce the reality of the moment.

It was a period of heavy rain and yet at the same time the nights were bitterly cold, so that the long stretches of darkness were a terrible ordeal for the companies, as we had to maintain fifty per cent, on sentry in each platoon and even then we lost two men to a German fighting patrol on the first night that we took over. With no moon and heavy banks of cloud the evenings soon used to turn into nights of impenetrable blackness which the 7th Parachute Division used to every advantage for their numerous patrols, and we found it so diffi-cult to stop them effectively that eventually the Commanding Officer gave out the order that sentries were not to be visited at night and that they were to shoot at anything suspicious without challenging. We strengthened up our defences with large numbers of trip-wires, flares and booby-traps, but even so it was impossible to stop up all the gaps in such a large frontage and the only real solution lay in bigger and better patrols from our side, which were organized as soon as possible.

When the second night came Oliver Wrightson took out a large fighting patrol. They occupied a small copse out in front of No. 3 Company, while the sappers mined it and put in booby-traps so as to make the wood as lethal as possible and close off this vulnerable approach up to our position. It was effective, too, as while the patrol were out they saw a lot of enemy; we put down some heavy fire on them, but it seems that they were out to repeat the previous night's performance, and soon after the patrol got in they heard some of the newly laid mines explode and all through the night a wounded man crying out for help until in the small hours of the night he grew weak and died – "a piner." The nights were in essence one long wait and listen, and almost all that we knew of what was going on was compounded out of sounds and noises.

Bursts of small-arms fire, or a stonk, were the intermittent and regular disturbers of the peace, and every time one had to try to assign some explanation – who was that firing, and at whom? Dick Fifoot was out with a reconnaissance patrol one night investigating some houses in the No Man's Land to the west of No. 1 Company, and soon after our other patrol was in we heard a great deal of firing from over in that direction.

Was it British or German?

It was definitely both.

Our patrol in trouble or a German patrol attacking?

The telephone bell at the command post gave an answering ring:

"Hallo – who is it? Ah, the very man! Do you know what all this noise is about? … Oh … . Hold on a minute … . It's David, sir; they've just been attacked by a fighting patrol; it's gone through towards Jack's company … . Hallo – did you get any of them? … Oh, a pity! … Have you had any casualties? O.K., I'll ring up Jack … . Hallo, 4 Company? Is that you, Jack? Yes, that's wha we wanted to ask about; they're making towards you … . Oh, not towards you, towards us? . . Um – well, we'll let you know.

The firing soon came to an end and then we lost all trace of them somewhere between Battalion Headquarters and Leunen. Where they eventually got to was never traced. It was a busy night with something happening pretty frequently, and no chance of rest for most of us. Often there were false alarms as our flares were set off by wandering pigs and livestock, which is funny enough in the morning but not in the night time when you have been waiting for hours for a German patrol to do it and expect more lethal visitors.

Then would come stand-to and a very slow daybreak to end the cramping thirteen hours of cheerless darkness. It was the moment for us at Battalion Headquarters to go round the companies getting in the details of the previous night and discussing patrols for the next one, and for the companies it meant the last of the torturous, watching hours with the promise of some breakfast ahead and a chance for some of the platoons to get back to the cover of a house for sleep and warmth. For the gunners it was the moment when they said: "We'll just wait for that S.P. gun to have his morning shoot at our church tower, then we must climb up and occupy the O.P."

There was only one proper route around the position, and although it had been laid with logs to form a corduroy road the mud was so thick and ever-increasing that the logs soon sank into the general quagmire and you had to struggle down a pathway that was like a river of chocolate mousse. Never can I forget the gloom of the road up to Leunen; it was a picture of all that one imagines of the last war battlefields, only at times it felt as though you were the last man left alive on the earth, a sudden victim of some wholly H. G. Wellsian state of affairs lost in the destruction and wreckage of the world. And Leunen was not a very pleasant end to any journey: you were almost bound to be shelled there – still, David Kennard, with his pipe in his mouth, stumping down the village street, was always a reassuring figure and if invited into his command post you could be fairly sure of a glass of rum. And then you could hear the story of the latest pig patrol while the night's victim was roasted outside, or meet the umpty-umpth dog which Ian Liddell had added to the company's menagerie and was probably house-trained at the expense of their headquarters.

The next day the weather became much worse and there were long periods of heavy rain that made our already dubious roads more unnavigable than ever before. We sent out patrols, but the results were not very good and the enemy, so far as we knew, attempted nothing. Conditions, in fact, grew worse day by day and our position was made all the more unpleasant by a very noticeable increase to the German artillery, and whereas before the main source of trouble was from field artillery this was now supplemented by nebelwerfers, which were increasingly troublesome. Some nights it was nothing exceptional for as many as a hundred rounds to come down on Leunen; inevitably there was a steady toll of wounded, but on the whole our casualties were not large considering the circumstances, and we felt more and more that we were setting the pace of events.

We had no more patrolling setbacks and Dick Fifoot, with an ambush, had an encounter with a German patrol that cost the enemy three killed. There were no papers on the bodies, but the uniforms that they were wearing were a sure enough guide – they had blue-grey caps with the Luftwaffe Hoheitsabzeichen – it was still the 7th Parachute Division (or in those days Division Erdmann). We had suspected this all along because of their aggressive tactics, but it was still a useful identification, as it was the first for a very long while. Was it still Regiment Grasmail? I suspect that it was, but that is a question that by now interests very few people. Not many of the embryo 1021st Parachute Regiment can have survived to the end of the war, and not many intelligence officers will remember the intricacies of their order of battle that we used to wrestle with. Still, there is a lot more to be told of the story of the 7th Parachute Division and this is an introductory mention.

We held this position near Venray for a week in all; we did what was asked of us and everything was understood. I must add that there are Coldstream graves near Leunen, just as there are graves wherever there is fighting. So much of this has been about the discomforts of the living that the sacrifice of those who died gets into a perspective that calls for a wider judgment and a greater tribute than can be made today. It was something that we knew and felt at the time but couldn't put into words; now one no longer senses so directly or clearly as at the time all that one would have wanted to say; it has become elusively beyond saying and the most that can be done is to state the facts and never to forget.

WINTER

OUR DAYS in the line at Venray were followed by a much longer period of defensive fighting in Germany, where, with a gap of ten days, we held a sector of the front for five weeks on end. With the winter already upon us, there appeared to be no immediate prospect of any large-scale offensive on the British sector, and the most important operation was on the American front, where preparations were going ahead to launch a big attack across the Roer River with the ultimate aim of reaching the Rhine and the capture of Cologne. The British contribution was to take over a large portion of the American front and for the Division this entailed a sector stretching from Sittard in Holland across the German frontier to the far side of Gangeld – a long, thinly held strip of land running parallel to the road to Geilenkirchen, which was then still in German hands. Sittard was easily within range of the German guns, but it was obviously a very exceptional thing for them to shell it, as it was practically undamaged and life seemed to carry on as though the war were twenty miles away. The shops were beginning to sell Christmas cards, a local cinema advertised coming attractions, and the inhabitants crowded about in the streets without any signs of anxiety. They were in very sharp contrast to their more harassed compatriots in Nijmegen, and though occasionally deserted streets warned one that a few shells had been arriving you usually found Sittard as peacefully preoccupied with daily life as though nothing ever did disturb the day's business.

At the far side of Sittard there was a signpost which pointed to "der Deutsches Grenze" and a few miles farther on a cluster of Customs houses marked the frontier of the Reich. Beyond this one came to a little village called Wehr, where we had our headquarters; then there was Susterzeal, and the tree-lined road ran up a hill towards Gangeld, about two miles away, where the next battalion to us was. Someone put up some notices that read "This stretch of road is under enemy observation – beware of shelling – keep on the move," but I motored down it many times in the next few weeks and nothing ever happened. Perhaps the military police, who signposted the road, were less lucky.

In front of Wehr there was a big, oblong hill covered with plantations of fir trees. The trees came to an end just short of the crest, and along the front edge of the wood lay the company positions, mostly well hidden on the reverse slope, with the Germans also more or less out of view in the valley below. Their defences centred upon a series of little villages with the unmistakably German names of Hongen, Kleinwehrhagen and Grosswehrhagen. In Wehr one could read German inscriptions on the shop fronts and everywhere that one went there was something to proclaim "This is Germany at last."

The whole area had been captured during the initial American rush across the German frontiers, so that hardly a shot had been fired to capture it and little had occurred in the succeeding months to disturb the undamaged air of quiet that lay over this backwater of war. At one stage the German inhabitants were gathering in a potato crop from some fields well in front of the forward company position and in Wehr all the houses were still occupied by civilians when we arrived; but, however uneventful things might be, we could hardly share the front line with enemy inhabitants and a few days later we had them evacuated elsewhere. It was rather a pathetic exodus; Wehr was only a peasant community, by now mostly reduced to the aged and children. They were given permission to leave one room in each house as a lock-up for what they didn't take away and had twenty- four hours in which to pack up. A very tearful population left in a series of T.C.Ls. the next day. Whatever one's feelings about the Germans, there is always something very tragic about evicting people *en masse* from their age-old homes, and yet I doubt whether an enemy village has ever received as much consideration as they did. In Hogen, opposite us, where the Germans carried out a similar evacuation of their own countrymen, several people who proved recalcitrant about leaving were shot: and the inhabitants regarded the German Army as perhaps the worst enemy of all. We took over the Customs house as an intelligence post, with Sergeant Todd and Sergeant Montijn, our Dutch interpreter, presiding over the Douane as chiefs of immigration and emigration, exports and imports, and everything else that goes on at a frontier.

Apart from the need for removing German inhabitants as an elementary measure of security, we also wanted the houses as billets. Only two companies and a bit of Support Company were needed to hold the positions up in the woods, and the remainder were a reserve that could rest back in billets in the village where shells were unknown and life a peaceful day-to-day existence.

The Germans held the front opposite us even more thinly than we did, and our chief preoccupation was to make sure that they didn't suddenly withdraw without our noticing it, or, rather less likely, reinforce their front and turn aggressive without due warning.

With so little to be seen and the defences so widely scattered, shelling played no great part in our daily routine, and though we put down occasional stonks in the hope of catching anyone who had become unduly careless it was more of gunner pastime than a serious programme of shoots, and the Germans' guns were even less active. Not more than about ten to twenty shells per day would come down on the woods, and generally this would happen just after dark or in the early morning, so that the day time was usually undisturbed.

Patrols were the chief centre of activity around which everything revolved, and we sent out at least two every night. Early each morning I used to go to a conference at Brigade Headquarters, where we discussed the results of the night's patrolling and Michael Rosse gave out what the Brigadier wanted each battalion to do on the following night; then back at Wehr the Commanding Officer used to brief each patrol commander, explaining on an air photograph what route they were to follow, and what we already knew of the enemy positions in the area. Then with anyone new to the position I used to take them up to an O.P. and point out such landmarks as there were and the minefield gaps. It all worked according to a carefully thought-out system, and though we must have sent out over fifty patrols while we were there David Fletcher, who was killed in an enemy minefield, was the only person whom we lost. By the end we had built up a most detailed picture of how the German defences lay and all that we had to do was make sure that they were still there each night; but at first it was much more difficult, as we had practically no information at all and our troubles were added to by the presence of numerous minefields, both German and American, none of them charted with much certainty. The Germans also used to patrol at night, but not so intensively, and though we laid numerous ambushes to try to catch them they didn't come off. It's extraordinarily difficult to hit anyone at night. Time and time again our patrols would find an enemy post, be fired at and get away without a single casualty. The Germans did the same to us once or twice, and one night Peter Strutt led a patrol that bumped into a German one. Both sides opened fire and the Germans withdrew, but though they left some belongings behind there was no proof that anyone had actually been hit.

We used to pass on a warning of any German patrols that visited us to the reserve companies just in case they got through anywhere, and the reserve company in Susterzeal used to pass on the warning to a rather unprotected little detachment of Military Government, who also lived in the village. On one occasion David Kennard forgot to pass them the "all clear" and the next morning as he was casually walking around the area he found them all still barricaded inside their farmhouse and prepared for a siege at nine o'clock in the morning. The only thing that they were really angry about was missing their breakfast!

The most isolated place of all was Michael Willoughby's officers' mess. It was the last house in the village before the open stretch of road to Gangeld, and there was nothing in the way of a defensive position between him and the Germans. If you went to dinner there it was always comforting to carry a revolver, as the road had acquired a sinister reputation after the disappearance of a Grenadier contact patrol. They set out from Gangeld one night to contact our outposts and were never heard of again; presumably they grew careless and were surprised by the enemy on the way. It was a very big gap that lay between us, and one morning two Belgian slave workers making a bid for liberty arrived in Susterzeal, having passed through both the German positions and our own without meeting a single person or obstacle of any kind.

They were extremely surprised and relieved when daylight came to discover that during the night they had crossed between the lines without realizing it, but we were very aggrieved to get hold of two people who had been through such an interesting experience and yet could give us no information about the German positions at all, though later on the story had a long sequel. It transpired that in a town a few miles away they had come into conversation with someone who claimed to be part of a secret German underground movement. He took them to a crossroads about a mile behind the German lines, pointed out a distant searchlight beam (part of the Monty's moonlight behind our own lines) and told them to keep walking straight towards the beam. In return for this information they were to carry a cigar with a message inside it to be delivered to a British officer when they were safely at the end of their journey. In due course the cigar was carefully dissected and a tiny crumple of paper discovered that when heated in front of the fire bore a message that was clear for all to see and couched in terms as melodramatic as the rest of the adventure. It was the sort of thing that one has smiled knowingly at in many a novel, and yet subsequent events proved that it was perfectly genuine. However comic opera the proceedings, there really was at any rate one little bit of underground movement in Hitler's Reich, and it was later put to good use, but it would probably still be indiscreet to tell the rest of the story which treads upon a world of immemorial secrecy.

The American offensive never got to Cologne; for various reasons it came to a halt along the line of the Roer River with very heavy fighting in Julich and Duren. Farther north British troops captured Geilenkirchen, after which it was planned to erase the remainder of the German salient across the Roer, which meant an attack on our front. In the middle of December we handed over the woods to the 7th Armoured Division and concentrated back in Wehr waiting for Operation "Shears," which was the name for this particular attack. We had everything ready, but it rained hard, making the ground too soft for tanks, and in the end it was cancelled. We returned to the woods once more.

Nothing very much could be done to relieve the tedium of life for the forward companies, but despite the abominable weather a lot was done to improve the comfort of the place. Trenches grew into deep dugouts with roofs, and in some areas improvised chimneys stuck out of them where a stove had even been installed. We organized what was left of the local livestock into a farm, which was a great help in improving the usually monotonous meals. On the same system as the British officers who hunted foxes behind the lines of Torres Vedras, we had a small but select shoot in a reserve company area, so that occasionally some game was also added to our diet. But despite everything that could be devised it was still the front line, and however quiet it was in comparison with other places that we had been in it was by no means an easy or comfortable life and after five weeks of tedium there we were delighted when the news arrived that for Christmas we were to be taken out of the line and go back to an area near Louvain for training. On the 17th of December our advance party went off to find billets, but the next day Rundstedt started the Ardennes offensive. I spent the morning searching damp acres of fir trees for specimens of the propaganda leaflets that were fired at us during the night. They were very much in demand as souvenirs. Most of them made play with the saying about being home by Christmas. There was one of a very jaunty British soldier passing a signpost with "Caen" written on it and "Home by Christmas" written underneath; then on the other side a picture of a snow-covered British grave presided over by a very disconsolate raven and inscribed "December 25th, 1945." Another was of sentimental little children sitting round the Christmas fireside saying: "It will be lonely without Daddy this year." Then there was the usual Jewish profiteer making love to a soldier's wife, and photographs of Russian atrocities. In the evening the Brigadier came to dine at Battalion Headquarters and eat a meal much disturbed by the uncertainty of the future. There was a possibility that the Germans would go over to the offensive on our front; however, we hoped that the next day we should leave peacefully for Louvain, and yet on the other hand there was the rumour that we should have to go south to the Ardennes. By the end of dinner the conflicting series of orders and messages had sorted themselves out into a final answer – the cry was "Go south, young man."

The 20th found us manning a road block at Opheylissem, just south of Tirelemont in Belgium, and vaguely prepared to go almost anywhere at any time. The Belgians muttered dark things about 1940 and started to pack, but by the 24th we were told that the worst of the crisis was over and we would be spending Christmas in Opheylissem. Christmas rations were issued by Sidney Cooper, the Quartermaster, and in the evening a large party of us went into Tirelemont in search of gaiety. It was an unplanned evening and we ended up drinking Avocat at the headquarters of the local ping-pong club, where they were holding an impromptu dance. I spent a lot of time drawing diagrams, explaining in incomprehensible French that the situation was well in hand, and that at any rate it couldn't be as serious as all that while we sat idly doing nothing in Opheylissem. When we got back at two in the morning we thought that perhaps the Commanding Officer had been waiting up to bid us "a merry Christmas." Actually he was waiting to explain with long-suffering patience that it had been difficult to organize the Battalion for a move when all the Battalion Headquarter officers were away at a party and that the order for Christmas Day was to be breakfasts at 0500 hrs. and then move soon afterwards to Namur, where we were to hold the bridges over the Meuse. When we drove off the next morning it was freezing hard, and very soon all the windscreens became frosted over; it was so cold that my hands and ears completely lost any sense of feeling and people with moustaches grew a curtain of icicles like mock impersonations of Old Man Winter. It hadn't yet begun to snow, but the fields were all white with hoar frost and the sky had turned into a great blanket of cloud that could hardly be expected to hold up much longer. Even with malicious forethought one could hardly have conjured up a more miserable Christmas morning; it was one of those situations that are so unspeakable as to be really rather funny, and the impending prospect of a battle seemed wholly irrelevant beside the loss of our Christmas dinners and our warm billets at Opheylissem. We found Namur stirring with uneasy life. Steady streams of cars were beginning to leave for safety, lugubrious groups of people watched our progress from the pavements, and a few of the more faithful made their way to church, but everyone was obviously extremely anxious. There were two bridges for us to guard; one of them an ancient stonework structure with massive grey arches that dipped into the icy waters of the Meuse like a natural continuation of the towering cliffs on either side, the other a very unsubstantial framework of girders that carried the railway line. The most important point seemed to be to make sure that no one blew the bridges in a premature moment of panic, and to guard the demolition charges against sabotage. The sudden arrival of any Germans was a very unlikely event, and apart from the sentries that we posted to look after this most of the Battalion was able to find refuge from the biting cold in nearby houses. There was a company guarding each bridge and the remainder of us sat about three miles back in the village of Congelee to await further news. Most of the news was good, and though we drove about in the country on the far side of the river planning what would have to be done if a battle developed there, few of us ever expected that there would be one. On the second night there was an air raid on Namur and a bomb hit the railway bridge, detonating some of the charges, which blew up, partially demolishing

Winter Quarters at Opheylissem, 1944/45. On church parade with the Regimental Band.

the bridge and thus saving us the trouble of guarding it any longer. Two men were wounded as a result of this. It was our only active contact with the Ardennes offensive. The next day the 6th Airborne Division took over from us, and we drove back to Opheylissem.

It had begun to snow heavily and when we got back we found the village already draped in the Christmas-card guise under which it was to remain for the rest of the time that we were there. It consisted of only two streets, and they were narrow pave covered ways, full of unexpected potholes and very slippery under the coating of ice and snow. The houses straggled unevenly along on either side, half cow houses, half residential, with a communal drainage that ran down the runnels of the street and gave the whole place a curious and distinctive smell that hung upon the frozen air and for the time being signified home for us. Most of the village lay on the side of a hill, which was a good thing from the drainage point of view, and at the bottom of the hill there was a large chateau, very Gallic, and wearing an air suggesting the French Revolution, the Tuileries, and anything else that those times bring to mind. In the chateau there lived Monsieur le Comte, and in the village there was, of course, Monsieur le Cure and Monsieur le Mayor; in fact, it was a complete entity of its own. Everyone was very kind and helpful to us. It was undoubtedly the happiest month of the war that we ever spent and at the end there were several marriages, so that for some it must have been very romantic and for all of us it was a haven of rest and recuperation.

Our most serious occupation was to carry out road checks. The German offensive was accompanied by an enormous sabotage campaign equivalent to any normal ideas on the subject multiplied by ten and run riot. The famous Colonel Scorzzini was rumoured to be at the head of it, and there was a story to the effect that he was personally gunning for General Eisenhower. Disputes arose as to whether saboteurs who turned out to be clad in German Army underwear could claim to be in uniform and under the Geneva Convention, or whether they should be shot outright, but none of these gentlemen ever came our way and most people looked upon the whole thing as highly comical.

On the 1st of January there was a huge dinner party at the chateau for all the Coldstream officers in the neighbourhood. Centred between the two wings of the chateau there was a hall as big as a church, surmounted by a vast dome, rather too large for aesthetic perfection but very imposing and filled with the chill of centuries. Three days before the big event we lit a fire in the hall proportionate to its size and consisting of whole tree trunks cut to fill the length of the gigantic fireplace; then when the evening arrived the Regimental Band was fitted into a corner and instructed to play music on a similar scale to the rest of the gargantuan arrangements. Lighting was a grave problem, as neither gas nor electricity had ever made an appearance in the fathomless darkness of the chateau, but by massing together the full resources of the Battalion's batteries a sufficient glow was produced for the Band to read their music and the diners ate by candle-light. We sat down to dine eighty-one strong with eighty-one bottles of champagne, jereboams of punch, dozens of roast turkeys and a general air of plentiful festivity such as can seldom have been seen since the Middle Ages. In every sense one can say that it was a huge success, and afterwards we sent telegrams of loyal greetings to the King and the Colonel of the Regiment – after all, there might never again be such an occasion; in fact, there never was and probably never can be. And should anyone cry "Shame" or "Rations," I'll fill the rest of the chapter with talk of bully beef and biscuits.

We stayed on at Opheylissem until the end of January.

The first of the leave parties set out for England and we started training programmes that involved long, cold days of floundering about in the snow, but at night we had warm, comfortable billets to return to and we were more than contented with the peaceful backwater into which the stream of our existence had found its way. It was a gala period for entertainments. While the Regimental Band was staying with us there was a concert at the chateau practically every day, and in the evenings there were company dances and cinema shows. The spirit of the moment seemed to say, "And so the war ended and they all lived happily ever after."

THE RHINELAND

IN THE middle of January I went on leave. I left the Battalion still resting in billets at Opheylissem and almost submerged by the heavy snowfalls. Everything was white, from the little lean-to shacks in the fields with drifts completely covering them, to the roofs of the clustering village houses which had become quite altered in shape by the accumulations of snow. England was also cold, but the cold was not so intense as on the Continent, and most noticeable of all the war seemed less intense. I never realized until then how wholly or completely I had become bound up with the experiences of the past six months. I had changed so that England now seemed different; a disappointment to my expectations. For us there was only one war – the fighting in Europe – and in our scheme of things England's part was that of a distant and sympathetic audience, there to applaud and appreciate but with no other role to play. Instead, I found that everyone was deeply absorbed by a war of their own that centred around flying bombs and the black-out, rationing and restrictions. They too had changed: altered by the anxious weariness of life in England and a common fund of experiences that drew them all closer together around their own focus of war, but it was a different focus from ours. We had been moving along parallel but separate roads of experience so that outside one's own family there was little of what we felt that could be shared or exchanged, and the misunderstanding gave me the impression that to many our hopes and fears in Europe were a matter of indifference except in so far as they contributed to the ending of the war in general. There seemed to be a gulf between the two worlds that was wider than the Channel but perhaps need never have been there if I had not made it so in my own mind. All the time that I was on leave I was really on the other side of the sea. I felt that the bridge should be built to me, and was annoyed when it wasn't; and when the time came to bundle myself on board the troopship at Dover and make the long, uncomfortable journey back to the Battalion I felt no inclination to get left behind or miss the train. I arrived amid streams of baggage laden soldiers at the Bourg Leopold transit camp to be greeted by a distribution of messages from Monty and news of the beginning of the Operation "Veritable," but I again felt no desire to drag out the hours between then and rejoining the Battalion. I had no illusions about my own courage. I knew that I should be frightened and hate every minute of possible danger that might lie ahead, and yet something impossible to explain urged me on as though the whole course of events depended upon my sudden and personal intervention in the battle.

I managed to scrounge a vehicle and then, after making a few erroneous calculations as to where the Division might be, made off at top speed for Nijmegen. It was pitch dark long before we got there and the roads were jammed with convoys moving up to the battle. In the distance I could hear the almost continual rumble of artillery supporting an attack in the Reichwald area, and the whole horizon was lit up by flickering light as the guns fired. All the paraphernalia of a big offensive met one at every turn. The new signposting, the converging multitude of transport, the carefully police-controlled cross-roads, everything breathed the air of the moment so that however mundane one's own circumstances one could not fail to catch a feeling of exhilaration from the scene. You can catch the same fleeting moment in this extract from a captured German letter (he was writing before the Ardennes offensive):

"DEAR RUTH,

My daily letter will be very short today. I write during one of those great hours before an attack – full of unrest, full of expectation for what the next days will bring. Everyone who has been here the last two days and nights (especially nights), who has witnessed hour after hour the assembly of our crack divisions, who has heard the constant rattling of panzers, knows that something is up and we are looking for a clear order to reduce the tension ... ." Hurriedly on the back of the envelope he had scribbled in pencil "18 December 1944. Ruth! Ruth! Ruth! WE MARCH!"

Only a German could have written that, but the air it breathes is authentic, despite the fact that the Englishman feels constrained under the same circumstances to say: . . well, darling, I have no more news now and must end this letter before I go to bed. Love from Bill."

In the same spirit I feel constrained to say that when I did find the Division their panzers were not rumbling down the road; they were harboured fifteen miles farther back than I had expected, and I found my fellow-officers pyjama-clad and preparing to go to sleep in the dining-room of the convent at Haaren, which had been turned into a dormitory for the occasion. They were tired after a long and exhausting day, and all I gathered of the future

203

was that the plan for Operation "Veritable" was to clear the ground between the Rivers Maas and Rhine preparatory to the big assault into Germany later on. The first move was to clear the Reichwald area just south-east of Nijmegen; then there was to be an armoured break-through towards Wesel which was to be our particular job. As soon as they were ready the Americans would do a similar attack to the south of us, and then over the Rhine and the end of all things. Seven divisions were to take part, five of them British, but for some political reason the operation was nominally Canadian. Four days had been the original timing, but it had been raining, there were bad floods in many places, and undoubtedly it would be slower. "Reveille" the next day was to be at four-thirty, as we might have to move at six o'clock, but that was, as always, a big IF, and anyway it would only be a move up to another concentration area closer to the battle.

Actually the war diary for the next day reads as follows:

"0800 hrs. Order received; no move till 1800 hrs., then at 1 hrs. notice.

"1400 hrs. Order received; no move till 2400 hrs., then at 1 hrs. notice.

"1800 hrs. Order received; no move till 0600 hrs., then at 1 hrs. notice."

This may all sound very inconvenient, but actually we received each successive postponement with sighs of relief. Meals that we had feared would be hurriedly eaten haversack rations became properly cooked hot food, and hours that we expected to spend driving through the night in convoy were spent wrapped up in our blankets.

Eventually we left at a very civilized hour in the morning and moved up towards Nijmegen. The day itself was not so smooth; our original harbour area turned out to be uninhabitable and a last-minute change was made to get us into Nijmegen instead; but, welcome as this was, the alteration led to a few confusing incidents, it was not until dark that we found our area, and the rain began to pour down as we arrived. Despite this, we were very grateful for our two nights in Nijmegen, which were both warm and comfortable.

Situation reports on the latest news of the battle reached us regularly and the more we heard the less pleasing the general picture became. Owing to the floods and the state of the roads a considerable delay had been imposed on the operation and by now the Germans had mustered four new divisions from other parts of the front, so that where before we had had to compete with only one and a half divisions there were now about six. Added to this only two roads were available for the advance, so that our troops already committed became more and more bogged down in a situation that couldn't possibly become anything but the world's greatest traffic jam should our armoured division be launched into the fray. In the end, as happens on these occasions, the tanks were left behind and the infantry battalions sent off under the 32nd Brigade to assist the 51st (Highland) Division near Gennep. But this alteration in the nature and course of events naturally happened in a much more gradual and complicated way than I have outlined, and in the interval we whiled away our time at Nijmegen having baths at the hospital, investigating the local amenities and jumping out of our skins every time the battery of heavy guns in the allotment just behind us fired a salvo. The second day we moved down to Groesbeek, which we knew well in the days when we were under the command of the American 82nd Airborne. It had had the reputation of being a bad shell-trap and on second acquaintance proved to have had every single tile knocked down – it was just a collection of walls and lattice-like roofs. We retiled most of them in the few hours that we were there and the work was amply repaid by a tolerably dry night spent under our own handiwork. Some of us picked our way across the fallen-in trenches and barbed wire of the old battlefield to the top of the hill just beyond us which was reputed to be the highest in Holland. In front you could see a huge, flat wilderness of war and then beyond that the dark, lump-like hill which is covered by the Reichwald Forest, and to the north of it the Rhine and the vast acres of flood beside it. You could see exactly how the opening attack had been made and there were still landing craft and ducks plying to and fro amid the flood land where the Canadians made their amphibious attacks. On some of the little strips of land batteries of guns were in action firing out beyond Cleve and on to the farthest edges of the forest.

There was a windmill there in what had once been a tea garden, and I remember Colonel Roddy saying: "When the war is over I shall bring my children here and bore them with long stories of how the battle happened." But when we passed by later on not a stone was left upon a stone – the windmill had vanished.

Before it was light the next morning the "O" Group went off to the 51st (Highland) Divisional Headquarters near Ottersum to get the details of an attack we were to do just in front of Gennep. There was a small bridgehead across the River Niers just here which was important, as the floods had turned this comparatively small stream into a very large obstacle, and once across it it was essential to push on and expand our hold as fast as possible.

We found Ottersum plastered with S.S. slogans proclaiming "Keine Pupricht nach dem Feind," "Der Feind ist ein Lupp," [8] and similar rudery, together with a great deal about dying for the Fuehrer.

After various deliberations and reconnaissance's we went back to Gennep, where the Battalion had by this time assembled, and Colonel Roddy gave out his orders. It was a beautiful, sunny day and I remember that despite the shell-torn condition of the town we found a very comfortable room full of warmth, easy chairs and broken glass, where we munched our sandwiches while poring over maps and preparing for the attack.

We left Gennep at one o'clock and marched to our start line about three miles away behind some sand-dunes. The whole of our area was sand-dunes and the general impression that the attack made upon me was that it was as if we were taking part in an exercise at Aldershot. Only one really unpleasant thing happened and that was before we crossed the start line – one of the tanks lined up behind us accidentally fired its Besa, shooting-up everyone in front. Miraculously only one person as killed, but it was an extremely alarming incident. While we were waiting, news came in that the enemy had gone, so our attack turned out to be a walk-over and we advanced on to our objective almost without a shot being fired. Then the Micks passed through us and went on to capture Hommersum.

While I was going round the company positions with Colonel Roddy a few mortar bombs came down in our area, but they did no damage. Everyone was well dug in among the sand-dunes almost within the first ten minutes of our arrival, and with the ground so soft the mortar bombs merely dug deeply into the sand, sending up great showers of dust and dirt, and causing no damage at all. For our part we

---

8 "No pity on the enemy," "The enemy is a coward."

were able to do far more useful shooting. The dunes ended abruptly in front of us and the land became a flat carpet of meadowland dotted with isolated farmhouses and almost entirely treeless. The tanks shot-up each little house in turn and on each occasion it resulted in a few prisoners emerging with white flags and their hands up, so that we collected over twenty before the light gave out. They were not a very impressive collection and several confessed that they had purposely stayed behind when their units withdrew, in order to give themselves up in the most convenient manner possible.

The next day at ten o'clock we were told to prepare ourselves for an attack on Hassum, the next village down the road from the Irish Guards in Hommersum. I went off, full of foreboding, with Colonel Roddy and George Mackean to have a look at the ground we would have to attack over. The German artillery had been much reinforced during the past four days and all the morning we had been watching Hommersum being steadily pounded into dust by heavy and repeated shelling. We set out down the road from the Mick headquarters towards the far end of the village amid ominous quiet. "The trouble about this stretch," said the Mick commanding officer, "is that you can be seen," and he had no sooner said this than away in the distance we heard the nebelwerfers fire – erwerp, erwerp, erwerp. There was just time to get off the middle of the road and then a screaming downpour of annihilation crashed all around us – not in one single crump but successive, insistent detonations like rapid hammer blows. And with each explosion a hail of metal would go sizzling past us, followed by a great shower of earth and acrid waves of cordite fumes. We were right in the centre of the target, so that each stick of bombs neatly straddled us, leaving one squirming like a worm in the vain impression that one posture was perhaps a little less exposed than another, and each time we tried to make for a better place we were just too late and the eeeeeeeecrump, CRUMP, CRUMP, CRUMP, CRUMP would drive us down on our faces once more. It's extraordinary that no one was hit. As soon as there was a pause Colonel Roddy set out for the bridge. Someone shouted, "He's mad! He'll kill himself. Come on back!"

We never did see the start line, as the bombardment started all over again, and before we had time to wait for a period of quiet the Commanding Officer was told to report back to Brigade Headquarters with all haste. I was miserably unhappy about the thought of starting an attack from Hommersum. With the whole Battalion marching down the road a repetition of this morning's incident would inevitably cause a lot of casualties, however carefully the Battalion was dispersed, but happily there were a lot of other good reasons for not attacking Hassum and the Brigadier changed our objective to a collection of farmsteads centred around a large farm called Mull and about a thousand yards south of Hassum. We would end up with Huns to the left of us in Hassum and Huns to the right of us in a large wood to the south, but this would later be remedied, as ours was only the first of six attacks lasting from midday on the 16th until four o'clock the next morning, by the end of which our situation would be less exposed.

When the next day came the mist was so thick that we could see nothing at all of the land in front of us, and had to alter some of our arrangements, but by lunch time it was a clear, blue-skied day. The General came up to watch the attack. In the few agonizing minutes while we waited for the moment to move off I remember discussing with someone what we would really like to do on such a day and coming to the conclusion that best of all would be to go to a race meeting. I had had the intention of writing one of those sort of letters that one labels "Not to be delivered except in the event of my death"; now I felt most annoyed that I had not done so. Perhaps I should get killed and no one would ever know my last testament. I had visualized it as a penetrating analysis of the vanities of the world written in a rather matter-of-fact way, suggesting that I didn't really mind dying at all and considered today as good a time as any. Now that I minded acutely I was sorry not to have put something on paper to say the exact reverse, and I thought, "Of course, now that I've missed the opportunity I really will be killed." Then I noticed that the leading companies, Nos. 1 and 4, were already half-way over the dunes and that it was time to go off and pick up Colonel Roddy with the carrier.

By the time we got to the start line everything was under way. Our artillery were firing with a compact rumble, rumble, rumble that sent their salvos singing overhead like drumming snipe, a sort of sighing rushing through the air, and then not far ahead one could see the spurts of flame and mushrooms of white smoke billowing up around the selected targets. The companies were perfectly spread out, as though the big square fields with their stunted hedges had been neatly peppered with moving figures going steadily on towards the smoke and the burning farmhouses. The clank, clank, clank of the carrier's tracks and the noise of the engine as we negotiated the stickier patches drowned the sound of almost everything else, so that I saw the enemy shells fall rather than heard them – sudden smudges of black that seemed to fountain up out of nothing so quickly that you felt the rush of hot air and smelt the cordite almost as you saw them burst. There was a good deal of small-arms fire, as we knew from the reports of No. 4 Company. I couldn't hear this with the earphones on, but I could judge from what I saw that we were having casualties. There were three men lying in lifeless heaps just beyond the first field and some stretcher-bearers attending to the wounded.

We saw with dismay that most of the Welsh Guards' tanks supporting us were hopelessly bogged down in the sticky going and only the two tanks following our carrier on the track were still mobile. I think the Germans must have been able to watch us all the way along, as everywhere we stopped to set up a temporary command post there was a heavy stonk that drove us on somewhere else.

I could hear No. 4 Company on the wireless all the way. Most of the time the signaller gave me reports: "Hullo, Roger Six. Sunray is not with me at the moment, but we are still going forward O.K. There's a big house ahead which I think is our objective," and then soon afterwards Jack Hamilton came up on the air and announced that they had captured Mull.

The Commanding Officer got hold of Derek Eastman on the wireless and told him to pass No. 3 Company through Jack on to their objective, which was a little hamlet called Startenhof, just beyond. No. 1 Company we couldn't get in touch with at all, but eventually we came across them farther down the track after we had been mortared out of one hide for the third time running. Actually we had in the confused mass of farm tracks strayed off our way, but it was quite fortunate, as we found David Kennard and got No. 1 Company's news. He had one platoon on one[1] side of the track in Germany and one on the other side in Holland; the third was heavily engaged and unable to get on. The whole position was under fire in one way or another and conversation was continually interrupted by an S.P. gun

Operation Veritable, crossing the Dutch border into Germany on 14th February 1945 at Hommersum.

which was firing at us. I remember I had two unsuccessful attempts to talk to our Sapper officer, who had just arrived. Each time we stood up on the bank to point out how things lay there was an appalling bang that sent us both down into the ditch. Then a clump of nebel-werfer shells came down behind us which killed most of the Pioneer Platoon.

I saw one man jump into a ditch that turned out to be about four feet deep and full of water. I don't think he cared, but everyone thought it was the funniest thing they'd ever seen.

After settling the No. 1 Company situation the Commanding Officer set off on foot with a wireless set to see No. 3 Company, which was meeting with a lot of opposition in Startenhof, and I was sent off to Mull to gather Battalion Headquarters together and start a command post. Some of our own men who'd just been killed lay sprawled across the track, completely blocking it. I suppose they wouldn't have minded, but even on a battlefield you can't drive over the dead bodies of your friends, and when we turned off on to the plough the carrier's tracks immediately sank in and bogged us. It was a maddening situation. I couldn't leave the wireless set and at the same time I had to get to Mull as soon as possible. Eventually Nevin Agnew, now Adjutant, got a jeep to rescue me and we struggled through the mud to a suitable farmhouse for a headquarters.

Three hours the complete attack lasted, but it was by no means the end of things, as the enemy artillery increased and they put down a lot of smoke so that we expected a counter-attack.

Guardsman Brewer, my Intelligence Section D.R., was killed. There were only three originals left by now and in numbers our casualties had already been one hundred per cent. It was a very costly day for Battalion Headquarters, though the total casualties were not quite so heavy as we expected.

And when the night brought a slight respite from shelling we had to put all our remaining energy into getting up a hot meal and supplies. Carriers were the only vehicles that could begin to negotiate the quagmire tracks up to us, and in the dark with frequent pauses to tow one another out of impassable stretches it was after midnight before they could reach the command post.

I managed to sleep for a few hours propped up against a sack of corn, but I hadn't got my greatcoat with me and towards the morning it became too cold to lie still any longer. It was strange to walk outside in the growing half-light before the dawn and to see where only a few hours before there had been so much noise and destruction a scene of such deserted calm. I knew exactly where there were platoons, antitank guns, mortars, the whole lay-out of the Battalion; and yet even when the full daylight arrived there would be little enough to see and you could pick out nothing. Only the dim outline of fields and hedgerows shrouded in

Breaching the Siegfried Line. Digging in at Müll on the advance to Goch.

mist, the muddied ruts where tracks had sunk deep into the mire, and their confused signature scribbled over the soft turf. The tileless skeleton roofs of the barns in which we slept showed up against the sky like an elaborate trellis, and the uneven brickwork was all chipped and freshly scarred. Carriers and jeeps were parked in the courtyard – we would have to get them more dispersed before the light came; now they were just a collection of hulks full of indistinguishable equipment and bodies sleeping wrapped in camouflage nets for warmth.

There was a sentry awake just outside the courtyard doing his best to keep warm, and inside the half-track which hums with the noise of the wireless set and emits stray chinks of light there was a signaller also awake; but the general impression was as though the night had swallowed up all the actors of the day before and left me in a wilderness with nothing but shadows, a hang-over from the urgency of yesterday. And the day will not be a period when one is awake and refreshed, but a time when you are tireder than before and must somehow arrange to get some sleep.

We were at Mull from the 17th until the 22nd of February, and though it was on the whole a quiet position we had several more casualties. We lost Dick Symons and Guardsman Andrews on a patrol, and the next night a large German patrol got right in between No. 4 Company Headquarters and Battalion Headquarters, and another officer was wounded. It rained a great deal so that everyone became drenched through and caked in mud. It was so bad we even feared that it might become impossible to relieve us, and all our supplies had to be brought up in Weasels.[9]

On the 21st the Irish Guards did a very similar attack to ours which cost them over two hundred casualties and they had to be withdrawn. It's remarkable how little can sometimes sway the margin between success and disaster. When all the pros and cons are added up I believe that in the end all that can be said is that we were lucky and they were unlucky. It's one of the most unpleasant things about doing an attack. In defence casualties are very roughly predictable, whilst in an attack even the most careful arrangements will not guarantee the result and the greater part of a battalion may become casualties in a way that could never have been foretold.

From Mull we moved back to a reserve position in Hommersum. where we had one night of grace before moving off early in the morning and prepared to take over a position from the 51st (Highland) Division just east of Goch at a place we called Schule because Battalion Headquarters was in a school and the companies in a series of tumbledown wrecks too indefinite to have a name. It was a nasty place, just as mud-ridden and impassable as Mull, only much more tiring, as the whole position was on a forward slope, visible

---

9   Vehicles with special wide tracks for bad going.

to the enemy and constantly shelled. We had to take once more to an existence of night life, getting all our supplies to and fro by dark and keeping strictly silent during the day. When we went round No. 4 Company's position we found a badly wounded pig eating a dead horse in a deep gully full of unburied mines. Most of the farmhouse buildings were destroyed and stank of burnt cattle.

As we were walking back we were shouted at by a very vociferous little Scotsman: "Yourrre underr enemy observation, serr – yourrre underr enemy observation, serr!" He might have been an umpire on an exercise, and by that time we cared as little as though he was.

We were at Schule from the 23rd of February until the 3rd of March, but the last few days were quiet enough, as on the 26th Operation "Blockbuster" began which at this stage was largely concerned with the capture of Udem, just opposite us. Our only part in the battle was to receive the "overs" during the first two days, and after that we were left in peace, well behind the front.

We killed a lot of chickens, which improved our diet, and I remember having a bath in the tin tub that we

Stretcher bearers at Müll bringing in the wounded

scrounged from somewhere. It was the only bath that I got during "Veritable." March, I suppose, is the moment when birds automatically sing more than usual; at all events, they sang as though the war had ended, and the louder the guns fired the more eloquent they became. It was rather an "all quiet on the Western Front" touch.

Then on the night of the 4th we drove into the ruins of Goch and joined up with the 1st Battalion tanks at midnight. The whole Division was now going into battle. At Kappeln the Grenadiers were already in action, and during the night we went down the well-known route via Goch, Weeze, Kevelier and Wettin to join them.

The battle centred around a great oval lump of tree-clad hill about five miles long referred to as "the high ground at Bonninghardt." We were launched into an attack on the west edge of the woods at about five-thirty and had as our objective a cluster of farms about a mile in, called Metxekath. It was not at all an easy attack, and looking through the war diary I see that our information ran as follows:

"The Bonninghardt woods are being strongly held by units of 8 Para. Div., who have been putting up a very stubborn resistance. They are supported by several S.P. guns. On the left Sonsbeck is still held by the enemy and on the right 53 Dv. have been pushed back to Issum by a counterattack."

At the last moment I was suddenly sent for by Brigade Headquarters and told that on our particular sector there were two battalions of enemy, not one; it was hardly the sort of information to cheer people up with, and I got back just in time to be shelled by our own guns. It was one of those things that are always liable to happen. Five field batteries and three medium batteries were supporting the attack and one of them, it was impossible to tell which, instead of bringing down its fire a couple of hundred yards ahead of the start line dropped the whole lot on us as we waited to move forward. Several people were killed outright and a lot more wounded; it wasn't a propitious start, and soon afterwards we heard that Derek Eastman, who was commanding No. 3 Company, the leading company on the left, had been wounded. It was a difficult battle to follow, as the advance was all through fir woods until at the very end, when we reached Metxekath in a clearing. Added to this, the little cluster of vehicles comprising the command post, which was making its way down a track between the two companies, ran into a patch of mines. First a tank set one off, then a few minutes later a carrier behind me was blown up, so that we had to halt and wait for the route to be cleared. The Commanding Officer went on foot and I was left behind with the scout car rather in the dark as to what was happening except for the sound of very heavy small-arms fire over on the right, where we knew No. 4 Company to be. They were actually about to rush the first lot of houses, but had great difficulty in doing so, as the front edge of the wood that they had to emerge from was being fired at by some well- placed anti-tank guns that were too well supported by infantry to be easily overcome. It was an extraordinarily stubborn position and one of the Germans, when finally he saw that he was about to be captured, shot himself as the position was overrun. Michael Wall, who led the attack which successfully captured the farm, was awarded the M.C.

It was nearly dark before we finally cleaned everything up and the total of prisoners captured came to a hundred and five, four of them officers. At about midnight I set off back down the centre line to visit Brigade Headquarters and get a forecast of events for the morrow. The path back through the woods was totally deserted and wrapped in the sinister quiet of impenetrable darkness. Farther back searchlights were weaving about in the sky and to the north an attack was going on that lit up the night with uneasy patches of flickering light as the guns fired, but I could only see this through the narrow strip of sky showing between the tops of the trees. It was just possible to distinguish the white tapes where the road had been cleared of mines and the dark outline of the broken-down carrier; then we came out of the wood and past some burning cottages. The fires were practically out by now, leaving little but a hulk full of red-hot embers and eddying sparks; the usual trade-mark of a battlefield. Beyond here everything was entirely different – the narrow track was jammed with trucks and carriers and ambulances, all trying to go in different directions and mostly getting stuck. The great art is to keep as much on the crown of the road as possible and force the traffic coming the other way to get stuck in the ditch, but as always happens eventually we met a bigger and more purposeful vehicle and were forced unwillingly into an inescapable slough. I abandoned the jeep and made for the R.A.P. to get a lift on an ambulance.

Doctor John had practically finished his work and asked me to have a cup of tea with him. The whole place exuded ether and disinfectant, and round the room on blanket-covered stretchers lay a lot of German wounded who kept up a continuous moaning as though they were souls in hell. I would have said "No, thank you," to the tea, but by this time it was too late and he handed it to me with blood-stained hands. I gulped it down and fled on the first available ambulance. The next doctor that I went to beg a lift off was half-way through an operation. After all that one had seen during the day it was extraordinary to be still capable of squeamishness, but that's how it was and I swore never again to defy the Geneva Convention and make use of medical transport. The dead I can become accustomed to; the still living are a different matter.

The news back at Brigade was reassuring. Other battalions were to finish clearing up the Bonninghardt feature and at the worst we might have to hold an unenergetic defensive position. After that no one could tell. It was anticipated that the Germans would try to hold a bridgehead across the Rhine at Wesel, but we had some five divisions on hand at the moment, and as to which would have to finish the job no one could say. Perhaps we would be squeezed out – how often before has one hoped in vain for that?

We had three days of comparative rest while the remainder of the high ground was cleared up, and our only commitments were to hold various reserve positions and patrol through the forest for stragglers. Then on the evening of the 8th Colonel Roddy went off to an "O" Group at 32nd Brigade Headquarters upon which our fate was to depend.

The Bonninghardt feature looks north-east on to a great expanse of flatness that is crossed by a large main road about two miles away running parallel to it, from Xanten to Rheinberg. Through the middle of the forest runs the main road to Wesel, which is on the far side of the Rhine where it curves away in a big loop. The cross-roads formed by the two roads was more or less the centre of events and the future depended upon whether it could be captured by an American attack from the south early the next morning, or whether our Division and the 52nd Division to the right of us would have to descend from the hill and capture it if the first attack failed. In this event the 52nd Division would advance down the Wesel road and the 32nd Brigade would attack parallel to them, the first attack being made by the Scots Guards, and the second one, to cut the Xanten – Rheinberg road, by us. We had little exact information about the Germans except that the bridgehead was being held by the 7th Parachute Division and that they had received a personal letter from Der Fuehrer saying that the position was to be held at all costs to the last man.

Our headquarters at that time was in a house known as "the Hunting Lodge"; it was almost undamaged and quite the most comfortable home we had ever had. As we drove back that evening I felt that somehow there was bound to be some connection between the Hunting Lodge and the possibility of the attack the next day. It is almost inevitable in war that the minute you find somewhere really pleasant you immediately have to go off and do something bloody.

It was three o'clock in the morning when I went to bed, and I wasn't very anxious to go to sleep even then; the room was cosy and soothingly unlike one's usual surroundings. It seemed a waste of time to be asleep in such a pleasant atmosphere. The light from a big wood fire made great shadows that moved to and fro upon the pale-green walls and the mathematical rows of antlers carefully nailed above the mantelpiece. I was warm, full of rum and reminiscences. I don't think I have ever felt less inclined to take part in a battle and when I woke up the next morning the sense of foreboding was even stronger than before.

Still lying on my camp-bed, I remember watching Neville Whitmee, who was our Gunner officer at that time, shaving in front of the mirror and singing to himself. He only knew the first verse, which consequently had to be repeated over and over again. It went like this:

"Take it easy, take it easy,
Take it easy, take it easy."

It was about two days before I could stop myself humming it; it went well when there were shells falling and such like, so that now it seems to evoke memories more strongly than anything else that I carry unbidden in my mind.

At eight o'clock all the company commanders assembled at the Hunting Lodge and the Commanding Officer gave out his orders. We still did not know the result of the American attack, but the plan was made on the assumption that it would not succeed, so as to avoid any delay in the second alternative, and on this basis the Scots Guards[5] attack was to start at half-past four, with our attack as soon after as possible. They would debouch over the front of the escarpment that makes the end of the hill and capture a little hamlet called Wegers- dorf and the ground as far as a railway embankment running across their front; then we would form up behind the embankment and continue the attack up to the main road about a thousand yards beyond. Nine field batteries, three medium batteries, and two heavy batteries were to help us on our way, but we gathered that owing to the general converging process the Germans also mustered a very strong force of artillery.

At two o'clock we learned that the American attack had not reached the cross-roads, and that everything would accordingly continue to plan. At about four o'clock we said good-bye to the Hunting Lodge, with its massive thatched roof and the red-and-white shutters. We rumbled down the road through Bonninghardt village and parked ourselves on the aerodrome beyond ready to move forward after the Scots Guards as soon as we got the word, but in the end, though the Scots Guards' attack went in successfully, ours was cancelled, as the 52nd Division on their right had been unable to capture a large building called Haus Loo, which completely covered the ground over which we were to advance. The sun went down behind the peaked line of fir trees and when it was dark the Germans hit a Scots Guards' ammunition truck and the scene was lit up from the opposite direction by huge detonations of flame and coloured fireworks. We could hear crump after crump coming down on their position and shook our heads anxiously. A few bad shots landed in our area and some of the Scotsmen in charge of their "F" Echelon came down to share the shelter we had found under an old aerodrome hut. They said that their casualties had been heavy and that the shelling was worst just by the stream below the embankment, where the sappers were putting across a bridge to take the tanks in the morning. We slept wrapped up in greatcoats on some straw. Cold and rather gloomy.

When the morning of the 9th came we were still uncertain as to when our attack was to take place and the Commanding Officer went off to Brigade Headquarters immediately after stand-to in order to get the latest news. He found that two attacks were to take place before ours. A further 52nd Division attack to capture Haus Loo and later the famous cross-roads starting at eight o'clock; and at ten o'clock a Canadian attack some distance away on our left. We would not start until eleven, and in any case not until Haus Loo had been captured.

We had been teed up so long waiting for the attack to happen that I was coming to the stage when one feels, "Well, with any luck the whole thing will be cancelled. They can't go on putting it off indefinitely." There was little that we could do by way of further preparation and I seem to remember spending most of the morning looking at the air photographs. Every detail down to which little blob of houses we would put the command post in had been arranged. One could see exactly what the shape of the garden was, and if you lacked anything better to do it was even possible to count up the number of fruit trees in each orchard. Surely by some clairvoyant means one should be able to decipher what the inscrutable photographs held in store!

Almost as much as anything else we were worried about feeding arrangements – would we be able to have a hot meal before starting, or would we suddenly have to set out just as the meal was ready? And as time wore on we were worried about Haus Loo, which was reported still held.

Soon after eleven the meal problem was solved by a message giving H Hour as 1430 hrs. Haus Loo was not mentioned, and I was sent off to discover whether it had or had not been captured.

At Brigade Headquarters I was hurried off to the Brigadier's caravan to receive the news.

"No, Haus Loo was still in enemy hands and would probably remain so. If we waited any longer we might not be able to finish the attack in daylight and it was impossible to put back the artillery programme any later. It was all very difficult, but we would have to go now or not at all, and if things became too hot the Commanding Officer was to select objectives a little farther back."

So that was that. I climbed down the steps feeling that I ought to have made some bright remark showing jaunty indifference or deep stoicism under difficult circumstances; wondering what Colonel Roddy would think about this change in circumstances, and what he would construe as being "too hot."

When I got back we had only about ten minutes left before moving off to the start line. Spread over the vast flatness of the aerodrome little groups of vehicles were beginning to form up in rough sequence so as to be ready when it was time for their serial to make for the start point and be joined into the main column. There was a squadron of 1st Battalion tanks to be parcelled out between the two leading companies, S.P. anti-tank guns, carriers with the Battalion mortars loaded on to them, company jeeps, the R.A.P. half-track ambulances, company carriers with wireless sets, a medley of odds and ends comprising Battalion Headquarters and a lot more besides. While I gulped down a slab of chocolate and some rum out of a flask I watched the first company in the distance marching down the road towards the escarpment all laden with Bren guns, ammunition, mortars, stretchers, wirelesses, and all the paraphernalia of a rifle company. It was surprisingly warm and sunny for March – hot enough to melt my chinagraph pencils, and when the tanks moved forward the dried-up surface of the road swam with the haze of dust and fumes.

Half an hour later everything was on the move, and most of the companies safely beyond the escarpment. It was an anxious moment, as it seemed inevitable that the Germans would spot the column as it wriggled its way down the exposed front of the hill; they had caused a lot of casualties there earlier in the day and to increase the danger the tanks had to slow up to cross the bridge below, so that there was a momentary jam of traffic right on the crest. It was one of those places where you particularly dislike having to stop, but fortunately the view was not so good as it might have been; burning houses and the constant shelling had produced a thick haze all over the low-lying land, and in places the smoke hung like banks of fog so that it was not at all easy to pick anything out. You could distinguish Menzelen about a thousand yards beyond our objective, and the factory area with its tower like an onion on stilts, but the road itself and the line of the railway seemed to be lost amid the checkwork of confused fields and orchard-ringed farms.

Perhaps the smoke was thick enough to hide us; at any rate, we got safely into our forming-up area behind the embankment without being shelled, and everyone began to dig in so as to have some sort of cover during the thirty minutes still left until the start.

I went off to go round the companies and explain the Haus Loo situation. I found Billy Straker Smith, who was commanding No. 2 Company, sitting in a big trench in an orchard at the back of a farmhouse. I suppose some Germans must have dug it, and the greater part of company headquarters seemed to fit into it. They had steel helmets on and after the march were dripping with sweat. I have an idea that Billy had been saying something to them – no doubt short and to the point. My news must have been a very bad blow for them, as they were the leading company on the right and would have to pass right in front of Haus Loo; but it might have been a question of discussing a winner for the Derby. Billy said he was sure that they would be O.K. We discussed this and that, and then I left, very much wondering how it would all work out. They were nearly all killed or wounded later.

There was a gun still firing from well this side of the embankment. I think it was an 88. Occasional rounds kept falling in our area, and as I made my way towards No. 1 Company I could hear the ominous brrrrrr-ah, brrrrrr-ah, of a German machine gun somewhere very close at hand. It seemed an immense distance to the farm that they were centred about and I remember thinking how foolish I was

Advancing up through Kappepellen near Wesel with difficulty.

to set out on a journey of that sort by myself. If I got hit no one would see, and I should probably be left lying with my face in the mud until I died.

When I got there I couldn't at first find anyone at all and for a short moment of panic I thought that I had lost the way; then someone shouted at me not to stand about in the roadway, as there was a sniper firing at them from the embankment. I sheltered behind some tanks and found Allan Pemberton, who said;

"You'll find David somewhere along the embankment beyond the archway over there."

"Isn't that more or less where we are being shot at from ?"

"Well, not quite; I think it's a bit farther up. David got across there all right, but they seem to have moved since then."

"Oh! How about letting the news wait until he comes back here?"

"Well, I suppose that would do as well, but he might want to ask you something about it."

"Oh! … there's nothing more that I can add to what I've told you, and I think I ought to get on to No. 4 Company."

I was determined not to play hide-and-seek along the railway embankment. It wasn't very gallant on my part, but somehow I felt that the news was hardly worth all that and, anyway, I had rather hoped that Allan would offer to go and tell him. I'm sure Allan was aware of this – it was one of those moments for a good diplomatic compromise.

When I got back to the scout car everyone was beginning to consult their watches and count the minutes until the half-hour. I climbed on board and took up the headphones, ready to receive any messages that might come in from the companies. The grass slope of the railway embankment a few hundred yards ahead rising slowly towards the main line on our left, behind it two clumps of buildings with their claret-coloured brickwork and tileless roofs, the cabbage fields and the plough dotted with waiting figures standing knee-deep in their temporary trenches – for a moment the scene imprinted itself on my mind as though it were something separated from the passing seconds and fixed in time; then four guns fired and almost instantaneously the whole force of our artillery opened up so that the ground shook with the concussion of reiterated detonations.

A troop of tanks went thundering past us, making for the raised track up to the embankment, and we followed along behind towards the shelter of a farmhouse. As it reached the top of the track the first tank was suddenly engulfed in a burst of black smoke and it stuck abruptly with one track blown up by a mine while the other tanks fanned out to the right, looking for a negotiable section of embankment. The leading companies were all across in the first few minutes and soon afterwards I heard Billy's voice on the wireless:

"Hullo, Baker Two. We're going ahead all right, but we are being heavily fired on from the right. Baker Two over."

I had to jump out of the scout car and run across to where Colonel Roddy was watching, as the noise was too great for him to hear what I said, and then the message went back:

"Hullo, Baker Two. Go slow till the tanks can get up with you and help. Baker Three, out to you," and to No. 3 Company, following behind them:

"Hullo, Baker Three. Do not cross the embankment till you are told to. Baker Three over."

And back from No. 3 Company came a rather distant "Baker Three wilco out."

I could distinguish the noise of firing from Haus Loo quite distinctly from the all the other sounds – the incessant crump, crump, crump of our artillery coming down along the line of the main road or the firing of the tanks like batteries of pneumatic drills at work – the German machine guns fired twice as fast as anything else, in repeated bursts of staccato vibration with a curious note at the end: brrrrrr-ah, brrrrrr-ah, brrrrrr-ah, and every now and then there was the equally distinctive sssss-bang of an enemy S.P. gun.

After another ten minutes No. 2 Company reported that they were still going ahead and about half-way to their objective, with the enemy firing hard both from Haus Loo and the main road.

The artillery fire was due to stop in a few more minutes, so the Commanding Officer ordered another fifteen minutes' worth and we prepared to move ourselves forward after the advance.

The way over the embankment was blocked by the blown-up tank, so while Colonel Roddy set out with a wireless on foot I went off in the scout car to try to get round by an archway over on the left. We had to drive flat out to prevent sinking in the soft plough, and once under the railway we kept to the pathway, though I didn't like this, as I felt sure it would be mined.

The attack was nearly over now, but the fireworks were by no means finished. A brickworks with a chimney and a large out-house marked the left-hand corner of our area where No. 1 Company were and they were still having a lot of trouble there with an S.P. gun. The buildings vomited dust and smoke out of the windows every time it fired at them and two of our tanks were knocked out. The line of the main road and the scattered, whitewashed houses along it was in our hands, but the Germans had only pulled back to the next line of cottages and continued to fire from them, spraying the gaps and the open fields behind. Our own S.P. anti-tank guns arrived and began to rumble down the track towards No. 2 Company, but they met with more mines; the leading one blew up and immediately afterwards an enemy S.P. gun put two shots into it that set the whole thing on fire.

The Germans had been seen to withdraw from Haus Loo as the attack ended; now it stood bleak and white with its surrounding trees completely stripped like so many hop-poles; but strewn across the green field that the company had advanced over lay the lifeless bodies of the men killed in the attack – there seemed to be an awful lot of them.

The house behind us was on fire and someone broke in through the stables to let out a panicking horse. The R.S.M., Dusty Smith, was busy organizing the defence of the command post, urging people on to dig deeper and faster, and presiding over the general set-up, his pipe billowing smoke like a factory chimney – one couldn't be quite sure whether he was about to curse someone or give them a fatherly pat on the back.

There was no need to urge anyone to dig in; regular batches of shells kept coming down, seldom concentrated in one place, but roving here and there as though they were ranging, and it was difficult to walk about in the open without finding yourself unconsciously keeping an eye open for the nearest trench or ditch. Added to this, large numbers of nebelwerfers came into action – it's curious the way they always seem to wait until the battle is over.

I felt like a patient coming to after a dangerous operation. It was three hours since the attack began, but I felt as though I had been ministering to the queries and commands of the wireless net for about three days; and yet there was a certain feeling of exhilaration now that the worst was over – we'd been through it all so often before – we'd never failed *yet* and here we were again – nothing could ever stop us, I felt.

Colonel Roddy came back from his tour round the companies; he seemed tired and rather depressed. He thought our casualties had been pretty heavy and he brought back with him Billy Straker Smith, who had been wounded.

Johnny Gull came up with his A.R.Vs.[10] to tow in knocked-out tanks, but we had to send him rudely away, as everywhere his A.R.Vs. stopped produced a hail of fire from the German S.P. guns, and we didn't see why both of us should be hit.

As darkness came on huge banks of black cloud came up from the east and the night shut down on us suddenly and completely as though someone had switched the lights off. The nebelwerfers and S.P. guns, however, became more active than ever. Nevin Agnew, who had gone up to No. 2 Company to help Peter Strutt, kept on requesting for more and more shoots to try to discourage them until finally something jammed the wireless net. I could hear an angry voice repeating: "For God's sake, get off the air whoever it is; you're jamming the net!" A long silence while we tried in vain to discover what had happened; eventually we found that it was Nevin himself who had caused the jam.

Soon after it was dark we heard that we were to be relieved about midnight and were to go back to our old area; after that we were prepared to put up with anything.

Not long before the relief was due to arrive we thought that we were about to be counter-attacked. There was a lot more shelling and David Kennard reported that there was

---

10 Armoured recovery vehicles.

a great deal of movement going on very close in front of him. We fired our D.F. tasks and waited, but nothing more came of it, and towards midnight the troops of the relieving battalion began to arrive. It wasn't an easy take-over, as they had had no time to see the layout of the ground before it became dark and off and on there were some very heavy stonks arriving.

Several buildings burnt like torches in the blackness, but it was not sufficient to light up the scene and it was extremely difficult stumbling about in the darkness to connect up the guides with the correct incoming companies. Two guides were hit and the proceedings were continually interrupted by a warning fizzz, a flash, and a deafening explosion that eliminated you couldn't be sure who, so that endless checking and delay took place.

The Commanding Officer always leaves the position last, not on the sinking ship principle but because he has to see that everything has been properly handed over. It was midnight when we set out and darker than ever before. We had a terrible time manoeuvring the scout car across the ploughed fields in the blackness, but by then I had ceased to care about anything. I had before me a mental picture of the inside of the Hunting Lodge with the fire lit, and a hot meal of stew or bully or anything at all, so long as it was hot, and also I seemed to remember that there was still some whisky ration left. On this carrot-and-donkey principle the journey back passed very quickly and when I found my blankets I slept as though I were dead.

Towards the early morning quiet set in around the bridgehead; there were two thunderous explosions as the Rhine bridges were demolished, and at first light it was found that the Germans had withdrawn. Operation "Veritable" finally ended almost without a shot being fired.

Months later a German officer who was a prisoner of ours gave me a quite considerable postscript to this, but at the time we didn't bother much as to why, after a Hitler order and such a stubborn resistance, the bridgehead had been so suddenly abandoned: we were only too pleased to be still alive, to know that we had a rest ahead, and to find that it was a glorious spring morning without compare.

"Veritable" was over. We'd made the last attack; no one could ask us to do more than that, and if anyone had asked us which was the best battalion in the Division we would have said that we were, not out of a sense of pride but because we felt there could be no doubt about it – our morale was terrific. And even more than the sense of accomplishment it seemed splendid beyond all measure to be alive and well, to have survived.

It was nearly midday before I woke up that morning. I remember that we spent a long time nursing the luxury of shaving and hot water, and as we dressed we composed a little rhyme about the battle. It went to a kind of Western Brothers' chant and the opening verse was as follows:

"Don't let's die today, boys,

Don't let's die today.

We've given all we're going to give,

We're very, very keen to live,

To hell with umpty umpty Div.!

Don't let's die today."

It wasn't at all a good rhyme, but as we made it up it seemed an epic, and in a way it was. I wonder if the ancient bards chronicled their own times with similar glee? They were probably less ribald.

GERMANY

BY ONE of those curious twists of fate that always seem to bring you back to the scene of old battles and past memories we spent the period of rest between Operation "Veritable" and the Rhine crossing just outside Mook. Nothing very much had changed, and though by now life in Nijmegen had become a slightly more ordered affair, and the hundreds of old gliders still strewn in the neighbouring fields had become more like the skeletons of primeval monsters than ever, the general impression was as though we had only been away a few weeks and were back once more in the autumn of last year. More than anything else the Battalion itself had changed; of the men who first landed on the beaches of Normandy no more than a smattering remained, and we had reached a stage when the odds for and against survival could be calculated with almost mathematical exactitude. A platoon commander would on average see about two months of war before being hit, a company commander somewhat longer, though less than three. It was about an even-money chance on survival for a Guardsman and about two to one against for an officer. And if you were hit the chances of living then amounted to about three to one. Some people never saw more than a few days of fighting and there were others who seemed to have outlived all the natural expectations of war, but taking everything into account you could only come to the conclusion that fighting was an experience which few in the end could ever hope to get through unscathed. I must point this out because such constant play has been made of the difference between the casualties in this war and the last, as though battles had been reduced to more harmless affairs where only the unlucky get hit. The sum totals are undeniable, but it should always be kept in mind that during this war the larger part of the Army consisted of administrative and maintenance troops who paid only occasional visits to the front and were most unlikely to become casualties, so that for the troops in the frontline the prospects of life were not so vastly different from the last war. In the last war the odium of the fighting troops was reserved for the Staff. It has in this war never been more than whispered that any such feelings existed, but the truth of the matter is that there was a good deal of odium towards the L. of C., who, indispensable and magnificent as their contribution was, seemed in comparison to live such a happy life while the P.B.I. bore the heat of the day. We were never in any sense either embittered or morbid, but the price of the war was visibly and inescapably heavy, and the only sum worthy of attention is the lives that were being constantly added to the cost. And in this connection it should be noted that, though in the histories of the war this last phase will no doubt appear to be no more than the pursuit and engulfment of a routed army, for us the impression was often very different. Between the crossing of the Rhine and VE Day we suffered a considerable number of casualties, and though there were many towns and villages which surrendered without a fight the most remarkable thing was the degree of resistance that the Germans were sometimes able to put up even at this stage. Only four days before the war ended a staff officer of the 15th Panzer Division wrote in his diary: "Our morale is as high as it has ever been, we have more ammunition and supporting weapons on hand than we have had for many months, and though there is no doubt of the final outcome, if we are attacked in our present positions we can only be overcome at a very considerable cost to the enemy."

We took no part in the actual Rhine crossing which took place on the 24th of March, and couldn't be brought into the battle until there was a bridge built strong enough for the tanks to cross by. The morning of the 29th found us sitting on a hill just outside Udem and waiting for the order to move. It was a depressing area – an old battlefield of "Veritable," with the fields forlornly uncultivated and the ruined houses more dilapidated than ever. Everywhere there were minefields and we had five casualties as a result of this while we were in our area; then the next day we drove down to the river and crossed over at Rees. All the succeeding advance was made as the Coldstream Group, with ourselves and the 1st Battalion tanks moving and fighting as one command, and by now we had become so proficient in this mixed capacity that it required hardly any additional effort to co-ordinate the two battalions. We knew exactly each other's needs and methods, and the team worked better than ever before. With this group system the Division consisted of four more or less autonomous fighting forces, two to each brigade, and as a rule each brigade had a centre line so that in theory on each centre line there was a group leading and in action, and another following in reserve, which gives prospects of alternate days of fighting and rest as the group in the lead is changed each day. In practice this system cannot be followed so conveniently. There were constant hold-ups due to stubbornly held villages, blown bridges and other obstacles, so that the reserve group continually had to launch out on to a new centre line and try to find other routes for the advance, which meant that the days of peaceful follow-my-leader were actually very few and far between.

Bridges were our chief difficulty. There seemed to be more rivers and canals in this part of the country than anywhere else in the world, and every bridge that had to be built was liable to impose half a day's delay or more, not so much because of the time taken in building but because of the procedure necessary. First an attack has to be made to win the far bank and form a bridgehead so that the sappers can build in safety; then the bridge has to be built, and finally the advance has to be reconstituted against an enemy who meanwhile have probably had time to reorganize themselves for the next stand. Added to this, the length of bridging available was not unlimited, and so it was imperative wherever possible to find ways which

Crossing the Rhine at Rees on 30th March 1945

didn't require bridging and where there were crossings still intact.

Often the greater part of the day would be spent in forcing a way through stubbornly defended villages that blocked the only routes available, searching miles of canal bank for an intact bridge, and small-scale fighting that was often costly without much apparent result except the capture of large numbers of prisoners. Then, just before nightfall, a clear way would be found and we would be able to rush forward some fifteen miles before darkness. Perhaps the line had at last been broken? Perhaps tomorrow we would really be able to get under way? We always felt that if only we could make a break-out and do one big advance the elaborate system of defence and withdrawal would break down, but it was never possible. Every inch was disputed, and while on other parts of the front the signs of resistance became less and less we found ourselves involved in an advance that was agonizingly slow and invariably opposed.

The night we crossed the Rhine we harboured in a little village called Dinxperloo, just across the Dutch frontier, and during the following four days we made a great loop north into Holland, then east and into Germany. It was pleasant to find little villages and towns not wholly destroyed by war and friendly inhabitants ready to welcome one into their houses when the night came. It was a change from the usual heaps of rubble populated by stray and sullen Germans who lived an unbelievable cellar existence, scuttling into and out of the ruins like human rats and searching the debris for food or loot- ghost towns like Goch or Cleve that seemed to dim the fate of Sodom and Gomorrah. In Holland we often found large and comfortable farms for our brief night's rest. They usually centred around a huge main hall that acted as kitchen-sitting-room and a great deal else besides. If they had a drawing-room it was far too ornately ugly and carefully preserved to be of any use, but the main room was as a rule both attractive and practical. As often as not the walls were lined with blue-and-white willow-pattern tiles; inevitably there was a vast stove of painted porcelain, and the only unwelcome feature was that the cow-barn invariably was a portion of the same house, which meant that the happy smell of cooking was sometimes disconcertingly mingled with cow.

A night under a roof was always an inestimable boon, but even then we had little enough rest. We were lucky if the day finished before dark and by the time the various "O" Groups fixing the arrangements for the next day were over it was. probably near midnight. From the remaining portion of the night two more hours must be subtracted to allow for one's turn on the wireless as duty officer, and then while it was still dark we would have to be up so as to eat breakfast and shave in time to start the new day's advance, which would begin as soon as it was light enough for the tanks to see the way. From Dinxperloo we fought our way to a little village called Neede, which held out too long for us to capture it that night, and the next day we liberated Enschede, which is quite a large town and required a full Battalion attack to clear it. Finally the opposition petered out after a fierce engagement along the canal bank in front of it, during which a lot of our tanks were knocked out by 88's on the aerodrome opposite.

After the capture of Enschede the Scots-Welsh Group[11] led the advance and crossed the frontier into Germany near Nordhom. There was some stiff fighting to clear Nordhorn and after this they made a night dash and reached the River

11 2nd Bn. Scots Guards Infantry and 2nd Bn. Welsh Guards Tanks

Ems just opposite Lingen. It was only due to bad luck that they failed to jump the bridge, a section had actually crossed when it was blown; but blown it was, and we now expected a fairly considerable delay, as there is a double obstacle at this point, the Ems and the Dortmund – Ems Canal both running parallel and under a mile apart straight across the line of our advance. It was the obvious obstacle for the Germans to try to hold us on, and in expectation of a large-scale river-crossing operation we were ordered to occupy Mittelohne on the near bank while the 3rd Division were brought up for the actual task of forcing the crossing.

We got to Mittelohne at about midday and I was just going to get some lunch when news came through that the Household Cavalry, who had been investigating the banks farther downstream, had discovered an unblown bridge about four miles away. It was hoped that a squadron of tanks might be able to rush it, and with them were to go No. 3 Company, commanded by Ian Liddell, to defend the bridge when it had been captured. I followed along with them through a maze of fir woods and heath and eventually we got to a big square plantation about a mile back from the river which had been agreed upon as the assembly area. From here onwards most of the way is open heathland until you get to a fringe of trees that runs along the top of a small escarpment about four hundred yards away from the river. It formed a perfect viewpoint and from a shack half-way down the slope you could get an excellent idea of the German positions. There was a small, sandy road running down to the river; it crossed a stretch of open meadow, then ran up a small incline to the bridge, which was closed at the near end by a road block consisting of neatly stacked tree trunks packed one on top of the other and completely sealing the way across. The bridge itself was a modern concrete one which looked as though it would blow up easily enough, and placed along the roadway there were several large aerial bombs that had obviously been put there for that purpose. Immediately beside the far end of the bridge there was a static ack-ack post, all banked about with protective sandbag walls, and no doubt full of well-dug trenches. Inside the post there were three 88's as large as life, manned by a crew who at times were also as large as life. It was obviously not a place that tanks could rush, and the only prospect was the hope that we could give the Germans such a surprise that it might be possible for some infantry to get across before it could be blown. It would take time to blast away the road block and meanwhile it presumably only required the turn of a switch and the bridge would go sky-high. Colonel Dicky Gooch,*[12] who was in command of the operation, decided that the best hope was to try to panic the defenders with a sudden heavy stonk and then for the company to put in an attack across it while the tanks shot-up everything on the far bank from the escarpment.

Huge dark clouds drifted across the sun so that it became quite dark, and as the company marched down the road from the plantation we were suddenly drenched by a storm of hail and squalls of rain. I walked along with Ian, sheltering behind the occasional straggly bushes of juniper while he explained to me what the company were to do. As soon as the artillery fire was over two platoons were to get into position behind the small bank on either side of the bridge, and while they and the tanks fired for all they were worth he was going to climb the road block, then cut the wiring of the bombs with a pair of wire cutters. If all went well the third platoon would then rush the far bank with

---

12 Commanding Officer of the 1st Bn. Coldstream Guards.

him. I thought: "My dear Ian, even if they don't blow the bridge when the first shot is fired, surely they won't let you walk about on it cutting wires under their very noses!" I said: "Do you think it will work?"

"Well, it's the only way it can be done. Oh, yes; I think it will certainly work – as long as I don't forget the wire cutters!"

I went to join Colonel Dicky and we waited for things to happen. The sun came out and soon afterwards we heard the eeeeee of our shells going overhead and the umph, umph, umph, umph as they landed just beyond, all around the bridge.

The tanks began to nose their way forward into the belt of trees along the escarpment, and as soon as they could see they loosed off a stream of Besa at the far end of the bridge and fired Typhoon rockets. We waited anxiously, expecting to hear the bridge go up, but all that we heard

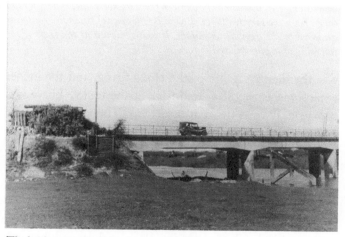

The bridge over the Ems river at Altenlingen. Captured single handedly on 3rd April 1945 by Ian Liddell for which he was awarded the Victoria Cross. Below the jeep can be seen supporting tanks on the west bank.

'Part of the fuse-wire attached to the demolition bombs.'

'Ian's Bridge' as it became known seen from the west side. A photograph taken from the family album. Below it is a piece of fuse wire that was attached to the demolition bombs, it was removed at the time of the storming of the bridge as a souvenir!

was the increasing din of the tanks firing, and the louder explosions as the 88's fired back at the tanks. There was some small-arms fire, but it seemed to be much too high, and there was also some type of quick-firing gun in action.

On the wireless net we could hear the squadron commander directing the fire of the tanks, then a warning to be careful, as the platoon was coming up to the bridge. It was all over extremely quickly, and within a few minutes a troop of tanks managed to knock down the road block and was up with the platoon, by now clearing the woods beyond.

When I counted up the damage at the end I discovered that over forty Germans had been killed, and we held forty-two prisoners, among them the commander of the position. He was a young captain, very shaken, and profusely anxious to explain why the bridge had not been blown – it had all been very difficult; he was in the wrong dug- out and couldn't get back to the one where the switch was; when he managed to, it was too late, nothing happened. He set out with his straggling band of followers escorted by a carrier like a rather ruffled version of Don Quixote. I thought: "Hardly anyone would believe it possible to get away with a thing like that, and yet that is really the reason why it succeeded." It seemed extraordinary how Ian had survived the attack. It was a unique feat and it won him the V.C., but before he ever knew this he had been killed in a battle a few weeks later.

The 3rd Division did the canal crossing later on in the night, and I led some of them up to Ian's bridge in the darkness. I had been over the route twice already, but I was still extremely uncertain of the way. Fortunately all went well – there is nothing so humiliating and disastrous as for a guide to lose the way. In the night the Ems looked quite small, a turbulent, fussy little stream reflecting the red glow of a burning house that cast great dancing shadows over the bridge with its litter of broken road block and spent cartridges.

After the canal crossing we had to clear a large stretch of country between the canal and the river while the 3rd Division forced their way into Lingen. It was not until the 6th, two days later, that we were able to advance once more, and then all that the day produced was a rather scrappy advance that ended up with the capture of two little villages called Baccum and Remsel, about ten miles on from the canal. We didn't leave Mittelohne until four o'clock, and by the time we put in our attack the light was

Ian Liddell was to die of wounds three weeks later near Rothenburg Germany on the 21st April 1945 without knowing that he had been awarded the decoration.

already beginning to fail. No. 1 Company made the attack through a big clump of woods, and having allowed, as we thought, due time for the attack to take place I drove up the road with Colonel Roddy to see how the land lay. The village cross-roads was ominously silent, but there was a lot of firing going on a little farther to our left, and the Commanding Officer thought we would probably find the company in that direction. Almost simultaneously some wounded Germans staggered backwards out of a house farther down the road with their hands up, and we saw a section dash across into the houses opposite, followed by the rest of the platoon. It turned out that we had arrived at almost exactly the same moment as the company – a little unorthodox, but, as it happened, harmless.

The next day centred around the capture of a village called Lenger- ich, which the Scots-Welsh Group at first made several unsuccessful attempts to capture; it was stoutly defended and with quite a lot of supporting artillery that knew well enough the roads we were advancing on and kept up a continual harassing fire. Our task was to clear another village called Thuine, about five miles farther south, and on the route to be followed by the 5th Brigade. We cleared Thuine successfully that morning, then moved up into a big wood below Lengerich while we waited for it to be cleared, and the 5th Brigade took up the advance where we left off. As the time wore on Lengerich still held out and in the end the tanks found a cross-country route that wormed its way in between the German posts to the south of the town and brought them out on the main route behind it. It was typical of the fighting in those days. Villages of any size that sat across the main roads were turned into strongly defended nodal points that could only be captured

This photograph of Ian's bridge was found in Lump Windsor Clive's album; he was one of the supporting platoon commanders during the battle to take the bridge.

by a full-scale attack, and although in the end someone always had to clear them, in the countryside round about there was often enough scope for wide circling moves that would get a squadron or so far behind the enemy and add to his discomfiture, though the surprise that this gained was sometimes mutual.

On this occasion we successfully decamped the whole group across country and behind beleaguered Lengerich. As the last attack of the day was being pressed home I set out back the way we had come to bring up our supply vehicles. The route was by now completely empty and mostly down grass-grown lanes, but easy enough to remember, as the ground was all turn up by the tanks that had passed that way earlier on. Half-way back I saw a group of German soldiers marching towards us down the side of the road; it was a common enough sight to see and I presumed that they must be prisoners with a guard following them, but as the jeep drew up to them I was horrified to discover that they were all armed – in fact, it was a normal infantry section withdrawing from Lengerich and apparently unaware of the situation. It was too late to stop and turn; we could only hope that they would be as slow in the uptake as I had been. As we drove past, going as fast as the ruts would allow, one of the stolidly trudging figures looked up and I waved to him. Almost mechanically he raised his hand, then gaped in astonishment. I don't know what happened after that – we drove flat out for safety, waiting for a volley of shots to pursue us down the lane, but we got away with it. With the battle ranging freely over such large areas of ground there were continual incidents like this, but not many people were so lucky and many of them came to unexpected ends, travelling in what they had assumed to be more or less home ground.

The fighting part of the group when advancing into battle would stretch backwards down some three or four miles of road, and though we always blocked any roads coming in from the sides, and probably had small detachments scouting out to the flanks, it was not at all unusual to find that while the head of the column was engaged in clearing a road block, half a mile back there would be a stretch of road under shellfire, and perhaps a mile behind that a cross-roads where everyone was being fired on by an S.P. gun. But all along we held the initiative and such incidents, trying as they might be to the people actually involved, were pinpricks that couldn't have any decisive effect on the advance as a whole. To ignore these side-shows that were liable to take place far behind the main battle required a courageous singleness of purpose, but at the same time without that point of view we could never have made any progress at all. Ahead there was always a stubbornly held centre of resistance that would not give

The Sherman tanks of the Ist Battalion entering Berge in April 1945 as the war entered its final phase. The two battalions had fought almost seamlessly together since Normandy.

except to a determined assault that was as often as not costly and difficult. Berge, the town that we came up against immediately after Lengerich, was a typical example. They were all small actions that depended for their success upon the efforts of a handful of tanks, a company, a troop of guns. No headlines in the papers saluted the results, and yet they were often more costly and testing affairs than many a grand attack with a hundred-gun barrage and all the trappings of a strategic battle ...

After Berge we found ourselves in reserve again and the Brigade was faced by a network of waterways that once more imposed a severe delay. Berge was captured on the 8th of April and we went into action again on the 11th to force the crossing of the River Haze, which was important for the Division, if not for the total solution of the war; but it deserves special attention, not because of its intrinsic importance but because it was a typical battle of a particular sort, an individual vignette of war as complete and self-contained as anything can be.

We had breakfast at four o'clock in the morning, one of those unreal sort of meals that one eats of necessity rather than appetite. The room was still full of the stale smoke and the cigarette ends of the night before. I swallowed down chunks of bacon feeling nauseated and grimly determined as though I were a lorry being filled up to capacity for a long run. I had reduced the number of items to be taken into a battle to an absolute minimum, not by a calculated process of priority but because such items as torches, steel helmets, compasses, spare socks, and all the other things deemed essential in military handbooks had long since been lost. Now I only had to buckle on a revolver over my jeep coat and make sure that I had the right maps on my map board. Sandwiches I always forgot.

Outside it was pitch dark and by the time I found the corner of the field where the leading company was formed up I had completely lost the exit, which was awkward, as my jeep was to lead the way. However, we got on to the road all right and from then on all went well, though I was a little anxious at moments. After many years of practice I particularly prided myself on reading a map, but with all the skill in the world it is easy to take a wrong turn in the darkness and, though this can easily be remedied by oneself, when there are over a hundred vehicles following behind such a mistake is extremely difficult to remedy. The prospect was a standing nightmare to me, and I heaved a deep sigh of relief when we drew up in Menslage behind the Scots Guards' positions. Their outposts were no longer in contact with the enemy and ahead there stretched about two miles of straight road leading up to the river. It seemed almost certain that the Germans had by now all withdrawn and blown the bridge behind them, but we had no confirmation of this, and so we advanced down the road deployed ready

This rare photograph shows the Guardsmen in action, fighting through Berge.

to meet anything, with a series of prearranged shoots that could be fired if we ran into trouble.

A dense mist lay all over the flat, open fields, shrouding the occasional belts of fir trees and masking the dreary length of road ahead. We walked along about a hundred yards behind the leading company watching the sections advance across the open like a line of beaters, and listening anxiously for the sound of any firing. A troop of tanks went with us, ready to try to rush the bridge if we found it still there. At intervals there were heaps of felled trees across the road, but they weren't big enough to stop the tanks and we pulled them out of the way quite easily, though with some hesitation, expecting that they would be mined. The sun rose, the mist dispersed and almost before we realized where we were we came up to the river. Our maps were incorrect and the company on the left advancing towards a nonexistent wood found themselves almost up to the banks and under heavy fire before they realized what was wrong. There was no line of willow trees or variation in the succession of flat meadows to give one the line of the river, and with the Germans dug in all along the opposite bank we had some difficulty in taking up our own positions. We put the command post in a copse about a hundred and fifty yards back from the site of the blown bridge, quite close enough to have shouted at the Germans across the river if we had wanted to, and in places where there was cover close to the banks the leading sections were not more than fifty yards away from the enemy on the far side. You had to move about extremely cautiously, as at such close range you could hardly be missed if you stepped unknowingly into view, and several men were shot in the early stages while we were still uncertain of the exact whereabouts of the river. Our gunner officer was caught by a sniper as he was trying to get a view of the river, and all along the length of it intermittent firing was going on.

While we were uneasily getting into position someone came and told me that the Intelligence truck had been blown up on a mine farther back; the driver and most of them were not seriously wounded, but Sergeant Todd had been killed – it was the worst news that I could possibly receive. He had come through everything. He was the sort of person one felt, quite illogically, always would. Whatever the disasters of the day I always knew that I should find Sergeant Todd as philosophic and undismayed as ever, and by now we had worked together so long that I could hardly imagine any other state of affairs – it seemed so impossible that I could hardly believe it, but there was much too much to be done at that moment to go back and see exactly what had happened. I went off with the Commanding Officer to try to find somewhere where we could look at the river.

We already knew that it was not much use trying to the left of the road and so we went off to the right, where No. 1 Company were. Despite the fact that they were almost within hailing distance, we had to walk nearly a mile to get to them unobserved, and then eventually we made our way forward through a wood that ran right up to a little mound beside the river bank. You had to crawl up the near side, then cover about fifteen feet of exposed slope and you found yourself in a small hollow about twelve feet from the river. We crawled cautiously over the carpet of dead leaves to the top, where we found a great blood-stained patch and the wrapping of a field dressing. Colonel Roddy said: "Well, it's obvious what happened there." I was hoping that he would be put off by this, but he wriggled over the top, murmuring: "The great thing is to take it slowly, then you are less likely to be seen." I followed him like a seal after the last herring in the world, and as I reached the bottom there was a great burst of firing. I might have said: "My God, they've got me! actually I said: "I'm sorry; I think that was my fault." Even that was rather an exaggeration; it was something a little farther down that had attracted attention. The river seeded extraordinarily small – not more than thirty feet across, cool, brown and languid. "Full of trout" was the first thing that came into my mind; after that I wondered whether we would get back safely – we did.

The morning's work produced a very gloomy series of conclusions. If it was almost impossible to get a look at the river, what would it be like trying to cross it? The place that we had reconnoitred was the most feasible – the boats could be launched there, the banks and the trees would give some cover before the assault; after that it looked as nasty as could be. There was not the slightest possibility of using artillery with both sides so close, and the only way the crossing could be covered would be with Bren guns mounted along the bank, but even though we would muster a much more powerful force than the Germans had on the other side, every other possible factor was against us. It was obviously a feasible project, but almost inevitably it was going to be very costly. We would have to wait until dark before making the attack, and in the meantime all the preparations went ahead. Boats had to be brought up and assembled; white tapes laid to guide people in the darkness; No. 2 Company, who were to make the assault, had to be carefully briefed as to the exact place they were to cross; and careful calculations made as to what order the crossing would be made in. Who would carry the boats to the crossing, who was to row them to and fro, how casualties were to be got back – there were certain to be a lot of casualties and it would be difficult getting them into and out of the boats in the darkness. The more the preparations got under way the more gloomy I felt.

While we were despondently thinking of all this and munching our sandwiches in the wood Jack Hamilton suddenly brought the news that he had an escaping French prisoner of war at his headquarters who claimed to have crossed the river by an unblown bridge about two miles farther down. Nothing was marked on the map and it all sounded very doubtful, but it was a ray of hope and the Commanding Officer told him to set out with a platoon and the troop of tanks to see what could be done.

It turned out that there was indeed a bridge. It was held, but they forced a way across and while they pressed on into the village of Bokah beyond another company was hastily moved up to the crossing and the Commanding Officer went back to confer with the Brigadier – vastly different prospects were beginning to take shape.

The main road after it crosses the River Haze comes to a little village called Boen, about a quarter of a mile away. We knew that it was held and could see some of the houses in the distance. The imperative task of the day was to clear Boen and have a bridgehead that would enable the sappers to build on the old site during the night so that the Division could continue the advance at first light the next day. The assault crossing was almost certain to achieve all that was required, but it looked costly; the new possibility provided a tempting alternative, but it was a gamble. We would have to clear the two miles of river bank that lay between Boen and our crossing to the east; we would have to advance through two miles of thick woodland to get to Boen, leaving a long and precarious route up behind us, open to every sort of unpleasant surprise; and finally we would have to make a very hurried full-scale attack from the end of the woods to capture Boen. It might well result in the type of operation that turns out to be more than one battalion can compete with, and the time available was getting short, but with all the snags it was preferable to the river crossing; and by half-past three the four rifle companies had been moved up to the newly captured bridge, leaving a small outpost to watch over the state of affairs behind while the advance to Boen was under way.

The bridge when we got to it turned out to be only a tiny wooden affair; someone had tried, very ineptly, to destroy it and all that now remained was a few planks, over which we made a rather dizzy crossing – it must have been a nightmare attack. The dead still lay where they had fallen, and on the other side there was a little group of surrendered Germans, some of them wounded, vainly waiting for somebody to notice them. It was very hot, much too hot for April, and I remember thinking rather disconsolately as we crossed over the bridge that I had seen the last of anything helpful on wheels for many hours to come. To add to our discomfort, some S.P. guns started to shell the crossing; close enough to make us duck at first; then when we saw that they were falling on the other side of the field a mere grating upon the nerves that grew more unpleasant as they corrected the range, though where they could see us from remained a mystery. Bokah was now clear and No. 3 Company started to advance through the woods towards Boen – dark, thickly grown fir trees that formed a forest with the rather Wagnerian name of Buren Tannen.

The gunner wireless set lost touch with the guns and I was told to stay behind and bring them on when they were on net again. For a quarter of an hour they sent out calls in vain and it was getting very near the time we had arranged for the attack. Firing was still going on in the woods, but I was afraid that I might never find the Battalion if I let them get too far ahead. I abandoned the wireless party, still renetting in vain, and set out after the Battalion; then I was rather sorry that I had. Stray Germans will seldom shoot at a body of people, but a single person is a different matter, and though things looked deserted enough I had no doubts but that there were plenty of enemy who must have been cut off by the river and were now straggling back across our route. The whole thing made me hot and angry and rather on edge. I was glad to come to the end of the wood and find the companies settling down to wait for the attack to start in a few minutes' time. I suppose we had not been very far, though it seemed like twenty miles, and now nothing stood between us and Boen but a small hillock just high enough to shut out the view.

The attack had already been arranged for five o'clock and we reached our rendezvous with only a very small margin to spare. The guns were far away to the south of us. As it turned the hour we heard the rumble and din as they opened fire and we moved forward out of the wood. Colonel Roddy posted himself on top of a great heap of straw, but I felt myself absolved from making such a prominent appearance – a tremendous burst of small-arms fire came from Boen the minute we showed ourselves. It was only a very short advance, but there seemed to be something firing out of almost every window in Boen. We followed behind the leading companies.

Our bit of the village was still uncleared. There was something rather comic about the Commanding Officer, the R.S.M., the signallers and myself all turning ourselves into a section for the clearance of Boen. However, we captured a suitable-looking house in fine style and found that it was the enemy R.A.P. A German doctor rushed up, his mouth inarticulately forming a few short sayings about the Geneva Convention, but we had no intention of interfering with him, besides which his arrangements proved most useful for our own wounded. There was as yet no way of getting them back across the river and so we shared the same R.A.P., and at the back of the house set up the command post. The firing went on for a long while after we got into Boen. Individual houses held out and there was a great deal of sniping. It's hard to say exactly when the attack finished, as there were so many separated incidents taking place at the finish. A tremendous fight developed along the river bank, where the Germans found themselves caught between the water and the advance of No. 2 Company, and in the houses they also fought unusually stubbornly, but as it grew dark round about eight o'clock quiet set in and we reported that the position was consolidated. We captured a hundred and ninety-two prisoners at a cost to ourselves of about forty casualties, and, unlike most battles, almost every one of our casualties was due to small-arms fire, the shelling being mercifully negligible.

As soon as the river bank was clear we set up a ferry system to evacuate the wounded and bring up our supplies. I went down to the river at about ten o'clock to make a report on the day to Brigade Headquarters and found that amidst a clatter of hammering steel span of the Bailey bridge was being edged across the river. When I got back it had developed into the recognizable beginnings of a bridge The road back was deserted, one or two houses were on fire, but from a distance Boen looked completely empty. I thought of the lines:

"I have a rendezvous with death ...

At midnight in some flaming town,

When Spring trips north again this year … .

It would be fine to look upon war so simply as that, and for once I felt that I could. At times one's feelings were curiously disconnected from the immediate moment, and despite all the destruction and tragedy you could feel a sense of repose as near to contentment as anything can be.

The next morning the bridge was complete and while the 5th Brigade took up the advance we had a day of rest and buried the dead; a very simple little ceremony, and though along the road beside us the tanks rumbled past with incessant noise, over the crowd gathered around the graves there was a silence as absolute as though the tanks had no existence. Everyone was very deep in their own thoughts, hushed by a rite which proclaims unbroken peace, a rest that is eternal.

After the capture of Boen we had three very easy days. The Germans were all withdrawing northwards to the next area of canals, and all that we had to do was to fight a few small actions which brought us to a village called Emsteck. At Emsteck we were promised four days' rest before the Division was changed over to another corps, and, as a pleasing rumour had it, we were then to take part in the liberation of Denmark.

Alan Pemberton and I set off in a 15-cwt. truck for Brussels to replenish the Battalion's store of drink. We made the journey in one day, which seemed a terrific feat at the time, and the whole excursion rather savoured of an expedition to "Never-never Land." We drove through the Teutonburgerwald, its massive beech woods startlingly green in their new foliage, and all the way along the trees by the roadside were thick with blossom. It seemed as though we had never really seen the spring before. Only the towns reminded one of the war: Munster, Osnabruck, Wesel – all of them mere graveyards full of dust and smelling like a Normandy battlefield. Along the main routes the monster emigrations of the slave population were beginning to take place and strung out for mile after mile we passed Russians, Poles, French, Czechs, Dutch – all Europe seemed to be on the move: an uncontrollable rabble of scarecrows wheeling along their belongings in prams and handcarts, sleeping in the hedgerows, and living off the country as they passed. From Munster back to the Rhine we met one solid stream of transport vehicles moving up after the advance, and wondered how it was possible for an army to have so much baggage and what exactly was the use of it all. At Wesel we ate our haversack ration beside what had once been a company headquarters.

Already the roofs had been patched up and the walls rebuilt. In the back garden they were hoeing lettuces, and many of the fields had been freshly planted. Turning over memories of how it had all looked when we were last there, it seemed as though we were stepping into a world of myth and yet the knocked-out tanks were still there resting in the fields and if you looked in the ditches the empty clips of ammunition still lay where they had been discarded. Brussels was like another world: smart cars purred up and down the Boulevarde Max, where the street vendors stood beside their barrows laden with plums and apricots, crying: "Vingt francs le kilo – vingt francs le kilo." Cream-coloured trams tinkled endlessly and clamorously after one another, the shops looked chic and well filled: it was a world of sunshine, noise and glamour that seemed to live on oysters, champagne and rumour.

The war, they said, was over. It would obviously be over very soon, but the feeling that it really was over had never entered my head before. It was a sort of "jam yesterday, jam tomorrow, but never jam today," state of affairs. All the way back I felt tormented by the idea of how close the end really was and how monstrous it would be to be killed at the last stage. We soused ourselves in wishful thinking: "Perhaps it would be all over when we got back; perhaps we should never have to fight another battle."

Our dreams were rudely shattered. The Division, we discovered, was again in action somewhere between the Weser and the Elbe, and rumour had it that there had been some very hard fighting. We felt like naughty schoolboys who had stolen an illicit holiday, and as if to remind us that the war was still a very serious matter some Focke- Wulfs dived out of the sky and shot us up as we crossed the Weser. We found the Battalion at Neunkirchen in the middle of a battle that had been going on all day.

There was still a week of hard and continuous fighting to go. Bremen was about to fall, Hamburg was next on the list, and the Division was steadily pushing its way forward across the great autobahn that runs between the two. On the 22nd of April we captured Scheessel, by ringing up the town hall and demanding its surrender on the telephone. We drove in in triumph, with the Burgomaster on the leading tank carrying a white flag; it was just the way that all wars should be fought, but it was only an incident and the next town refused to surrender despite every possible threat and inducement that we could devise.

The next day Ian Liddell was killed as his company fought their way down the road to Rothenburg. It required a full-scale Brigade attack to capture Rothenburg, and though nearly a thousand prisoners were captured there was some stiff fighting and quite a lot of shelling afterwards. The troops who relieved us came marching in laden down with steel helmets and paraphernalia as though they were about to attack the Siegfried Line. It wasn't a very nice place to take over at that moment, but the sight amused us – we felt like aged, aged veterans. Two days later we took part in another big attack to capture Zeven. We were up against the confident 15th Panzer Division that I referred to earlier, and we were more heavily shelled than we had been for a very long while. We had a lot of casualties and amid one stonk I peered out of the scout car and saw a tremendous explosion occur just beside us that caught Nevin Agnew and left us without an Adjutant. The end of the war seemed to be as remote as ever, and during the next few days we fought our way through village after village that had to be reduced to heaps of rubble before it could be captured. Mines were more numerous than ever, and we shunned the edge of the roadside like a typhus ward. Then on the 28th there was a slight change in conditions and we altered our direction towards the Elbe, where there seemed to be more scope and big advances were being made. Stade, which is quite a large town right on the estuary, surrendered almost without a shot and the next day, the 3rd of May,

No. 4 Company occupied a village called Himmelp-forten; as someone pointed out, it meant "The Gates of Heaven," but at that stage my enthusiasm for "The Gates of Heaven" was at a record low ebb. That evening we held a big "O" Group. The bulk of the German forces had withdrawn across the Oste Canal. The bridge opposite a little village called Hechthausen was to be reconnoitred the next morning and if it was blown we would have to make an assault crossing on the 5th. I think I have seldom prayed so heartily for a bridge to remain intact in all my life. News of the first peace envoys had reached us; besides this I had been stricken with a germ that made it impossible for me to eat anything for the next two days and I had quite made up

Billy Straker Smith and Robert Lawrie lead 3 Company marching through Zeven on 24th April 1945

my mind that I was never, never going to attack anything ever again. The next morning the bridge was found intact and No. 4 Company moved up to cross over and occupy Hechthausen. As I was driving up to join them I felt the ground give a slight tremble and in the distance I saw a cloud of smoke rising slowly up into the air as though a volcano had erupted. The road had been mined with a sea mine; nothing remained of the tank that set it off and when I arrived I found a gigantic crater about sixty feet across where once there had been a road. The crew of the tank were all killed, and to our own list of wounded were added Guardsmen Brown and Preece; they were our last casualties of the war. We found Hechthausen deserted.

That evening as I lay in bed feeling more ill than ever I heard a great commotion and sound of voices going on around the wireless truck outside. It was caused by the announcement of the German surrender. I crawled out of bed to celebrate the event with a whisky and soda, but there was very little merriment going on. Everyone seemed flat, tired, uncomprehending, as though it would take us many days to realize what had happened. Now that the war was really over I felt as though it could only be a rumour. Peace was something I knew of years and years ago when I was almost a child, something fantastically remote and unreal. I had lived whole lifetimes since then, so that I had become quite a different person. Presumably life was about to blossom out into security, plenty, freedom, happiness and all the things that we had been told we were fighting for, but the notion was as remotely obscure, as if one had been announced as the next Dalai Lama. Whatever life might hold in the future, nothing would ever matter so much as what was past. I might live to a great age or be run over by a bus in Piccadilly, but whatever occurred would be curiously trivial in comparison. It would be wonderful never again to know fear and fatigue and discomfort as we had known them in the days that it seemed were over, and yet there was something missing. After the last war Siegfried Sassoon wrote: "Suddenly everyone burst out singing." … I don't think any of us felt like that, or that anyone could have solved the riddle of our thoughts.

The next morning we received an official message which read as follows: "Germans surrendered unconditionally at 1800 hrs. 4th May. Hostilities on all sectors Army front will cease at 0800 hrs. B time 5th May. No, repeat no, advance beyond present front line without orders from this H.Q."

On the 7th we moved up to an aerodrome just south of Cuxhaven to disarm the 7th Parachute Division. It was a curious drive: all the villages that we passed on our way up were packed with German troops. Armed sentries stood outside the headquarters, and at intervals on the road we passed smart German officers in staff cars and German D.Rs., presumably carrying the orders that had been given out by us for their disarmament. At a level crossing the crew of a German ack-ack train still stood by their formidable array of weapons and every now and then we met long columns of horse-drawn transport making their way slowly towards the aerodrome where they were to concentrate to be disarmed. That evening there was a slight hitch, as the 7th Parachute Division had not had time to assemble as we had expected, but by the next day everything was sorted out and the Commanding Officer ordered the whole Division to parade on the aerodrome at 1600 hrs. so that we could check up that all the units were present.

General Erdman, the divisional commander, was on the other side of the Elbe preparing for a battle that never took place, but we found all the other characters that we knew so well from the intelligence reports, and his place was taken by Colonel Mensil, his deputy. He was a curious contrast to his staff officer, and except for his badges of rank he might have been mistaken for an ordinary paratrooper. The staff officer was an immaculately dressed figure complete with field boots, who would have done very well as a Hollywood representation of a German officer, and indeed I had never seen anyone like that before except in a film. We drove slowly past each unit in turn. As we drew up in front of them the troops were called to attention and Colonel Mensil saluted Colonel Roddy and reported their designation and strength. So this was the 7th Parachute Division that we had fought for so long at Venray and Wesel and half-way across Germany ! The infantry regiments were very reduced, but the rest of the division seemed fairly well up to strength and their equipment covered acres and acres of ground, with the guns all lined up wheel to wheel. It was an impressively complete and formal ceremony. Here lined up in their hundreds in front of the empty hangars and along the cement runways were the surrendered troops whose defeat

End of the War. Bob Tomlinson, The padre with a celebratory cigarette at Cuxhaven, final page from Mike Bendix's album.

we had so long fought for. It was the tangible expression of something that would perhaps take many years before its full significance could be realized, but for us it was the end of the war.

I sat down on a lovely sunny evening to write the last edition of the Battalion news-sheet, feeling that I should like to say something wise and Olympian about the Battalion, but it proved too difficult and I abandoned the idea. I think now that I was right; after all, "War is only an incident in the history of the Coldstream Guards" – but, my, what an incident!

Appendix A

Enll of Honour

OF THE

5TH BATTALION COLDSTREAM GUARDS

2653669 L./Cpl. H. Allison	Killed in action	3/9/44
2655912 L./Sergt. R.Anderson	Died of wounds	14/9/44
2661177 Gdsn. R. Anderson	Killed in action	31/8/44
2661589 Gdsn. W Anderson ..	Died of wounds	10/3/45
2662705 Gdsn. W Andrews	Presumed died of wounds	21/2/45
Lieut. S. E. Argyle	Killed in action	8/9/44
2659783 Gdsn. A. Arnold	Died of wounds	8/9/44
2664660 L./Cpl. L. Ascough	Died of wounds	29/6/44
2659919 Gdsn. A. Ashton	Killed in action	21/7/44
14566016 Gdsn. K. Backhouse	Killed in action	9/3/45
2664831 Gdsn. T. Baker	Killed in action	1/8/44
2657441 L./Sergt. S. Barker	Killed in action	4/4/45
2665920 L./Cpl. A. Barrett	Killed in action	16/2/45
2666664 Gdsn. S. Bates	Killed in action	9/3/45
2658506 L./Sergt. C. Bayliss	Presumed killed in action	7/8/44 (at sea)
2667006 Gdsn. D. Beck	Killed in action	9/3/45
2666967 Gdsn. H. Bedford	Killed in action	26/4/45
14498250 Gdsn. T. Birch	Killed in action	11/4/45
2666205 Gdsn. D. Bowditch	Killed in action	29/6/44
Lieut. H. C. H. Bowser	Killed in action	20/7/44
5511006 Gdsn. N. Boyce	Killed in action	20/7/44
Lieut. D. L. Boyle	Killed in action	14/8/44
2654002 L./Cpl. R. Boynton	Killed in action	1/7/44
2663250 Gdsn. L. Brazier	Killed in action	28/6/44
2659069 Gdsn. R. Bretherick	Killed in action	3/8/44
2661276 Gdsn. C. Brewer	Killed in action	16/2/45
2666632 Gdsn. A. Brewis	Killed in action	7/3/45
14681109 Gdsn. G. Brown	Killed in action	22/4/45
Major W. S. Stewart Brown, D.S.O	Died of wounds	28/7/44
4698303 L./Cpl. T. Buckingham	Killed in action	19/4/45
2666373 Gdsn. S. Buckley	Killed in action	20/9/44

2663511 Gdsn. C. Bull	Killed in action	27/7/44
2656687 Gdsn. C. Burkinshaw	Killed in action	8/9/44
2662886 L./Cpl. R. Bums	Died (natural causes)	14/3/45
2663495 Gdsn. C. Burrows	Killed in action	8/9/44
14686885 Gdsn. W Burton	Killed in action	23/9/44
2666676 Gdsn. R. Capron	Killed in action	16/2/45
2663707 Gdsn. T. Carpenter	Killed in action	23/9/44
2659126 Gdsn. A. Carr	Died of wounds	1/8/44
2662982 Gdsn. W. Chalk	Killed in action	8/9/44
2665349 L./Cpl. R. Chapman	Killed in action	3/8/44
2665807 Gdsn. E. Childs	Killed in action	6/8/44
2656083 Gdsn. C. Clayton	Died of wounds	19/7/44
2663030 L./Cpl. N. Clifton	Killed in action	19/4/45
3861848 L./Sgt. W Clitheroe,	Killed in action	11/4/45
2662985 L./Cpl. G. Clough	Died of wounds	12/4/45
2664221 L./Cpl. G. Cobby	Killed in action	29/6/44
2655227 Gdsn. S. Cole	Killed in action	11/4/45
Lieut. J. N. M. Coles	Killed in action	6/8/44
2659037 L./Cpl. C. Cooper	Killed in action	3/8/44
2659235 Gdsn. H. Cooper	Killed in action	16/2/45
2662214 L./Cpl. S. Corke	Died of wounds	11/8/44
2658831 Gdsn. R. Crane	Died of wounds	23/7/44
2661909 Sergt E. Crockford	Died of wounds	7/8/44
2665825 Gdsn. J. Croom	Killed in action	11/8/44
14655719 Gdsn. G. Crown	Died of wounds	25/9/44
2659746 Sergt. A. Dale	Died of wounds	9/9/44
2667117 Gdsn. W Davies	Killed in action	11/4/45
2664342 Gdsn. G. Dawson	Died of wounds	25/9/44
2665611 Gdsn. T. Dean	Killed in action	29/6/44
2655379 Gdsn. B. Dennis	Killed in action	11/11/44
2659276 Gdsn. E. Diggines	Killed in action	4/7/44
2666633 Gdsn. J. Dixon	Killed in action	11/8/44
2664176 Gdsn. K. Dolling	Died of wounds	29/6/44
5735558 Gdsn. R. Dowle	Killed in action	31/8/44
2658205 Gdsn. D. Downs	Killed in action	3/9/44
5735196 Gdsn. H. Dyer	Killed in action	24/4/45

2662542 Gdsn. F. Edwards	Killed in action	3/9/44
2658474 Gdsn. D. Ellison	Died of wounds	28/9/44
2658465 Gdsn. W Elms	Killed in action	25/9/44
2660671 Gdsn. S. Eyden	Killed in action	12/8/44
Lieut. G. B. Faller	Died of wounds	12/8/44
Capt. P. L. Fanning	Killed in action	4/11/44
6202354 L./Sergt. J. Farr	Killed in action	22/7/44
2661746 Gdsn. F. Farrar	Killed in action	18/7/44
3525074 L./Cpl. A. Farrow	Killed in action	5/3/45
2660489 Gdsn. H. Felton	Killed in action	6/8/44
2/Lieut. D. H. Fletcher	Presumed died of wounds	16/11/44
2663876 Gdsn. F. Fletcher	Killed in action	19/7/44
2658332 Gdsn. G. Fletcher	Died of wounds	5/10/44
2663032 Gdsn. P. Foy	Killed in action	8/9/44
2659120 L. /Cpl. D. Freeman	Killed in action	5/3/45
2663294 Gdsn. E. Gillett	Killed in action	14/9/44
2660912 Sergt. S. Goff	Killed in action	1/9/44
2663719 Gdsn. L. Goldsworthy	Killed in action	24/4/45
2666376 Gdsn. R. Gooding	Killed in action	1/8/44
2660375 L./Cpl. T. Gough	Killed in action	25/9/44
2663718 Gdsn. J. Grainger	Killed in action	8/9/44
2656148 Gdsn. R. Grainger	Died of wounds	20/7/44
2658534 Sergt. D. Grant	Killed in action	8/9/44
2662871 Gdsn. J. Green	Killed in action	8/9/44
2654411 C.S.M. T. Griffiths	Killed in action	14/9/44
3854048 Gdsn. J. Hacking	Killed in action	28/6/44
2660399 L./Sergt. F. Halliwell	Died of wounds	15/9/44
2663248 Gdsn. W Harris	Killed in action	9/3/45
2665507 Gdsn. G. Harrison	Killed in action	24/2/45
Major The Marquess of Hartington	Killed in action	9/9/44
14420034 Gdsn. L. Heiliar	Killed in action	11/4/45
11053183 Gdsn. S. Hinks	Killed in action	9/3/45
2661325 Gdsn. F. Hodge	Killed in action	16/2/45
2659969 L./Cpl. G. Hodgson	Died of wounds	27/7/44
Major M. P. G. Howard	Killed in action	2/7/44
2658387 Gdsn. R. Hunter	Died of wounds	12/4/45

2666249 Gdsn. R. Howell	Killed in action	16/2/45
2658868 L./Sergt. J. Hoyle	Killed in action	8/9/44
2663973 L./Cpl. H. Hunt	Died of wounds	29/4/45
2/Lieut. K. H. Irgens	Killed in action	8/9/44
2656377 L./Sergt. J. Jacklin	Died of wounds	6/12/44
2663466 L. /Cpl. E. Jackson	Killed in action	24/4/45
2662553 Gdsn. B. Ielfs	Killed in action	8/9/44
2662474 Gdsn. J. Jennings	Killed in action	16/2/45
2661135 Gdsn. T. Johnson	Killed in action	29/6/44
2666095 Gdsn. D. Keatings	Died of wounds	8/8/44
2659930 L./Cpl. T. Keith	Killed in action	9/9/44
2663570 L./Cpl. H. Kelly	Died (natural causes)	4/10/45
2659176 L./Cpl. G. Kingston	Killed in action	3/8/44
2666310 L./Cpl. W Kneller	Killed in action	8/4/45
2666956 Gdsn. D. Lean	Killed in action	11/4/45
2662133 Gdsn. J. Lee	Died of wounds	6/3/45
2662502 Gdsn. S. Leighton	Killed in action	18/7/44
2663202 Gdsn. J. Levell	Died of wounds	16/8/44
2659562 L./Sergt. J. Lewis	Killed in action	1/8/44
2660931 Gdsn. H. Lias	Killed in action	3/8/44
Capt. 1. o. Liddell, v.c.	Died of wounds	21/4/45
2660840 L./Cpl. R. Lister	Died of wounds	24/9/44
Major Viscount Long	Killed in action	23/9/44
2657969 L./Cpl. C. Loring	Died of wounds	11/4/45
2662586 Gdsn. F. Lowcock	Killed in action	8/9/44
2664041 Gdsn. J. Maher	Killed in action	28/6/44
2667122 Gdsn. F. Maguire	Killed in action	11/4/45
2664845 Gdsn. J. Mansell	Killed in action	18/7/44
2663595 Gdsn. F. Martin	Killed in action	3/8/44
2667091 Gdsn. J. Metcalfe	Died (natural causes)	27/3/45
2658429 Gdsn. R. Middleton	Killed in action	3/8/44
2661545 Gdsn. D. Milburn	Killed in action	8/4/45
2663444 Gdsn. E. Miller	Killed in action	21/7/44
2657598 L./Cpl. W Miller	Killed in action	19/7/44
2664304 L./Cpl. O. Millman Lieut. T. A.	Killed in action	11/4/45
Mitchell 2659278 Sergt. W Moore	Killed in action	8/9/44

2665609 Gdsn. C. Morgan	Killed in action	16/2/45
2664222 L. / Cpl. J. Morley	Killed in action	1/8/44
2662244 Gdsn. A. Morris	Killed in action	9/9/44
Lieut. R. F. Montagu	Died of wounds	3/10/44
2654028 Sergt. A. Mumberson	Killed in action	5/3/45
2666986 Gdsn. E. Nolder	Killed in action	9/3/45
2664486 Gdsn. J. O'Brien	Killed in action	11/4/45
2656246 Sergt. T. Oliver	Killed in action	5/7/44
2661649 L./Sergt. J. Olney	Killed in action	11/4/45
2667086 Gdsn. L. Page	Killed in action	14/9/44
5104312 Gdsn. H. Palmer	Killed in action	19/4/45
5683025 Gdsn. C. Parfitt	Killed in action	14/2/45
2659162 Gdsn. H. Plows	Killed in action	9/9/44
2666656 Gdsn. A. Poole	Killed in action	8/9/44
2656350 L./Sergt. T. Potts	Killed in action	26/6/44
2666371 Gdsn. P. Pugh	Killed in action	8/9/44
2655599 L./Sergt. J. Putt	Died of wounds	11/8/44
2661136 L./Cpl. S. Quinn	Killed in action	8/9/44
2654130 L./Cpl. G. Rawson	Killed in action	1/8/44
2661474 Gdsn. A. Readhead	Killed in action	22/7/44
2666574 Gdsn. W Reading	Killed in action	21/7/44
2653255 D./Sergt. S. Reason	Killed (battle accident)	23/3/45
2667271 Gdsn. G. Robinson	Killed in action	14/9/44
2661467 L./Sergt. F. Robinson	Died of wounds	21/4/45
14499696 Gdsn. J. Robinson	Killed in action	8/9/44
2666445 Gdsn. W. Robinson	Killed in action	11/4/45
2653845 Sergt. T. Rollinson	Killed in action	3/4/45
2665412 L./Cpl. E. Rolph	Killed in action	14/9/44
2662092 Gdsn. S. Russell	Killed in action	20/7/44
2659863 Gdsn. T. Rutherford	Died of wounds	21/7/44
2666000 Gdsn. J. Sainter	Killed in action	5/3/45
2661391 Gdsn. W. Salmon	Killed in action	5/3/45
2666704 Gdsn. J. Schorah	Died of wounds	3/8/44
2666266 Gdsn. R. Schofield	Killed in action	3/8/44
2659473 Gdsn. A. Shaw	Killed in action	1/8/44
2661268 Gdsn. C. Shaw	Killed in action	9/9/44

2656996 Gdsn. D. Sherwood	Killed in action	3/8/44
14714212 Gdsn. R. Skidmore	Killed in action	9/3/45
2665958 Gdsn. J. Slate	Killed in action	8/9/44
2667381 Gdsn. P. Shorthall	Killed in action	9/3/45
2660142 L./Cpl. G. Smith	Killed in action	20/4/45
2664242 L./Cpl. J. Smith	Killed in action	16/2/45
2653958 Gdsn. L. Smith	Killed in action	9/9/44
2659937 Gdsn. T. Smith	Killed in action	28/6/44
2666357 Gdsn. W. Smith	Killed in action	3/9/44
2662018 Gdsn. H. Stebbings	Killed in action	9/9/44
664516 Gdsn. W. Steele	Killed in action	16/2/45j
2661256 Gdsn. A. Stockall	Died of wounds	5/10/44
2667418 Gdsn. E. Stoker	Killed in action	11/8/44
2660907 L./Sergt. H. Storrow	Died (battle accident)	9/6/45
2661936 Gdsn. V. Stroud	Killed in action	3/8/44
Lieut. T. R. Symons	Died of wounds	29/10/44
2660384 Gdsn. J. Surr	Presumed killed in action	21/2/45
2661445 Gdsn. A. Taylor	Killed in action	6/8/44
2661127 Gdsn. F. Taylor	Died of wounds	25/7/44
2660899 Gdsn. C. Taylor	Killed in action	1/7/44
2660094 Gdsn. G. Thacker	Killed in action	6/8/44
Capt. R. Thompson	Killed in action	19/4/45
2658395 Gdsn. D. Thorpe	Accidentally killed	5/ 1/45
2653581 Gdsn. E. Thorpe	Killed in action	3/8/44
905855 Sergt. G. Todd	Killed in action	11/8/44
14499212 Gdsn. N. Trosh	Died of wounds	11/4/45
6015083 Gdsn. G. Trundle	Killed in action	8/9/44
2656924 L./Sergt. E. Tulloch	Killed in action	19/4/45
2666157 Gdsn. W. Turner	Killed in action	31/8/44
2659947 Sergt. C. Tyers	Killed in action	11/8/44
2660707 L./Cpl. W Vaughan	Killed in action	3/8/44
2666592 Gdsn. S. Waitt	Died of wounds	7/8/44
2664751 Gdsn. F. Walkey	Killed in action	4/10/44
2663654 L./Cpl F. Walshaw	Died of wounds	11/8/44
2663252 Gdsn. J. Walton	Killed in action	21/7/44
2665758 Gdsn. J. Warburton	Died (battle accident)	20/9/44

2658027 L./Cpl. R. Ward	Killed in action	11/4/45
2666652 Gdsn. J. Wass	Died of wounds	8/10/44
2660577 Gdsn. J. Watson	Killed in action	16/2/45
2658857 L./Cpl. J. Wedderburn	Died of wounds	19/7/44
2666839 Gdsn. J. Weeks	Killed in action	16/2/45
2663371 Gdsn. W Welsby	Killed in action	16/2/45
2662181 Gdsn. J. Whaley	Killed in action	1/8/44
2664575 Gdsn. R. Wigglesworth	Died of wounds	12/8/44
2666750 Gdsn. B. Wilkins	Killed in action	5/3/45
2658822 Gdsn. G. Wilson	Died of wounds	19/4/45
2666575 Gdsn. P. Wood	Died of wounds	29/7/44
2658689 L./Cpl. E. Woolley	Died of wounds	24/4/45
2661925 L./Cpl. H. Wright	Killed in action	1/8/44
2660995 Gdsn. T. Wynn	Killed in action	9/3/45
2662863 Gdsn. F. Yates	Killed in action	31/7/44
2660911 Gdsn. G. Yates	Died of wounds	22/7/44

ORDERS OF BATTLE

11th OCTOBER, 1941 (FORMATION)

BATTALION HEADQUARTERS

Commanding Officer	Lieutenant-Colonel The Lord Stratheden
Second-in-Command	Major W.L. Steele
Adjutant	Captain M.P.G. Howard
Mechanical Transport Officer	Captain C. Burges
Quartermaster	Lieutenant S. Middleditch
Regimental Sergeant-Major	R.S.M. H. Hewitt
Regimental Quartermaster-Sergeant	R.Q.M.S. F. Tortoishell
Drill Sergeant - Drill Sergeant	P. Robinson
Drill Sergeant - Drill Sergeant	F. Roberts
Medical Officer	Captain J.G.A. Gilruth
Padre	Capt. Reverend R. Tomlinson

HEADQUARTER COMPANY

Company Commander	Captain Tennyson d'Eyncourt
Carrier Officer	Lieutenant A.S. Jackling
Carrier Officer	2nd Lieutenant C.W. Lambton
Signal Officer	2nd Lieutenant D.I.T. Eastman
Mortar Officer	2nd Lieutenant Lord A. Cavendish
Pioneer Officer	2nd Lieutenant K.D.E.H. Harrington
Company Sergeant-Major	C.S.M. F. Gibson
Company Quartermaster-Sergeant	C.Q.M.S. J. Dyer

1 COMPANY

Company Commander	Captain C.W.S. Blackett
Second-in-Command	Lieutenant D.H. Doughty
Platoon Commander	2nd Lieutenant E.R. Hubbard
Platoon Commander	2nd Lieutenant P.L. Fanning
Platoon Commander	2nd Lieutenant T.J. Gurney
Company Sergeant-Major	C.S.M. R. Hudson
Company Quartermaster- Sergeant	C.Q.M.S. G. Treadwell

2 COMPANY

Company Commander	Captain L.C.M. Gibbs
Second-in-Command	2nd Lieutenant H.G.P. Woodroffe
Platoon Commander	2nd Lieutenant J. Pereira
Platoon Commander	2nd Lieutenant D.R. Rooper
Platoon Commander	2nd Lieutenant J.W.B. Cole
Company Sergeant-Major	C.S.M. J. Denham
Company Quartermster-Sergeant	C.Q.M.S. F. Guerney

3 COMPANY

Company Commander	Captain Hon. A.R.G. Strutt
Second-in-Command	2nd Lieutenant W.A. Gillilan
Platoon Commander	2nd Lieutenant Hon. D.M.G.J. Willoughby
Platoon Commander	2nd Lieutenant R.G. Style
Platoon Commander	2nd Lieutenant J.H. Ponsonby
Commmpany Sergeant-Major	2nd Lieutenant L. Lambert
Company Quartermaster-Sergeant	C.Q.M.S. T. Moody

4 COMPANY

Company Commander	Captain F.M. Turner
Second-in-Command	2nd Lieutenant R. Barnes-Gorrell
Platoon Commander	2nd Lieutenant D.J.R. Ker
Platoon Commander	2nd Lieutenant R.O. Caroe
Platoon Commander	2nd Lieutenant A.R. Coventry
Platoon Commander	2nd Lieutenant C. Mills
Company Sergeant-Major	C.S.M. W. Stanley
Company Quartermaster-Sergeant	C.Q.M.S. L. Boddy

NORMANDY LANDING, 20th June, 1944

BATTALION HEADQUARTERS

Commanding Officer	Lieutenant-Colonel The Lord Stratheden
Second-in-Command	Major W.S. Stewart Brown, D.S.O.
Adjutant	Captain C.W. Lambton
Mechanical Transport Officer	Captain I.O. Liddell
Quartermaster - Captain (Quartermaster)	S.B.R. Cooper
Regimental Sergeant-Major	R.S.M. S. Lonsbrough
Regimental Quartermaster-Sergeant	R.Q.M.S. E. Lovejoy
Drill Sergeant	Drill Sergeant S. Reason
Drill Sergeant	Drill Sergeant W. Stanley
Medical Officer	Captain P.J. Deller
Padre	Capt. Reverend R. Tomlinson

HEADQUARTER COMPANY

Company Commander	Major C.H. Feilden
Signal Officer	Captain R.G. Style
Intelligence Officer	Captain J. Pereira
Pioneer Officer	Lieutenant R. Thompson
Company Sergeant-Major	C.S.M. T. Griffiths
Company Quartermaster-Sergeant	C.Q.M.S. F. Farnhill

SUPPORT COMPANY

Company Commander	Major B.E. Luard
Carrier Officer	Captain P.L. Fanning
Carrier Officer	Lieutenant R.G. Lomer
Mortar Officer	Captain J.T. Paget
Anti-Tank Officer	Captain G.B. Mackean
Anti-Tank Officer	Captain B. Blower
Company Sergeant-Major	C.S.M. D. Hamnett
Company Quartermaster-Sergeant	C.Q.M.S. G. Tilling

1 COMPANY

Company Commander	Major K. Thornton
Second-in-Command	Captain F. Brown
Platoon Commander	Lieutenant H. Graham-Vivian
Platoon Commander -	Lieutenant R.F.C. Parrington
Platoon Commander	2nd Lieutenant C.D. Lawrie
Company Sergeant-Major	C.S.M. G. Harrison
Company Quartermaster- Sergeant	C.Q.M.S. H. Stevens

2 COMPANY

Company Commander	Major J. d'H. Hamilton
Second-in-Command -	Captain Hon. D.M.G.J. Willoughby
Platoon Commander	Lieutenant K. Kendall
Platoon Commander	Lieutenant G. Faller
Platoon Commander	Lieutenant N. Coles
Company Sergeant-Major	C.S.M. G. Whyte
Company Quartermster-Sergeant	C.Q.M.S. B. Ayres

3 COMPANY

Company Commander	Major M.E. Adean
Second-in-Command	Captain A. Gibbs
Platoon Commander	Lieutenant Hon. J. Knatchbull
Platoon Commander	Lieutenant Lord Balgonie
Platoon Commander -	
Commpany Sergeant-Major	J. Cowley
Company Quartermaster-Sergeant	C.Q.M.S. R. Fowler

4 COMPANY

Company Commander	Major M.P.G. Howard
Second-in-Command	Captain D.I.T. Eastman
Platoon Commander	Lieutenant C.H.Bowser
Platoon Commander	Lieutenant M.W. Wall
Platoon Commander	Lieutenant G. Myrddin-Evans
Company Sergeant-Major	C.S.M. N. Reid
Company Quartermaster-Sergeant	C.Q.M.S. F. Marsden

ENTRY INTO BRUSSELS, 3rd September, 1944

BATTALION HEADQUARTERS

Commanding Officer	Lieutenant-Colonel E.R. Hill
Second-in-Command	Major W.S. Blackett
Adjutant -	Captain C.W. Lambton
Mechanical Transport Officer	Captain I.O. Liddell
Quartermaster	Captain (Quartermaster) S.B.R. Cooper
Regimental Sergeant-Major	R.S.M. S. Lonsbrough
Regimental Quartermaster-Sergeant	R.Q.M.S. R.W. Smith
Drill Sergeant	Drill Sergeant S. Reason
Medical Officer	Captain J.B. Ingram
Padre	Capt. Reverend R. Tomlinson

HEADQUARTER COMPANY

Company Commander -	Major A. Gibbs
Signal Officer -	Lieutenant Earl of Plymouth
Intelligence Officer -	Captain J. Pereira
Pioneer Officer -	Lieutenant R. Thompson
Company Sergeant-Major -	C.S.M. T. Griffiths
Company Quartermaster-Sergeant -	C.Q.M.S. S.J. Connelly

SUPPORT COMPANY

Company Commander -	Major G.B. Mackean
Platoon Commander -	Captain P.L. Fanning
Carrier Officer -	2nd Lieutenant E.R.S. Fifoot
Mortar Officer -	Captain J.T. Paget
Anti-Tank Officer -	Captain M. Bendix
Anti-Tank Officer -	Captain B. Blower
Company Sergeant-Major -	C.S.M. D. Hamnett
Company Quartermaster-Sergeant -	C.Q.M.S. G. Tilling

No 1 COMPANY

Company Commander	Major C.H. Feilden
Second-in-Command	Lieutenant C.D. Lawrie
Platoon Commander	Lieutenant B. Whitehorn
Platoon Commander	Lieutenant H. Philip
Platoon Commander	Lieutenant T.R. Symons
Company Sergeant-Major	C.S.M. F. Farnhill
Company Quartermaster- Sergeant	C.Q.M.S. H. Stevens

No 2 COMPANY

Company Commander	Captain Hon. D.M.G.J. Willoughby
Second-in-Command	Captain J.N. Agnew
Platoon Commander	Lieutenant D.E. Plater
Platoon Commander	Lieutenant K.H. Irgens
Platoon Commander	Lieutenant P.J. Wadsworth
Company Sergeant-Major	C.S.M. R. Skells
Company Quartermaster-Sergeant	C.Q.M.S. D. Ayres

NO 3 COMPANY

Company Commander	Major The Marqess of Hartington
Second-in-Command	Captain R.G. Style
Platoon Commander	Lieutenant Hon. J. Knatchbull
Platoon Commander	Lieutenant T. Mitchell
Platoon Commander	
Company Sergeant-Major	C.S.M. J. Cowley
Company Quartermaster-Sergeant	C.Q.M.S. T. Thornton

No 4 COMPANY

Company Commander	Captain D.I.T. Eastman
Second-in-Command	
Platoon Commander	Lieutenant C.N. Acheson-Gray
Platoon Commander	Lieutenant M.W. Wall
Platoon Commander	Lieutenant S. Argyll
Company Sergeant-Major	C.S.M. N. Reid
Company Quartermaster-Sergeant	C.Q.M.S. F. Marsden

CROSSING THE RHINE, 30th March, 1945

BATTALION HEADQUARTERS

Commanding Officer	Lieutenant-Colonel E.R. Hill, D.S.O.
Second-in-Command	Major B.E. Luard, M.C.
Adjutant	Captain J.N. Agnew
Mechanical Transport Officer	Lieutenant H. Whitwell
Quartermaster	Captain (Quartermaster) S.B.R. Cooper
Regimental Sergeant-Major	R.S.M. R.W. Smith, D.C.M.
Regimental Quartermaster-Sergeant	R.Q.M.S. E. Lovejoy
Drill Sergeant	Drill Sergeant R. Skells
Drill Sergeant	Drill Sergeant J. Cowley, D.C.M.
Medical Officer	Captain J.B. Ingram
Padre	Capt. Reverend R. Tomlinson

HEADQUARTER COMPANY

Company Commander	Major A. Gibbs
Signal Officer	Lieutenant A.K. Feiling
Intelligence Officer	Captain J. Pereira
Pioneer Officer	Lieutenant P.R. Spurgin
Company Sergeant-Major	C.S.M. A. Seatherton
Company Quartermaster-Sergeant	C.Q.M.S. F. Connelly

SUPPORT COMPANY

Company Commander	Major G.B. Mackean
Carrier Officer	Captain B. Blower
Mortar Officer	Lieutenant Hon. J.J. Ormsby-Gore
Anti-Tank Officer	Captain M. Bendix
Company Sergeant-Major	C.S.M. G. Tilling
Company Quartermaster-Sergeant	C.Q.M.S. T. Thornton

1 COMPANY

Company Commander	Major D.A. Kennard, M.C.
Second-in-Command	Captain A.B. Pemberton
Platoon Commander	Lieutenant J.G.B. Chester
Platoon Commander	Lieutenant E.R.S. Fifoot
Platoon Commander	Lieutenant T. Matheson
Company Sergeant-Major	C.S.M. F. Farnhill, D.C.M.
Company Quartermaster- Sergeant	C.Q.M.S. R. Paterson

2 COMPANY

Company Commander	Major Hon. D.M.G.J. Willoghby
Second-in-Command	Captain J.T. Paget
Platoon Commander	Lieutenant Hon. P.A. Strutt
Platoon Commander	Lieutenant D.E. Plater
Platoon Commander	Lieutenant C. French
Company Sergeant-Major	C.S.M. D. Ayres
Company Quartermaster-Sergeant	C.Q.M.S. E. Hayes

3 COMPANY

Company Commander	Captain I.O. Liddell
Second-in-Command	Captain Earl of Plymouth
Platoon Commander	Lieutenant E.I. Windsor-Clive
Platoon Commander	Lieutenant J. Northcott
Platoon Commander	Lieutenant R. Laurie
Company Sergeant-Major	C.S.M. S. Berry
Company Quartermaster-Sergeant	C.Q.M.S. A. Townsend, M.M.

4 COMPANY

Company Commander	Major J. d'H. Hamilton
Second-in-Command	Lieutenant M.W. Wall
Platoon Commander	Lieutenant D.L. Sheldon
Platoon Commander	Lieutenant T.S. Glaister
Platoon Commander	Lieutenant G.H.G. Doggart
Company Sergeant-Major	C.S.M. N. Reid
Company Quartermaster-Sergeant	C.Q.M.S. F. Marsden

VE DAY, 8th May 1945

BATTALION HEADQUARTERS

Commanding Officer -	Lieutenant-Colonel E.R. Hill, D.S.O.
Second-in-Command -	Major B.E. Luard, M.C.
Adjutant -	Captain J.T. Paget
Mechanical Transport Officer -	Lieutenant H. Whitwell
Quartermaster - Captain (Quartermaster)	S.B.R. Cooper
Regimental Sergeant-Major -	R.S.M. R.W. Smith, D.C.M.
Regimental Quartermaster-Sergeant -	R.Q.M.S. E. Lovejoy
Drill Sergeant -	Drill Sergeant R. Skells
Drill Sergeant -	Drill Sergeant J. Cowley, D.C.M.
Medical Officer -	Captain J.B. Ingram
Padre -	Capt. Reverend R. Tomlinson

HEADQUARTER COMPANY

Company Commander -	Major A. Gibbs
Signal Officer -	Lieutenant A.K. Feiling
Intelligence Officer -	Captain J. Pereira
Pioneer Officer -	Lieutenant P.R. Spurgin
Company Sergeant-Major -	C.S.M. A. Seatherton
Company Quartermaster-Sergeant -	C.Q.M.S. F. Connelly

SUPPORT COMPANY

Company Commander	Major G.B. Mackean
Carrier Officer	Captain B. Blower
Carrier Officer	Lieutenant B.I.J. Bridger
Mortar Officer	Lieutenant Hon. J.J. Ormsby-Gore
Anti-Tank Officer	Captain M. Bendix
Anti-Tank Officer,	Lieutenant J.G. Porter
Company Sergeant-Major	C.S.M. G. Tilling
Company Quartermaster-Sergeant	C.Q.M.S. T. Thornton

No 1 COMPANY

Company Commander	Major D.A. Kennard, M.C.
Second-in-Command	Captain A.B. Pemberton
Platoon Commander	Lieutenant R.C. Treasure
Platoon Commander	Lieutenant J.G.B. Chester, M.C.
Platoon Commander	Lieutenant E.R.S. Fifoot, M.C.
Company Sergeant-Major	C.S.M. F. Farnhill, D.C.M.
Company Quartermaster- Sergeant	C.Q.M.S. R. Paterson

No 2 COMPANY

Company Commander	Major Hon. D.M.G.J. Willoughby
Platoon Commander	Lieutenant C.N. Acheson-Gray
Platoon Commander	Lieutenant Lord Balgonie
Platoon Commander	Lieutenant Hon. P.A. Strutt, M.C.
Platoon Commander	Lieutenant D.E. Plater
Company Sergeant-Major	C.S.M. C. Egan
Company Quartermster-Sergeant	C.Q.M.S. E. Hayes

No3 COMPANY

Company Commander	Captain W.J. Straker-Smith
Second-in-Command	Captain Earl of Plymouth
Platoon Commander	Lieutenant Hon. J. Knatchbull
Platoon Commander	Lieutenant R.P. Laurie
Platoon Commander	Lieutenant E.I. Windsor-Clive
Commpany Sergeant-Major	C.S.M. S. Berry
Company Quartermaster-Sergeant	C.Q.M.S. A. Townsend, M.M.

4 No COMPANY

Company Commander	Major J. d'H. Hamilton
Second-in-Command	Captain R.E. Philips, M.C.
Platoon Commander	Lieutenant G.H.G. Doggart
Platoon Commander	Lieutenant D.L. Sheldon
Platoon Commander	Lieutenant T.S. Glaister
Company Sergeant-Major	C.S.M. N. Reid
Company Quartermaster-Sergeant	C.Q.M.S. S. Stewart

HONOURS AND AWARDS CITATIONS

VICTORIA CROSS

W.S./ LIEUT. (T./CAPT.) IAN OSWALD LIDDELL.

On 3rd April, 1945, Capt. I. O. Liddell was commanding a company of the Coldstream Guards which was ordered to capture intact a bridge over the River Ems near Lingen. The bridge was covered on the far bank by an enemy position which was subsequently discovered to consist of 150 entrenched infantry supported by three 88-mm. and two 20-mm. guns. The bridge was also prepared for demolition with 500-lb. bombs, which could plainly be seen. Having directed his two leading platoons on to the near bank, Capt. Liddell ran alone to the bridge. He scaled the 10-foot-high road block guarding it with the intention of neutralizing the charges and taking the bridge intact. In order to achieve his object he had to cross the whole length of the bridge by himself under intense enemy fire, which increased as his object became apparent. Having disconnected the charges on the far side he recrossed the bridge and cut the wires on the near side. It was necessary for him to kneel, forming an easy target, whilst he successively cut the wires. He then discovered that there were also charges underneath the bridge. Completely undeterred, he disconnected these further charges. His task completed, he climbed up on to the road block in full view of the enemy and signalled his leading platoon to advance.

Thus alone and unprotected, without cover and under heavy enemy fire, he achieved his object and opened the way for the advance across the River Ems. His superb example of courage and self-sacrifice will never be forgotten by those who saw it.

Statement by Major P. H. Hunt, M.C., 1st (Armoured) Bn. Coldstream Guards.
On the 3rd April, 1945, my squadron was ordered to attack and capture a bridge over the River Ems, in close support of No. 3 Company of the 5th Bn. Coldstream Guards.

Before the attack started six 500-lb. aerial bombs could be seen lying on the bridge, and therefore it was arranged for the infantry to clear these so as to allow the tanks to get across.

When Capt. Liddell had got his company within 100 yards of the bridge he halted them and ran forward alone under extremely heavy fire which was coming from two 88-mm.'s and approximately 150 German infantry, climbed over a 10-foot road block and went the whole length of the bridge, cutting the wires attached to the aerial bombs, which were primed and ready for blowing. During this time he was the sole target for all the enemy fire and at any moment the bombs might have exploded.

Having rendered the bombs harmless, Capt Liddell W bridge and, standing on the top of the road bloeh beckoned his company fw ward, and personally led them in a charge across the bndge and into entrenched enemy positions along the far bank. As soon as the tank g he directed their fire on all the enemy strong-points.

Without this extremely gallant action andcomplete disregard f ɾcnnal safety which was an inspiration to all ranks who saw him, that the bridge would have been blown and Capt. Liddell's company would have suffered extremely heavy casualties.

Statement by No. 2661585 C.S.M. S. Berry. 5 Bn. Coldstream Guards.

On the 3rd of April, 1945, No. 3 Company, 5th Bn. Coldstream Guards, 'of which I am the Company Sergeant-Major, was ordered to capture the bridge over the River Ems at Altenlingen.

The bridge, besides being heavily defended, was also prepared for demolition, having four 500-lb. aerial bombs on its road surface and another four 500-lb. bombs attached to its supports. In addition to this, explosive charges were underneath the bridge itself.

My Company Commander, Capt. I. O. Liddell, knew that our only chance ot success would be to neutralize the explosives before the enemy could take action.

He went forward alone, armed with a pair of wire cutters, and under extremely heavy fire from 88-mm. and 20-mm. guns and Spandau and rifle fire, succeeded in cutting the wires attached to the bombs on the bridge, and then dashed over and cut the wires leading to the bombs underneath.

Having neutralized the explosives, he recrossed the bridge and led the leading platoon over to attack the enemy entrenched on the other side.

The action of Capt. Liddell, besides ensuring the capture of the bridge, was a most inspiring example of bravery and leadership to those of us who had the privilege of witnessing it.

Statement by No. 2667018 Gdsn. T. Laws, 5th Bn. Coldstream Guards.

On the 3rd of April, 1945, 1 was in the leading platoon of No. 3 Company, who had the job of taking a bridge over the Ems at Altenlingen. The company commander,

Capt. Liddell, had gone forward to the bridge and seen that the bridge was all ready for demolition, two bombs wired up on both ends. He knew that the enemy would in all probability blow it while he attempted to cross it. Without any hesitation and before any of us could bring any covering fire down, he had scrambled over the barrier in front of the bridge, which was about ten feet high, and dashed about 100 yards across and cut the wires leading to the bombs at the far end. He then dashed back and did the same to the others on the home side. He was waving us forward when one of the section whose job was clearing underneath the bridge told him there were another four under the bridge, so he climbed over and cut the wires underneath. He then led the platoon across, and cut the wires underneath at the far side.

All the time he was on the bridge Jerry was firing everything he had. How he came through all that fire power unhurt was a miracle. At one time he was a sitting target about twenty yards from the nearest gun and the same from a bazooka, whom we finished off when we crossed. His heroic act inspired all of us that saw it.

DISTINGUISHED SERVICE ORDER
MAJOR (T./LIEUT.-COLONEL) EDWARD RODERICK HILL.
After crossing the Albert Canal at Beeringen on 8th September, 1944, a battalion of the Coldstream Guards which was under the command of an Armoured Guards Brigade for the operation, with armour and artillery in support, were directed on to Bourg Leopold. Immediately after crossing the bridge the Battalion became involved in most severe and difficult fighting against a determined enemy supported by anti-tank guns. Throughout that day and night at least three battalion attacks were put in and the Battalion suffered very heavy casualties in both officers and other ranks.

Lieut.-Colonel Hill commanded this group in an exemplary manner. Throughout this action his calmness and cheerfulness and acceptance of several unpleasant situations and his complete disregard of his own safety in going to see for himself were a splendid example of leadership, and there is no doubt that it was due to this officer that steady gains were made throughout a very difficult and expensive day and night. By pushing on relentlessly, the Battalion group opened the door for another operation, and thus made it possible for the battle to proceed successfully on a wider front.

BAR TO MILITARY CROSS

T./Major David Arthur Kennard.

On the 9th March, 1945, this officer commanded the left forward company in the Battalion attack on the Xanten – Rheinberg road which resulted in the clearing up of the Wesel bridgehead. His company came under heavy mortar and artillery fire in the F.U.P. and as soon as they crossed the start line under aimed small-arms fire as well. Before the operation started it was doubted if the final objective could ever be reached, but without hesitation this officer led his company forward to it and, despite loss, consolidated in the face of very heavy and accurate mortar and nebelwerfer fire. Once there his position was threatened not only from the front but also from his open left flank. He immediately altered his dispositions to meet the new threat and, despite everything the enemy could do, remained on his objective until the enemy wearied of assaulting him. There is no doubt that a large share of the credit for this completely successful operation must be given to the intrepid leadership displayed throughout by Major Kennard and his masterly handling of his company during the advance and subsequent consolidation.

His personal example was an inspiration to all ranks, and his power of command and leadership of the very highest order.

MILITARY CROSS

LIEUT. RICHARD GODFREY LOMER.

On 3rd August, 1944, this officer was acting as second-in-command to his company north of Le Busq.

Throughout the day he displayed the highest qualities of leadership and endurance, carrying forward Piat bombs to a forward platoon under heavy mortar fire which a little later it became necessary to extricate. This officer volunteered to go up again to organise the withdrawal, which he did with great coolness and efficiency. The last section to be got out suffered heavy casualties from German mortar fire. Lieut Lomer, who was bringing up the rear =, was painfully wounded by the same agency while going to the aid of the wounded men. Despite this and though barely able to walk, he carried two men a distance of forty yards each to comparative safety. He then returned to the remaining wounded and refused to leave them until all had been evacuated or died.

While waiting with the last man he crawled to a ditch with a Sten gun with a view to dealing with an anticipated German counter-attack.

Throughout the whole operation this officer set a magnificent example of cheerfulness and efficiency, and I strongly recommend him for the award of the Military Cross.

CAPT. DEREK IAN TENNENT EASTMAN.

On 8th September, 1944, the 5th Bn. Coldstream Guards was ordered to attempt the capture of Bourg Leopold. The attack was planned in four phases, and owing to very strong enemy resistance it was nearly dark before the third phase, the capture of Heppen, could be undertaken.

This attack was carried out by the company of which Capt. Eastman was second-in-command, and reached its objectives just after dark. The company commander was wounded, one of the platoon commanders was killed, another had been wounded earlier the same day, and the remaining one with his platoon had been directed on to an objective slightly to the left of the main position.

Owing to the darkness the squadron of tanks which should have co-operated in the assault were unable to locate the company and were ordered to return. When night fell, therefore, this company was over 1,000 yards in front of the rest of the position, in a state of some disorganization owing to loss in officers, and very close to the main German stronghold at Bourg Leopold.

Capt. Eastman at once asked permission to go forward to try to locate the company and reorganize it. In this task he was completely successful. He contacted the leaderless remnants of the company, joined them up with the platoon on the left, and brought them safely back, together with all the wounded. But for this officer's initiative and powers of leadership there is every reason to suppose that none of the company would have got back and certainly not the wounded.

At the time, like everyone else, this officer was extremely tired, the night was very dark and no one knew the exact location of the company in the very thick country in which they were operating. The only certainty was that there were a great many Germans still in the area.

W.S./LIEUT. MICHAEL WHINORAY WALL.

On the 5th March, 1945, this officer was commanding one of the forward platoons in the Battalion attack on Metzekath in the Bonninghardt. The line of advance of the platoon was up a road through some woods which came to an end before reaching the objective. On reaching the edge of this wood the platoon came under heavy fire from a 75-mm. anti-tank gun, small-arms fire and bazooka fire from a house farther on. At this moment the platoon mortar corporal was killed by a direct hit from the anti-tank gun, but Lieut. Wall managed to get a smoke screen put down by his 2-inch mortar to cover his advance across the open while he led one section to assault the gun. The assault was successful despite the fact that the gun crew fought to the last, the leader being bayoneted in the act of reloading the gun. Lieut Wall then led on to attack the house whence the small-arms fire came and which was equally stubbornly held, every German having to be killed and none surrendering.

Lieut. Wall then led on to his final objective, now for the first time taking prisoners as he went.

Throughout the whole attack this officer showed the greatest dash and leadership. His conduct was an inspiration to his platoon and there is no doubt that they would follow him anywhere as they have done from Normandy to the Rhine.

There is no doubt that it was largely thanks to this officer's great bravery and power of leadership that his company attack was able to keep up its momentum and thus the Battalion attack to be entirely successful in time for consolidation to be carried out before darkness fell.

W.S./LIEUT. HON. PETER ALGERNON STRUTT.

This officer started by commanding the reserve platoon of a forward company in the Battalion's attack on to the Xanten – Rheinberg road on 9th March, 1945. Early in the battle the two forward platoons were held up by extremely heavy machine-gun fire from the right flank. They were in the open and suffering heavy casualties. When he was ordered to advance round the left flank, this officer led his platoon with great skill and dash and, clearing the ground in front, led his platoon on to their most forward objective.

At this stage the company commander was wounded and most of company headquarters knocked out. This officer then took charge of the company and under intense fire from both small arms and heavy weapons organized and sited the consolidation positions. He saw to the evacuation of the wounded and personally directed fire on to the enemy who were in close contact.

Throughout the battle the fine example and courage shown by this officer were an inspiration to his company and one of the main factors in the success of the operation.

W.S./Lieut. Erik Richard Sidney Fifoot.

This officer has been an outstanding patrol and platoon leader ever since joining the Battalion in August, 1944. Every time he has had the opportunity to distinguish himself for bravery and devotion to duty he has done so. Outstanding examples occurred twice during Operation "Veritable."

In the Battalion attack on Mull, south-east of Gennep, he commanded the right-hand forward platoon which had to cross 3,000 yards of open country in face of heavy and accurate enemy D.F. fire and considerable small-arms fire from farmhouses and concrete "haystacks." Over all this distance this officer's fine example was of the utmost encouragement and resulted, despite heavy casualties, in complete victory.

Again on the 9th March this officer was commanding a forward platoon in the Battalion attack on the Wesel bridgehead. His platoon started to suffer casualties before crossing the start line, and on reaching that they were met with further heavy small-arms and mortar fire.

Despite all this, Lieut Fifoot led his platoon with conspicuous dash and gallantry. No sooner was the original objective reached than he was ordered to carry out a difficult manoeuvre to the flank to meet a threatened German counter- attack. Despite the intense and accurate mortar and nebelwerfer fire, he accomplished this with great skill, thus neutralising the threat to his whole company's position.

These are but two examples of this young officer's intrepid conduct as a platoon commander in the offensive operations of the last few months During the winter defensive fighting he was equally outstanding as a gallant and resourceful patrol leader. His outstanding conduct and devotion to duty have on many occasions been brought to the notice of his superiors.

W.S./CAPT. (T./MAJOR) JOHN D'HENIN HAMILTON.

On 11th April, 1945, the Battalion was ordered to force a crossing of the River Haze and establish a bridgehead at Boen, using boat equipment. The map, however, disclosed a small bridge two miles to the east and Major Hamilton was ordered to take his company with one troop of tanks under command to investigate this bridge and, if possible, seize it. On arrival the bridge was found to be partially blown and strongly defended on the far bank. Major Hamilton at once organized the best available fire plan and then personally led a platoon over the broken bridge in the face of accurate and heavy small- arms fire. Such dash and determination upset the defenders, who numbered about 150, and who were all either killed or captured or withdrew to a small village 500 yards to the north. Without a pause, Major

Hamilton followed them up, appreciating that he must clear the village too in order to make the bridge safe for the rest of the Battalion to use.

As a result of this action the whole Battalion (less any wheels) crossed the Haze before the enemy completed the destruction of the bridge by shell fire, and the subsequent attack on Boen was carried out with much less loss of life and time than would otherwise have been the case.

This was achieved by .the outstanding power of leadership and personal bravery of Major Hamilton.

W.S./Capt. (T./Major) Hon. Digby Michael Godfrey John Willoughby.

On 11th April, 1945, this officer was commanding his company in the Battalion attack to gain a crossing of the River Haze. Owing to the forcing of a bridge, at the last moment the whole plan was changed and the role allotted to the company was to sweep south of the village of Boen and clear the north bank of the river, not then thought to be any longer strongly held. The bulk of the supporting fire, therefore, was directed on to the village itself and beyond.

From the time the company debouched into the open it became obvious that all the objectives allotted to it were strongly held by a numerous enemy garrison who were able to shoot at it from front, flank and rear. Major Willoughby, with vigour and determination, directed his forward platoons on despite loss and then went himself to his reserve platoon, commanded by a sergeant, and personally directed its operation against the most troublesome enemy positions. As a result, over forty members of the 61st Parachute Regiment were then killed or captured and the whole situation softened up so that all the company objectives were soon afterwards seized.

Undoubtedly it was this officer's great gallantry and outstanding leadership which were responsible for the successful completion of the operation.

Major Willoughby has commanded his company in every action fought by the Battalion from Normandy onwards, except one, and has always been outstanding, but on this occasion the special circumstances conspired to give him his opportunity to excel.

W.S./LIEUT. JOHN GREVILLE BOGRET CHESTER.

On 24th April, 1945, this officer was commanding the forward platoon of the right forward company in the Battalion attack on Zeven. His first task was to take his platoon forward to gain the first objective before the rest of the Battalion moved and he had to remain there alone for three-quarters of an hour exposed to heavy mortar and machine-gun fire while a neighbouring battalion came up alongside. When once a further advance was permitted this officer's platoon led the company attack across a long stretch of open ground to the next objective. *En route* his leading section all became casualties, but Lieut. Chester immediately himself picked up the Bren and led the remains of his platoon into the strongly held wood which formed this objective.

Here due to his great bravery and power of leadership the attack never paused for an instant, and despite further losses Lieut. Chester led on into the town itself and ultimately reached his final objective on the other side of it. There is no doubt that the very fine performance of this company was largely due to this officer's entire disregard of his own personal safety and great devotion to duty throughout the long and arduous battle, of which he personally bore the full brunt.

It was thanks to him that the whole Battalion attack was able to keep up its momentum and to achieve complete success.

DISTINGUISHED CONDUCT MEDAL

No. 2658115 C.S.M. JAMES COWLEY.

On 9th September, 1944, the company of which this W.O. was Company Sergeant-Major was ordered to take part with another company and a squadron of tanks in an attack on the village of Heppen. The attack was successful, but by the time the company had cleared its half of the village none of the officers were left, the company commander having been killed in the street fighting. Coming after the loss of all platoon commanders in the last few days' fighting, the loss of the company commander came as a great blow to the company and there was a moment of hesitation. At once this warrant officer realized that it was his duty to carry on, and he at once rallied the men and consolidated the company well forward of the objective. He then reported the situation to the tank squadron leader, who was the senior officer present, and continued by his personal example to encourage the men despite the fact that a good deal of shooting was still in progress. When this had been overcome and it was possible to take stock of the position, it was discovered that this company's morale was entirely restored, that the position was very satisfactorily organized and that everything that should have been done had been done.

Credit for all of this and in very trying circumstances must be given to this company sergeant-major.

I attach report received by me from squadron leader concerned, which he asked to be allowed sent in.

"1ST (ARMD.) BN. COLDSTREAM GUARDS.
"11/9/44.

"MY DEAR COLONEL,
"I have no doubt you will have heard from other sources of the magnificent manner in which C.S.M. Cowley took over command of No 4 Coy. when his Coy. Commander was killed and no Officer remained unwounded

"I would like, however, to add my testimony to this Warrant Officer splendid example to the men – who had suffered heavy casualties. The way in which he handled the Coy. in seizing his objective and taking up a Coy. position in face of strong opposition showed courage, leadership and initiative of a very high order.

"I have no hesitation in saying that, in my opinion, his conduct deserves recognition.

"Yours ever,
"(Sgd.) **BILL ANSTRUTHER GRAY.**"

No. 2653987 R.S.M. ROBERT WILLIAM SMITH.
At last light on Thursday, 14th September, 1944, when the Battalion was in a defensive position north of the Meuse – Escaut Canal, one of the two Battalion ammunition lorries was hit by a salvo of German shell fire. It at once caught fire and the ammunition started to explode.

Without hesitation and with a very full realization of the risks involved, R.S.M. Smith walked up to the second lorry which had just been placed alongside the first for a certain purpose and drove it away well clear from the burning one.

During his walk to the lorry, his efforts to start it, and whilst driving it away he was in imminent danger of being blown to pieces either by an explosion from the burning lorry or by his own exploding also.

There is little doubt that but for this example of courage and devotion to duty the whole of the Battalion ammunition reserve might have been lost and a very much heavier toll of life taken place at Battalion Headquarters than in fact happened.

No. 828597 C.S.M. FRANK FARNHILL.

On 23rd September, 1944, the company of which this warrant officer was company sergeant-major led an attack on the village of Voekel.

Soon after crossing the start line the only officer platoon commander was wounded and almost immediately upon entering the village the company commander was killed. Despite being thus left without any officers and with the major portion of the operation still to be carried out, this warrant officer at once assumed control and by his ability and example pressed the attack through to a successful conclusion.

It was not until the final objective had been reached and after heavy fighting that it was possible for another officer to be sent up to take over command of the company. On his arrival he found that this warrant officer had already re-organized the company and had done everything that should have been done to ensure the complete success of the attack.

But for this warrant officer's presence of mind and personal example it is very doubtful whether the operation could have been successfully concluded.

MILITARY MEDAL

No. 2661603 GDSN. ALEXANDER EDWARD McINTYRE HENRY.

Gdsn. Henry is employed as a stretcher-bearer, and on two occasions he has gone out to attend the wounded while under fire. The first occasion occurred when his company were in a position in front of Cagny on 20th July, 1944. There was a wounded man in the front right platoon who was being sniped at by two snipers from the buildings and woods at Frenouville. They opened fire at any movement on this platoon so it was decided to put down a smoke screen to enable the wounded man to be evacuated. Gdsn. Henry left company headquarters and walked over to the platoon and was told by the platoon commander to get down and wait until the smoke screen had started. As this was a bit slow in coming down, Gdsn. Henry decided to wait no longer and proceeded over to the wounded man in full view of the enemy. The wounded man was eventually evacuated after being treated by Gdsn. Henry.

On the second occasion in front of Frenouville two men had been killed and two wounded by an 88-mm. shell. Again it was found impossible to approach the wounded men on account of machine-gun fire by the enemy, but again Gdsn. Henry walked right in and got the two men out.

These are but two examples of Gdsn. Henry's courage. Ever since the Battalion has been in action he has shown great devotion to duty and extreme gallantry in action regardless of self and is a great cheering influence on the whole company.

No. 2661926 Sergt. D. Brookes.

On 1st August, 1944, in front of St. Martin des Besaces, this N.C.O. showed magnificent personal courage and offensive spirit as platoon sergeant to his platoon. He personally attacked a number of the enemy in the open, using every available weapon, killing a German officer and others in single combat and generally leading the hand-to-hand fighting.

Later while his platoon was taking up a fire position behind a bank this N.C.O. stood in front of it spraying the oncoming enemy with a Bren gun, firing from the hip and inflicting such heavy casualties that the enemy withdrew.

In addition, he damaged an enemy tank by scoring hits on it with a Piat.

His work of an administrative nature was as outstanding as his gallantry in the field, and I strongly recommend him for an immediate award.

No. 2654115 Sergt. Ambrose William Townsend.

On the 9th September, 1944, Sergt. Townsend was platoon sergeant of his platoon in the attack on Heppen (west of Bourg Leopold), in which there was particularly strong resistance from small-arms and 88-mm. fire. When starting to cross some open ground his platoon commander was wounded; this N.C.O. immediately took command of the platoon and led on.

The situation at this stage was particularly unpleasant, and Sergt. Townsend, showing complete disregard for his personal safety, rallied and led his platoon across ground exposed to heavy fire, and there is no doubt that the success of the company's part in the attack was largely due to this N.C.O.'s personal bravery and leadership.

This is not an isolated case, for Sergt. Townsend has consistently shown himself exceedingly cool under fire and is always an inspiration to his platoon and his company.

No. 2663832 L./Sergt. Albert Verdun Lowe.

On 23rd September, 1944, this N.C.O. was commanding a section in the company which led the attack on Voekel.

Despite a preliminary mortar bombardment, many German machine guns were still alive, and this N.C.O.

showed outstanding dash, initiative and leadership in working his section forward under hostile machine-gun fire from both flanks.

It was as a result of his resolute action in continuing to gain ground that his platoon was able to reach its objective and that the company attack subsequently proved to be completely successful.

No. 2662218 GDSN. DOUGLAS BARTLETT.

On the 23rd September, 1944, this Guardsman was No. 1 on the Bren in his section. His company was leading in the attack on Voekel and became pinned to the ground by hostile machine-gun fire.

On his own initiative he jumped up and fired his Bren from the hip, putting out of action the German machine gun which was holding his section up. This action enabled his section to go forward and reach its objective, which in turn allowed the rest of the platoon to advance

No. 2664946 GDSN. WILLIAM BUTTERS.

During this period 4th – 12th November, 1944, the company to which this Guardsman was attached as a signaler was holding a very exposed part of the line south of Venraij. The whole area was under constant enemy observation and close in close contact with the Germans, who were most active with patrols during the night and artillery and mortar fire during the day.

As a company of a very wide front there were telephone lines to all the platoons as well as to the headquarters behind the mortars, etc. To add to the difficulties, the battalion had taken over here a very complicated signal layout, including many old lines , while all were constantly being cut by are own tanks and enemy shell fire.

During the whole of this time this Guardsman had to control the whole signal layout and to sally forth frequently into exposed fields around to mend the lines, which meant exposing himself to aimed enemy fire during the day or to risk of being mopped up by enemy patrols at night.

None of these things prevented Guardsman Butters from immediately going out as soon as a line ceased to operate, and it is hardly to much to say that if the company had been less well served in this respect their position, which was always somewhat precarious , might well have become almost untenable. That this did not occur was largely due to coolness, efficiency and devotion to duty of this Guardsman.

No. 3861848 L./Sergt. Wilfred Clitheroe.

On 16th February, 1945, this N.C.O. was commanding a section in the left- hand platoon of the left forward company in the Battalion attack on the German defences south of Hommersum. His platoon's objective was some farm buddings on the far side of a flooded stream which could only be approached by a causeway about fifty yards long through the flood water.

The bridge crossing the stream itself had been blown, leaving a gap 15 feet wide, crossed only now with lengths of light railway line. The causeway and bridge were covered by automatic fire from the farm on the far side, and the platoon plan was to support the crossing by the 2-inch mortar.

However, without waiting for this fire to become effective or even for the final order to go this N.C.O. led his section with great dash straight along the causeway, over the partially demolished bridge and into the farm buddings from which at this moment the enemy fled.

Throughout the whole attack L./Sergt. Clitheroe's leadership and example were a great encouragement to the whole platoon.

No. 2658364 CPL. (L./SERGT.) VICTOR RUDDICK.

Throughout the whole campaign inNorth-WestEurope this N.C.O. has been one of the outstanding section leaders in the Battalion and one of the few to come through ad the fighting unscathed. After each of our many battles his name has been brought to my notice for outstanding bravery and devotion to duty.

A typical example occurred on the 16th February, 1945, when his section was the leading one in his company, which on that day passed through the original forward companies in the attack on the strongly defended German defences at Mull, south-east of Gennep. The platoon objective was a farm 300 yards beyond the main German anti-tank obstacle, and having crossed this L./Sergt. Ruddick led his section for 300 yards over open country in the face of the fire from at least two German machine guns.

On reaching the farm he approached a door and fired his Sten into the house. The gun jammed and after throwing a grenade he rushed in, wounding two Germans and capturing ten more.

This is merely a typical example of this N.C.O.'s dash and initiative, which have at all times been of the utmost encouragement to the rest of his platoon and indeed to the whole company.

No. 14402668 GDSN. ROBERT GREIG.

On 16th February, 1945, Gdsn. Greig was a member of the right-hand section of the right-hand company of the Battalion attack on the German defences south of

Hommersum. After a long advance under heavy enemy artillery fire, this section was within a few hundred yards of its final objective when it was temporarily unsighted by a smoke screen put down for the benefit of the formation on the right. For this reason they did not see a German machine-gun post in their vicinity until it had opened up at short range, killing the section commander and one other man. Gdsn. Greig at once assumed command of the section and seized the Bren gun, but while he was doing this two more men in the section had been killed by the same German machine-gun post. Gdsn. Greig now single-handed, charged the enemy post, killed the two men on the machine gun and put the remainder to flight. He then fell wounded in four places in the leg.

As a result of his fine action he allowed the few remaining men of the section to continue their advance, thus covering the right flank of his platoon and, incidentally, of the whole company.

No. 2662917 CPL. (L./SERGT.) JOHN LINDSEY.

On the 5th March, 1945, this N.C.O. was commanding one of the forward sections in the Battalion attack on Metzekath in the Bonninghardt. The line of advance of the platoon was up a road through some woods which came to an end before reaching the objective. On coming to the edge of the woods the platoon came under fire from a 75-mm. anti-tank gun, small-arms fire and bazooka fire from a house. This N.C.O. was ordered to give covering fire while his platoon commander led the other sections in an assault on the anti-tank gun. Appreciating that the assaulting party would come under heavy fire from the house while assaulting the gun, L./Sergt. Lindsey on his own initiative led his section across the bullet-swept ground and attacked the house under very heavy fire. He fought his way in with grenades, being twice blown off his feet by blast from bazooka bombs while doing so. Undeterred, he led his section on, killing two of the enemy and putting the rest to flight. He then led his section in pursuit, capturing them all to the number of thirteen This action had the effect of helping the platoon attack to be successful and L./Sergt. Lindsey at once pushed on with the rest of the platoon to the'final objective and ordered his section to dig m. He then collapsed from the effects of the blast of the bazooka bombs.

This N.C.O. has taken part in every attack since the Normandy days, and this latest example of utter disregard for his own safety and complete devotion to duty is typical of his exemplary conduct during the whole campaign There is no doubt that his great gallantry on the 5th March, 1945, was largely responsible for the complete success of the Battalion attack

No. **2663989 CPL. (L./SERGT.) DENNIS FRANK JORDAN.**

On 9th March, 1945, the Battalion was ordered to capture the Xanten – Rheinberg road. Extremely heavy machine-gun fire was met by the right-hand leading sections as soon as they crossed the start line, and they suffered heavy casualties, yet this N.C.O., who was commanding one of them showed outstanding courage and skill in fighting his way forward. At one time he took on a German section single-handed and liquidated it, although he was under fire from paratroops in adjacent houses. It was largely due to this N.C.O.'s leadership and dash that the company was able to fight its way to its objective. On consolidation L./Sergt. Jordan had to take over command of his platoon and although under continuous fire from snipers and Spandaus he went round and personally sited the sections and helped them to reorganize.

This N.C.O. has in previous battles shown a similar complete disregard for his own personal safety and his example has been an inspiration to the company.

No. 2661863 A./Sergt. Charles Handley.

At the beginning of Operation "Veritable" this N.C.O. was platoon sergeant of a platoon. On the 5th March, 1945, prior to the Battalion attack on Metze- kath, the forward companies, which included his, were unfortunately heavily shelled on the start line. This N.C.O.'s platoon commander and a quarter of the platoon strength were killed or wounded at that time, but Sergt. Handley immediately rallied the survivors and, despite this unfavourable start and due to his outstanding leadership, he led them forward to fulfil the mission allotted to them in every respect and despite stubborn enemy opposition.

Four days later, on the 9th March, Sergt. Handley was commanding the platoon in the Battalion attack on the Wesel bridgehead. This time his company was in reserve, but as the forward companies had been ordered to bypass as much opposition as possible in order to reach their objective much bitter hand-to-hand fighting fell to the lot of the platoon before the area allotted to them as their objective was clear of enemy. During the whole period this N.C.O. displayed the utmost gallantry and dash in leading assaults on house after house, all of which were occupied by the enemy and defended by them to the last

Throughout the whole period under review, until he was himself wounded in the Battalion attack over the River Haze, whether as platoon sergeant or platoon commander, his example has been an inspiration to the whole platoon and has undoubtedly been a great factor in achieving the unbroken record of success against fierce opposition which is the proud record of this N.C.O.'s company.

No. 5335644 GDSN. JOHN FINNEY.

This Guardsman had always been employed as a stretcher-bearer with his company from June, 1944, until the 29th March, 1945, when he had a leg blown off in a minefield while endeavouring to rescue a British soldier from another unit who had against orders entered the minefield.

During the many previous months of fighting, from Normandy to Germany, the heroic actions of the Battalion stretcher-bearers were repeatedly being brought to notice, but of them all this Guardsman displayed the most outstanding devotion to duty.

In every battle in which the Battalion took part this Guardsman risked his life whenever by so doing he was able to lessen the sufferings of the wounded in his company, and the last act of his soldiering was merely one more example of what he had done so many times before. This incident happened when the Battalion was out of touch with the enemy and waiting to cross the Rhine. His company headquarters was located near a clearly marked overrun enemy minefield, but against strict orders a soldier of another unit entered the enclosure and at once became a casualty on a mine. As soon as Gdsn. Finney heard of the accident and without hesitation or orders, he went to the scene with a stretcher, reached the casualty and started to tend the wounded man. In so doing he had his right leg blown off.

This example'of complete indifference to personal danger Was typical of this Guardsman's behaviour on all occasions. He had invariably done much more than his duty as a company stretcher-bearer, and this last example, like so many before, was an inspiration to his whole company.

No. 2664442 L./Cpl. John Edward William Royal.

On 3rd April, 1945, this N.C.O. was commanding the section which led the assault on the bridge over the River Ems at Altenlingen. After the dash across the bridge, in the face of heavy fire from 88's and small arms, the section fought its way into a deep trench, but were held up at a bend by a party of enemy round the corner. Heavy enemy fire was sweeping the top of the trench from one direction, and our own supporting fire from our tanks from the other, but despite all this L./Cpl. Royal, without any hesitation, climbed out into the open and ran along the top of the trench for over eighty yards firing his Sten gun at the enemy in the trench who were holding up the advance of his section. Some he accounted for, some surrendered and the remainder who fled were killed by fire from the tanks.

This action enabled the platoon to complete the clearing of the trench and ensured that the bridge was captured intact.

There is no doubt that the absolute disregard of his own personal safety shown by this N.C.O. was responsible for the speedy elimination of enemy resistance on the far bank and the completion of the whole operation with such dash and determination that the enemy was never given a chance to reorganize his defence.

No. 2662048 Sergt. Norman Duckworth.

On the 4th April 1945, Sergt. Duckworth was the platoon sergeant of a forward platoon in the company of Coldstream Guards detailed to attack the large barracks west of Lingen. The attack went in at last light and the tank support was unable to keep up with the infantry owing to a stream. In the circumstances the clearing of the barrack building became a matter of great difficulty and smoke had to be used to get the sections across the gaps between, as all were covered by Spandau fire. In this instance the forward sections were across, but the remaining one attempted to follow, the section leader was killed and the section paused. At one this N.C.O. ran back to them and without any smoke protection ,rallied them and bought them across the gap. With this extra support the pillbox which was holding the platoon was captured and the advance continued. One hundred and forty two prisoners were taken by the company.

This N.C.O.'s unhesitating acceptance of all risks and great power of leadership (which has been invaluable to the platoon ever since Normandy) undoubtedly resulted in keeping the impetus of the attack and the entirely successful completion of the task.

No. 2660552 Gdsn. (U./L./Cpl.) Hector Dodds

This N.C.O. was in charge of the stretcher-bearers attached to the rifle company of his Battalion throughout the campaign and during that time there is no doubt that, thanks to his utter disregard for his own safety and very high sense of devotion to duty ,he saved lives of many of his comrades and lessened the suffering of many others. Of the many cases possible to cite for outstanding bravery two must stand as illustrations.

During his company attack on the Siegfried Line at Mull on 16th February, 1945, his headquarters received a direct hit from a shell which wounded two of the stretcher-bearers and badly shook this N.C.O. However, he at once rendered first aid to his companions and then proceeded to the right forward platoon, who had just suffered the loss of one complete section by enemy medium machine-gun fire. CpL Dodds had to cross this hostile fire himself before he could reach the wounded men and this he did without the slightest hesitation. On arrival a heavy smoke concentration was put down on to this platoon locality, but despite all this Cpl. Dodds continued moving from man to man until all had been dealt with.

On 11th April, 1945, this N.C.O.'s company were lining the bank of the River Haze prior to forcing a crossing at another place. The company were under heavy and accurate small-arms fire, and movement appeared impossible. Casualties were being suffered and each time the call came for stretcher-bearers this N.C.O. went without any hesitation and amidst a hail of bullets from at least two enemy medium machine guns from across the river.

Apart from these exploits on behalf of his own company the opportunity twice came for him to help the men of other regiments, and on both occasions his action was gratefully brought to my notice by the commanding officers concerned.

The first occasion was the expensive attack by the Irish Guards through us, south of Hommersum, and the second was on the 9th March, 1945, when the Scots Guards began the assault on the Wesel bridgehead when their centre line v/as cut and their R.A.P. staff separated from their forward companies. This corporal did all that could be done to make good their loss.

No. 2663510 CPL. (L./SERGT.) SAMUEL VINEY.

On the 19th April, 1945, this Battalion carried out an attack on the town of Visselhovede. This N.C.O. was commanding one of the leading sections ordered to clear up the main road leading out of the town to the north. As his section reached this road they came under heavy automatic fire, wounding some and forcing the remainder to cover. This N.C.O. immediately reorganized his depleted command, dragged the wounded men from the road back to cover and then immediately led on to clear the nearest post obstructing his advance. In this he was successful and the momentum of the company attack was thus never allowed to diminish.

During the whole of this time this N.C.O. had been operating under heavy and accurate small-arms fire and there is no doubt that it was due to his utter disregard of his own safety and great power of leadership that the above satisfactory results were achieved. This N.C.O. has invariably behaved in this outstanding way in action and his example has at all times been an inspiration to his section and indeed the whole platoon.

Appendix D

SPEECH BY MAJOR-GENERAL ALLAN ADAIR AT THE BATTALION'S FAREWELL PARADE, COLOGNE STADIUM, JULY, 1945

"Now that the war is over we come to a period of change and reorganization. The old firm has to be broken up. We have said farewell to our tanks and now tonight we have to say farewell to the fighting 5th Battalion. It is in many ways a sad moment, but don't forget that the war is won and such reorganizations are inevitable.

"Now, I feel no one is more qualified than I, who had the great fortune to command the Division throughout this campaign, to say to you, 'Well done.' I have seen you fight in every battle throughout the campaign.

"For a moment let us turn back to those many battles you fought, and I would say here and now that the 5th Bn. Coldstream Guards have fought in more battles than any other battalion in the Division, and the Battalion has gone from strength to strength. Turn back for a moment to that time when the Battalion landed on the beaches of Normandy under the command then of that fine leader Colonel Sandy Stratheden, who we are delighted to see fit and well and with us here this evening.

"You had that tough fighting in the beach-head at that horrible place by the airfield at Caen, where minnies dropped, Cagny, and on to the bocage country; all those many fights there – tough ones nearly all – and then we had that glorious time when we crossed the Seine where you led the way with the tanks on to Arras and Douai, and then on to Brussels, where after a short pause for light refreshments we continued on to the Albert Canal at Beeringen, and I always think that battle you fought at Heppen, near Bourg

Leopold, was the key to the whole subsequent operations. Those Boche paratroopers were fighting fanatically and unless you had succeeded in widening the bridgehead to the west any subsequent advances would have been extremely difficult.

"Then we went gaily on to Nijmegen, where you supported the 82nd U.S. Airborne Division, and when the centre line was cut you went and cleared it, and when we wanted more food you went and took Oss and provided the Division with more food, including some horrible ersatz coffee!

"Now I pass on to Operation 'Veritable.' That battle of yours in smashing the Wesel bridgehead has become world-famous. That relentless advance on a very narrow front – it had to be narrow – against strong opposition, backed up by the tanks as usual, somehow has struck the imagination and indeed it was a very fine action.

"Then on the 30th March we crossed the Rhine and the end of the campaign was in sight. But as you know well plenty of tough fighting remained for us

I need not detail to you that gallant action of No. 3 Company on the bridge over the Ems, the seizing of that bridge under the magnificent leadership of Capt. Ian Liddell. We, everyone in the Brigade of Guards and in the Division, are proud of his memory and proud of those who took part in that operation. You were strongly helped there, as always, by the tanks and the results were inevitable and magnificent.

"You passed on and captured Rotenburg, you went on to capture Zeven, and finally you crossed the Oste Canal, and VE Day came along. What could be a more fitting climax than the disarming of your old opponents, the 7th Parachute Division, by yourselves and the 1st Battalion! It was a fitting climax to a great campaign.

"Now in a few minutes you will be marching off to the strains of 'Auld Lang Syne.' Old teams will perhaps be broken up in a few days, old friendships **for** the moment severed, but remember each one of you wherever you may be or wherever you may go that you have been sent with a very high standard of conduct and achievement in this Battalion, and it is always up to you individually to keep that standard up.

"I congratulate Colonel Roddy Hill, who has led you so well, and I congratulate every one of you. You have added a proud chapter to the history of your Regiment. And I say you have proved that the 5th Battalion is well worthy of your motto 'Nulli Secundus.'"

EPILOGUE

Jocelyn Perier's time at Cambridge was curtailed by the war and he was to follow his father's footsteps by joining the Coldstream. After the war Jocelyn embarked on a career as a geologist having qualified at the London School of Mines. He worked for Rio Tinto Zinc with his first posting was to British Guiana in South America; this was followed by many years in Australia prospecting for minerals. He married twice (his first having wife predeceased him). In the 1960's he retired back to London. He was a man with a brilliant mind, an intellectual of the first order with a passion for quantum physics.

His book *A Distant Drum*, a leather-bound copy of which was given to King George VI, became recommended reading for students of the Staff College after the war.

Jocelyn Periera died in 1985.

Jocelyn Perier